BLACK AFRICA

Russell Warren Howe

BLACK AFRICA

Africa South of the Sahara from Pre-History to Independence

Volume I

From Pre-History to
the Eve of the Colonial Era

 Walker and Company · New York

Library of Congress Catalog Card Number: LC 67-14265

First published in the United States of America
in 1966 by Walker and Company, a division of
Publications Development Corporation

Published simultaneously in Canada by the
Ryerson Press, Toronto

Printed and Bound in Great Britain by
Bookprint Limited, London and Crawley

To
NAOMI

CONTENTS

vii

Author's Note

THIS BOOK, which is divided into four parts and is being published as two volumes, is intended as a historical introduction to Black Africa, a background to the news despatches coming from the four fifths of the continent which lie to the South of the great Sahara sand ocean.

In recent years, there have been a vast number of books on Africa. There has been, in particular, a studious effort to piece together the purely indigenous history, a difficult process because of the widespread absence, in the past, of African nations that could read and write. Using largely Arabic records, and the often intelligent – but sometimes highly conjectural – guesswork of Delafosse, E. W. Bovill, in his *Caravans of the Old Sahara*, published in 1933, heralded a major 20th Century search for a documented, reasonably accurately dated account of pre-Colonial Africa. A number of scholars began re-reading the narratives of ibn Battuta, Leo Africanus and al-Bakri, or of Middle Eastern, European and Chinese writers associated with southern and eastern Africa. The 'Fifties saw the appearance of several works, mostly in English; more recently, there have been some scholarly books in French.

A considerable contemporary literature has come down to us from the period of European penetration, from the *épopée* of the navigators, traders, explorers, missionaries and finally the soldiers and administrators. Other writers have dealt with the African communities with which the traders treated. Unfortunately, most recorders of Africa's recent centuries unwittingly or wittingly take sides, ignoring either the contribution of the Europeans or that of the indigenous realms and cultures to the sum of African – and world – history; this is especially true of some of the later historians of African cultures who – writing in the atmosphere of the decolonization period – have often emotionally rejected European penetration as a brash intrusion, an unscientific approach incompatible with history. Indeed, in an effort to prove the truth – that Africa had a history, and specifically a history before the European came – some emotional paternalists have constructed African pasts from obscure and unproven data, doubtful or inflated facts: their polemical pretense to an almost Athenian nature for some warrior empires – comparable in reality to the rule of Genghiz Khan or of Charlemagne – has tended to respectabilize, rather than to disprove the emotional arguments of that other school which sought to show for reasons of current politics that Africa had 'no past at all.' In this book, I have felt that the useful task of freeing African history from the shackles of ethnic prejudice could best be served by avoiding any attempt to read more into existing knowledge than is there.

*

On the imperial period of Africa's story – the subject of the second volume – there is already fairly abundant published material, mostly area or country studies, considerable travel narratives, plus a small literature on the philosophy of colonialism, and a still-growing wealth of anthropology. The nationalist movements are also fairly well documented, both by nationalist writers and outside observers and historians. In recent years there has been a flood of direct-account books about specific places, and several on contemporary Black Africa – or Africa – as a whole, or concerning great expanses of it. Several books have also examined the continent's modern problems, from pan-Africanism and economics to medicine and community development.

What this four-part book (which, like all books, is inevitably subjective and incomplete) attempts to do is to bind all the ancient and modern history of Black Africa together in one general introductory work. It attempts to avoid involvement in contemporary attitudes, to be clinically critical, and to regard each aspect of Africa's story, each cultural interchange and metamorphosis, as an essential ingredient of the whole; and Africa's story itself as one contributory aspect of the world past and the world present.

Since these volumes are addressed to the diplomat, the correspondent, the international businessman, the university and high school student (both in Africa and abroad), and to the broad nonfiction reader, rather than to the specialist who needs a finer view of a smaller canvas, I have avoided the laborious use of footnotes and the tedious quotation of sources – with two exceptions: those writers or works of centuries past forming, themselves, a part of African history, and certain distinguished modern Africanists who merit, I think, special mention. I am particularly indebted to the French Islamist, Professor Vincent Monteil of the University of Dakar, an indispensable source of knowledge of the ancient empires; to the earlier-mentioned British writer, Bovill; to the American scholar, Dr. James Duffy, for his unequalled knowledge of Portuguese African history; to the Nigerian historian, Professor K. Onwuka Dike of the University of Ibadan, for his painstaking reconstruction of events in the Niger Delta; to the Australian writer Alan Moorehead for his work on the Emperor Theodore and the Napier invasion of Ethiopia; and in the later volume to my friend the late George Padmore of Trinidad, gentleman-revolutionary, whose records of early pan-Africanism are unique.

Apart from the classics of times past, the modern books or manuscripts of Robert Ardrey, Robert Cornevin, John Drysdale, J. E. Flint, Harry Gailey, Brian Gardner, Gordon Gaskill, Charles-André Gilis, Thomas Hodgkin, A. H. M. Jones and Elizabeth Monroe, Lawrence A. Marinelli, C. W. Newbury, Arthur Porter and even Sir Roy Welensky were particularly valuable for their original material.

In determining what works to cite in a selective bibliographical list at the end of each volume, I have included many 'minor' sources, including such writers as Blixen, Delius, Gide, Greene, Barbara Hall and Keppel-Jones, whose books, like those of Bosman and Captain Adams in earlier centuries, were more precious for the feel they gave of an era, a country or a régime than just for concrete historical data. It would be difficult to write a convincing history without such witnesses as these. Similarly, Madame Mrabet's apparently inapposite book is cited as the most intimate portrait available of that remarkable Black African colonist, the Arab male. I have omitted from the bibliographic list a few sources of minor information when these books also contain substantial inaccuracies or palpably selective omissions and which might, in my subjective view, mislead students.

In composition, an African history cannot observe chronology alone, as would be the way with most histories of Europe, America or Asia. To begin with, there are no equivalent deadlines to Magna Carta, the Renaissance, Columbus or the French Revolution. The exploits of Portuguese navigators – navally but not politically comparable to the first European voyages to the Americas – only influenced limited stretches of the African shoreline. Nineteenth Century Bornu was not greatly different from Eleventh Century Almoravid Ghana. Yet Seventeenth Century Sofala or Saint-Louis-du-Sénégal must have been on a par with much of Mediterranean Europe in their day. Each Black African region had its own pace of events, ignorant as the actors inevitably were of events in other parts of the continent. Whereas politics in Italy 'cross-pollinated' those in France, which affected those in Holland or of Portugal; whereas British affairs were influenced by those of Spain or Germany, the Niger Delta lived out its history unaffected by Angola or Ethiopia, which in turn was uninfluenced by Kamerun or Senegal. There is no chronological 'sequence,' until recent times, to the continent; each country's or region's earlier history tends to exist in a sort of partial vacuum, with Europe or the Arabs as an occasional connecting link in limited cases.

The first part of this book deals with pre-European Africa, where one of the two aspects of history – conquest – was much in evidence, but the other, human progress, largely limited to the spread of Islam (which was not always an unmixed blessing). Part 2 deals with pre-colonial Africa, and therefore begins, on the coasts, a few centuries before the first part ends up-country. In the second volume, Part 3, on the colonial period, also requires turning back the calendar again, in the case of Portuguese Africa, and even of Sierra Leone. With the last part, there is a return to chronological accounting.

A history of Black Africa could well be several thousand pages in extent: in selecting what to omit or include, I have tried to resist the temptation merely to reveal how clever modern scholars have been in unearthing the ancient past; I have concentrated on what appear to me significant events. The Ghanas, the Malis and Song'hai were all much alike, and the changes of power between them made scant difference to the story of Man. I have treated as the most significant piece of ancient history, in the West Sudan, the forlorn Moorish attempt to invade Song'hai; for this Black African military victory had obvious lessons for the future, and determined the next few hundred years of Western Sudanic history.

Similarly, I have spotlighted such events as Napier's invasion of Ethiopia, which opened up that country to the outside world, and the incredible First World War campaign in East Africa, when the fate of the world was partly decided in Tanganyika. On the West Coast, I have attached less importance to the military campaigns and more to trade, the *raison d'être* of Coastal civilization. I have regarded as particularly significant the Niger Delta, the thin end of the British wedge, and to a lesser degree the special colonial status of Senegal – France's spearhead.

Except for a brief analysis of residual colonialism, inter-African strategy in relation to that and other problems, and the issue of African unity, I have ended each country's story, in the second volume, (the older states of Ethiopia, Liberia and South Africa excepted) at independence.

Contemporary proper names and well-known place names are rendered either in the local-usage spelling (Abidjan, Accra, Diori) or, where it exists, the established English spelling (Timbuktu, Addis Ababa, Salee). I accept that these local and English spellings, all based on 'colonial' language laws, are often quite illogical, and that it is absurd to have to know the pronunciation of European tongues in order to pronounce the name of an African tribe (a Kwanyama, for instance, is a Cuanhama in Angola, a Couaniama in Brazzaville, a Kuaniama in ex-German South-West Africa). But some of the 'European' spellings are too established to drop as yet, and clearly a politician – like anyone else – has the right to misspell his name. It makes more sense, in a book in English, to misspell a word Englishly than Frenchly or Portuguesely, if an English misspelling exists. I have written, for instance, Antananarivo, not Tananarive. But for lesser-known places, the phonetical orthography of the International African Alphabet (Nwakshot, Kamerun, Konakri) is universally employed – partly on the assumption that IAA orthography, already used in all vernacular literature, will inevitably become general.

R. W. H.

1 SAND AND SWORD

The Age of African Empires

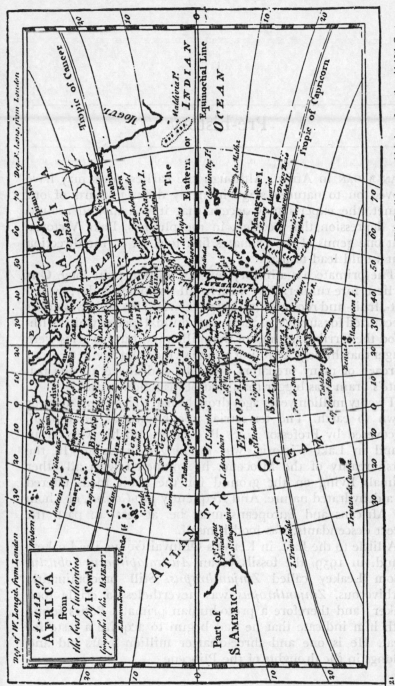

21 The first maps of the full African coastline appeared in the early 16th Century and were a Portuguese state secret. This English map, which dates from the mid-18th Century, shows how little was known of the African interior in the early centuries of trade. The Senegal River is described as the Niger. The Congo is assumed to rise in the Monomotapa's realm, which is assumed to reach almost to the Atlantic. The Nile is assumed to rise North of the Niger. The dates of later maps can be best assessed from the accuracy or inaccuracy of the tracing of the Nile, Senegal, Niger and Congo courses.

Author's collection

Pre-history

MAN BEGAN in Africa. Although the earliest apes may have moved on to nature's stage in many different parts of our planet, the experts now accept that it was in and around the depression that became, in the pluvials, Lake Victoria, that one genus of the primates first took off in the direction that would lead to man.

The primate has a history seventy million years long. Our earliest fore-runner, like nearly all primates today, was a nut-, fruit- and root-masticating vegetarian; his body was not as specialized for survival as most other animal species which withstood the terrible testings of the millennia; but his arms were longer than his legs, enabling him to swing from tree to tree, out of reach of many predatory animals; and above all, the primate's brain was bigger than that of his fellow-beasts.

Twenty million years ago, drought had driven our ancestor down to earth. The terrestrial ape known as *pro-Consul*, discovered by Professor L. S. B. Leakey and his wife on an island in Lake Victoria, was no longer brachiate. In the harsh reality of the Miocene, he competed with all other animals living on the ground for the scant foods offered by a dehydrated nature. And frequently *pro-Consul*, of whom we Africans and Europeans must be, at least in part, the direct descendants, was food himself.

A little to the East, in Kenya's Olduvai Gorge, the Leakeys found, in 1959, the fossils of an *Australopithecus robustus* whom Leakey called *Zinjanthropus*. Still predominantly herbivorous, *Zinjanthropus* was nevertheless a crude toolmaker – and therefore a proto-human primate. Bones found with him indicate that he had begun to acquire a taste for meat. He is one and three-quarter million years old and belongs in the droughts of the Pliocene.

Over thirty years before Leakey's great discovery, at the southern point of the continent, in a mined and destroyed limestone cave, an even closer relative of ours was found. His scientific name is *Australopithecus africanus* (African southern ape) and he is recognizably a man. This thin-featured, eight hundred thousand-year-old African predator was about four feet tall and weighed seventy pounds or so – a sort of Causasian pygmy. His brain was a little bigger than his ancestor of Olduvai – even further away from him, in time, than he is from us – and *A.a.* was so far removed from the high security of the trees, so involved with the daily scramble for life on the treacherous ground that he had, like us, a head that fitted on to his spine in such a way that it could comfortably stay upright. He had our flat feet, for he no longer needed hands on the end of his legs to skim up trees, and he could no longer use his arms to help him sprint. His arms had become short – free for other purposes than locomotion. He had our big behind, concentrating a powerful pattern of muscles that enable us to swing and twist our bodies with far more agility than our fellow apes. Only his agility and his brain saved our ancestor from extinction.

Australopithecus africanus had the dentition, like us, of a carnivore. Absent are the immense molars, thickly covered with three millimeters of enamel, which characterize the eternal chewer, the herbivore. His canine fang had atrophied; as with us today, its roots remained large and bulky, but in length the eye tooth itself, with him as with us, is little bigger than the other front teeth of the upper jaw. *A.a.* was the first truly carnivorous ape. He used the front *humerus* legbone of the antelope as a club, and the teeth-bearing jaws of other beasts as knives. With these weapons, he slew his neighbors and ate them raw. He was that essentially human, un-animal creature, a weapon-maker. He had neither deadly fangs nor claws, for his pads had become sentient and sensitive to feel and touch; but he killed with his brain, his co-ordinating powers, and his elementary, home-made, brain-guided weapons.

Over six hundred fossils of this proto-man exist, thanks to Professor Raymond Dart – an Australian – who also discovered *Australopithecus robustus* earlier than the Leakeys, although not examples of such venerable age as the ape of

5

Olduvai. Since then Leakey has discovered an older cousin of Dart's human ape, another carnivorous, weapon-bearing pygmy whom he calls *Homo habilis*. He is a contemporary of the less human *Zinjanthropus,* one and three-quarter million years old, living in the Pliocene.

Peking or Java man, *Pithecanthropus,* belongs to only four hundred thousand years ago. He may have come from Africa, a wanderer across the millenia, or he may have followed a different but similar evolutionary path from a different but similar – and later – evolutionary beginning in furthest Asia. The earliest known European man dates from only a quarter-million years ago; he presumably moved over from Africa when the glaciers withdrew from Europe; modern man, with his large brain, developed chin and straight profile, comes from only yesterday.

The Pleistocene – the last million years – has been peculiarly favorable to human development, and our species, which had survived twelve million years of quasi-constant African drought and dryness, began to advance fast. In the paleontological flash of a mere quarter-million years, *A.a.'s* brain tripled in size, an extraordinary mutation, and we began not only to forge ahead of the other apes, but to bring about a world largely of our design in which our brother apes would find it difficult, and perhaps impossible, to survive.

❋

The story of Black Africa is the story of many different, frequently disconnected worlds, divided by natural barriers and scattered over a continent over three times as big as the United States. It is also the story of many different external influences from Europe, the Americas, Asia and the Mediterranean.

Little, except science's discoveries of the link between ape and man in eastern and southern Africa, and some highly speculative theories about migrations, is known of Africa's past before the first of these influences, that of Mediterranean Africa, met and conquered the Sahara challenge. The men of the Barbary Shore established considerable empires in the Western Sudan – principally in what is now Mauritania, Mali and Niger. Culturally, religiously,

6

linguistically and politically, North Africa was eventually to become a close extension of the Middle East – that is, of the eastern end of the Mediterranean. In recent years, only a few tenuous Islamic links, and more recently a common international front on certain colonial issues, have created a bond between the two shores of the sand ocean. But in the early centuries of the previous millennium, the face of Mediterranean trade looked both North and South, not only to the ports of Rome, Greece and the Levant, but also across what still remains today as one of the most formidable barriers known to man. Beyond the sea horizon was less daunting a journey. It was not by chance that when the camel, with its in-built food and liquid storage system and its vastly superior speed to the mule, entered the pattern of trans-Sahara trade, it was baptized the ship of the desert.

No Black African nation established itself as a seagoing power, and the (partly religious) dread of the sea was matched by the (well-founded, physical) dread of a desert journey. The relative absence of a spirit of adventure among African nations of the past is historically important. It helps to explain the one-way nature of culture-fusion under colonialism, and even colonialism itself. It determined that moves across the Sahara should be from North to South.

Just as the sands leave no trace of man's passage, so much of Africa's early history is also untraceable. But enough remains to have a general picture of the Upper Nile, the kingdoms of East Africa, the early power struggle in the Western Sudan, the motives of conquest and the fate of the major empires.

*

The history of Black Africa is to a large degree determined by its geography. Africa north of the Sahara is a geographic and cultural mirror of the world to which it is most closely linked: the other Mediterranean shore. The Spaniards, the Greeks, the Sicilians are, in effect, Arabs whose religion theoretically teaches charity instead of the sword. South of the Mediterranean's southern wall comes the arid desert. Further south of this, a new continent commences: stubby grassland rises, then savannah country – tall grass, bushes, occasional trees. Gradually, the forest develops in vast patches

7

– Liberia, the southern Ivory Coast, Ashanti. From the Niger Delta, East and South, it becomes a quasi-permanent reality. There are rain-forests in the Congo as large as the main countries of Europe.

South and East of this Equatorial area great mountains and plateaux reach for the azure sky, cleft by majestic lakes and immense watercourses, determined by the fissures of the Great Rift. Here the climate is often only sub-tropical. These were the areas that for long repelled the African, with the notable exception of certain Nilotics and related peoples – Ethiopia's Amharics and Gallas, the Baganda, the Batutsi – and at once attracted the European.

This is the broad picture of Africa: it is, of course, incomplete. Just south of the damp Ashanti forest lie the semi-arid plains around Accra. Just south of the fair hills around Salisbury lie the humid forests of Natal. Kenya offers the semi-desert of the north, the cool highlands of the center, a sweltering green coast. Until the age of petroleum, much of Africa could be looked upon as inimical to man, and useless. Of eleven million square miles, four and a half million are desert sand.

The sea, as well as the land, affected Africa's development. The rough Atlantic, in the west, may well have seemed unbreachable for centuries – and it is fairly sure that only the sailing prowess of strange peoples from far away, beginning with the Phoenicians, bred the Africans to the sea. The Indian Ocean coast is less formidable. Here the rollers are rare; reef-sheltered shorelines make for calm seas and shoals rich in giant fish. But nowhere is the African, in history, a navigator.

*

In Gamblian times (10,000 BC to the start of the present era) the human type appears to have been boskopoid, in Capricorn Africa. This type of man persists today in the person of the South African bushman. Pygmies may have been contemporary with the earliest Boskops; possibly, they may have come a little later. The Negro – nature's most modern human creation – seems to have made his appearance only as recently as 5000 BC, apparently beginning in East Africa. All these early peoples lived exclusively off hunting.

8

They had known the use of fire since approximately fifty thousand years ago.

In the dry periods between the Kanjeran and Gamblian pluvials, man penetrated the Congolese and Guinean rain-forests. Numerous relics of these inter-pluvial periods have been found, including more varied tools than axs – and more axs than in any other continent. Spearheads and assorted missiles have been unearthed, as well as bone needles, and evidence of string and cosmetics. Possibly the world's earliest bows and arrows date from this period.

In the sixth and seventh millennia BC, evidence of the Capsian culture of the 'proto-Hamites' appears South of the Sahara. These people, who were predominantly caucasoid, are thought to have been of Palestinian origin; the most notable archeological site associated with them lies north of the Sahara – at Gafsa, in Tunisia. With them came a great step forward in human evolution: settled agriculture. Exclusive use of natural recipients was gradually replaced by the fashioning of pottery.

The Sahara, once green and inhabited, began to lose its fertility about six thousand years ago. The rivers dried up, leaving only the tortured *wadis* seen today from the air. Before this desiccation process was too developed, hunting had been partly replaced by pastoralism. Tamed horses appeared – presumably from Arabia – around 1200 BC. By then, raiding and trading were the motives of existence for the more developed communities. The Fezzan route across the desert had been traced and proven, and from the eastern wall of the Mediterranean the Phoenicians – ancestors of to-day's Syrians and Lebanese – were bypassing the Sahara, sailing ships to the west coast of Africa; but knowledge of these maritime routes died with the cultures which had pioneered them.

It was the Sahara which, more than anything else, decreed the arresting of development in Africa, where man began with a few millenia of advance on Europe, and probably on Asia too. The cultural advance stolen by the Middle East, which spread to Europe, would have spread to sub-Sahara Africa as well, if the sand curtain had not determined other-wise. In any case, Africa would have been vast and varied, and most of Africa's climate would have kept the principal

9

areas of inhabitation behind the temperate zone in development, in recent times: but Mediterranean civilization would have spread further than it did, were it not for the Sahara. It is also probably true that the generous availability of land and game discouraged Black Africa, for a long time, from founding fixed civilizations.

*

Three main racial groups are clearly evident in Africa South of the Sahara. These are the Bushmen of the South, the Negroes and the Hamites – the latter being a Caucasian ethnic group. The Hamites, and probably the Negroes too, came from Asia – although both, of course, interbred with Africa's original human species, and with each other. The Bushmen are the direct descendants of African proto-man, which in its day was the most advanced creature – the only human – living.

Interbreedings of these types, and especially between Negroes and Hamitics, are varied and numerous, particularly on the eastern side of Africa. Some of these may be fairly recent, for originally Africa's human population must have been extremely small, and communications over wide areas difficult. Nevertheless, migration was an early dynamic.

Today's Boskops are sometimes taller than the early Bushmen. They and the Pygmies are still hunters. Both are dying out. The Hottentots, another South African group – believed by some researchers to be a Negro-Bushman hybrid – are also on the way to extinction, party by absorption.

Tribal organization, then as now, must have offered a plethora of systems and social laws, repeatedly enriched, modified or transformed by migratory cross-pollenization. Relatively few people in Africa are today where they have 'always' been. Most tribes migrated to their present tribal homelands only within the past few centuries. In these nomadic historical circumstances – exaggerated in the forest areas, where movement was a quasi-annual occurrence – a stagnant culture within a frequently complex social framework was inevitable. Man does not build cathedrals on the way from Stream-where-antelopes to Bad-water-chief-died.

Where a culture of some consequence *has* developed, this has been exceptional; but we are obliged to ascribe much to these exceptions, because by comparison they are notable – and because, if man broadly failed in Africa, he must have failed for circumstantial reasons which the more exceptional African peoples overcame. It is, of course, important not to exaggerate the peaks achieved by these exceptions. Comparisons with Asia and with Europe's past are necessary. The exotic notion of an Africa, dark and benighted, is still basically – as generalizations go – a fair conception; but within this limited context, there was a ferment which had the remarkable quality of being isolated. With only a minimum of pollenization from *extra*-African cultures, the African tribes derived the most complicated religions from their contemplation of fate and nature; ethics and disciplines, usually harsh and hidebound but also often exquisitely involved and sometimes even sagaciously understanding, were handed down, modified by oracular jurisprudence drawn from departed spirits and jealous gods, from father to son, from mother to daughter. A complex herbal pharmacopœia was – almost everywhere in Black Africa – at the service of the countless sick; mining and metalworking were African discoveries; but the greatest developments in the diet were a contribution from the seamen of Portugal and Asia, and the diet changes were a major turning point of African history equally as important as the casting of iron.

Of the five hundred main plants and trees of the modern Congo, three hundred and seventyseven are of Asian and one hundred and seven of American origin: only sixteen are indigenous. One hundred of the five hundred are common foods in the Congo today. The imports include many types of flora generally believed to be African: although modern bananas are seedless, this is due to selective breeding; at one time they must have been propagated by seed and there is therefore very good reason to believe that the banana is, in Africa, an importation. There are wild yams in Africa but these are only different sub-species of the Malayan *dioscorea alata*, *dioscorea bulbifera* and *dioscorea esculenta*. Similarly, the cocoyam, *colocasia antiquorum*, is not found in Africa in a wild form.

Food-growing and stock-breeding probably began to replace hunting in the Nile Valley in the fifth millennium before our era. In the second half of the fourth millennium BC, there

11

were goats in what is now the Sudan – but apparently no crops. In the third millennium BC, the Negroes of the savannah had begun to farm; but the poor, nomadic forest tribes only made the switch from hunting and fishing in the beginning of the Christian era.

The oldest crop is millet, notably in the form of fonio, sorghum or guinea corn – a fact commemorated on the flag of the independent kingdom of Burundi by the presence of a sheaf of millet. The development of farming and improved diets increased longevity and health and raised the continent's population.

In the 16th and 17th Centuries, Portuguese ships began to introduce maize-corn, cassava, groundnuts and fruits, including citrus – mostly from the Americas; from Asia, a little earlier, had come yams, cocoyam, rice and probably the banana. All these made forest-area farming possible, and primitive tribes of huntsmen became sedentary. Today, cassava, yam, rice and maize-corn are the main staples of Africa.

Deep-sea fishing was only introduced by the Nova Scotian Creoles, beginning of course with Sierra Leone. The seine net is first mentioned by Lieutenant Clarkson in 1792, as a Sierra Leonean import from Europe. It reached the Gold Coast in 1907 and is today the hallmark of the nomadic Fanti fisherman.

Language, in Africa, appears to be about five thousand years in age – although clearly there is no definite demarcation lines when the elementary means of primate communication became sophisticated enough to be dignified by reference to linguistics. Early Africa presumably spoke with an even greater number of tongues than Africa employs today – approximately six hundred languages and two thousand dialects. The earlier languages were, of course, inadequate and primitive means of communication by modern standards; but they appear, for the most part, to have developed individually, little influencing each other until comparatively recent times. There were four main groups: in the North and North-East, the languages were Hamito-Semitic; at the southern and south-eastern end of the continent were the languages, characterized by throat-clicking, of the Boskops and later the Hottentots. Elsewhere, the languages could be divided into West Sudanic and East Sudanic. Languages, in other words, could be divided along the same lines as the physical groupings, as one would expect, with the first area of fusion being between Hamitics and Negroes in the East.

Today the broadest set of similarities exist between the various Bantu tongues of the southern half of the continent – which are probably only about two thousand years in age, and presumably originate from the West Sudan. (Some incorporate clicking characteristics.) In modern classifications, linguists differentiate between Bantu, West Sudanic and a middle group, found for instance in Kamerun, of crypto-Bantu or 'semi-Bantu' languages.

Characteristic of nearly all African tongues is the use of suffixes, prefixes and infixes, the employment of tonality to change tense, positivity and other factors, and certain elements of syntax. In modern times, the great vehicular languages of West Africa – Hausa, Bambara – are influenced by Arabic, while the even more important lingua franca of eastern Africa, ki-Swahili, is a 'Bantu' derivation of Arabic. African tongues are rich in material, particularly zoological and botanical, words, but weak in metaphysical and abstract concepts. In recent times, the Senegalese scholar Sheikh Anta Diop has translated a page of Paul Langevin on relativity into Wolof (by using root-meanings, based on the root-meanings of scientific words of Greek or Latin origin) to prove that African languages have unsuspected riches; but it is probably fair to say that African tongues match other inadequacies in African civilizations, where these occur – and that enrichment of African languages has come in recent centuries by contact with Arabic and with various European tongues. Except for Arabic, an impartial and objective view can only doubt whether African languages will survive the technological centuries to come.

Punt and the Zimbabwes

THE EARLIEST BLACK AFRICAN CIVILIZATION was probably in Punt, an area now part of modern Sudan or Somalia. Egypt sought slaves in the black lands at the end of the Red Sea coast, and thus began the southward cultural move from the Middle East. The patterns of trade grew along with Egypt's wealth.

The records of this period are sketchy and incomplete, but we do know that in the 4th Millennium BC, Amratian was importing gold and copper from the Red Sea hills; the ports were built with slave labor. Little is known, either, of the mentality of the people, but both wealth and a preoccupation with the after life are reflected in the burial rites: persons were interred with considerable goods. In Punt, houses with glass windows were built in this period. By the 3rd Millennium BC, silver and lead were being imported from the Aegean Islands, and shipwrights were erecting vessels for sixty oars. Quinquiremes roamed these relatively tame seas seeking ebony, ivory, gold, electrum and perfume materials.

During the 1st Millennium before Christ, an offshoot civilization grew up in Kush – now the Northern Sudan. Here, considerable quantities of bronze were worked. Kush was originally a Caucasian community, but a considerable Negro population, both slave and free, was absorbed as it burgeoned south. The administration and leadership of the state was Caucasian, and the religion was Egyptian.

The power of the state soon challenged that of its great neighbor lying to the North. Finally, Kashta of Kush invaded Egypt, and his son, Piankhy, completed the conquest about 725 BC, to found the twentyfifth or 'Ethiopian' dynasty of Pharaohs. In the following century, the Kushite occupiers were driven South to their own lands by the Assyrians.

Later, possibly to escape the desiccation of the encroaching desert, the capital of Kush was moved from Napata to Meroë, about a hundred miles North of modern Khartum. Impressive ruins of Meroë remain, and huge slag-heaps of the smelters. But today the sands have overtaken and much remains to be unearthed.

In the 4th Century AD, Meroë was conquered by Axum, the Ethiopian kingdom. By this time, Kushite religious beliefs, now a localized variant of the Egyptian faith, and Kushite methods of smelting had spread westward into the desert and perhaps beyond; some modern Nigerian scholars trace Yoruba traditional religion to Kushite origins. About this time the influence of Christianity appears in the area, becoming firmly established in Ethiopia. In its epic period, Kush was in commerce with Arabia, India and even China, and cosmopolitan influences penetrated.

The kingdoms and chieftaincies to the South of Kush, in Ethiopia and East Africa, were similar, and relate to Semitic invasions from Arabia several centuries BC. The survival of Christianity among the Amharics dates from the 4th Century of our era, when the early Ethiopians were converted by Byzantine priests of the Roman Empire. The Lion of Judah, as Ethiopia's reigning Emperor is always known, does not descend from Solomon and the Queen of Sheba, as a fanciful legend seeks to prove; but his official title of 'Negus' (*Negusa Nagast*) goes back at least to the 3rd or 4th Centuries AD, when it was the style in use by the King of Habashat and Axum. Apparent Ethiopian influences which are found much further South today, and even down to South Africa, are terraced farming, drystone building and hilltop fortresses.

The Azanian iron-age 'civilization' of Kenya was more humble in its achievements – but it endured until a few centuries ago. Here the Semitic framework of society was thinner. The vast ruined town of Engaruka is the most notable known vestige of Azania. It seems likely that the kingdom originated further North and was driven South by Islam. Azania finally broke up under pressure from the warriors of such Nilotic tribes as the Luo, the Masai, the Bahima and the wa-Nyika.

The Bahima, like the Batutsi of Rwanda and Burundi, imposed a feudal system similar to medieval Europe's. The

15

upper caste owned cattle as symbols of wealth and prestige, and engaged in gentle arts like spinning poetry and cloth. The Bahima's client class was the Baïru tribe; the Batutsi had the Bahutu. The Rwandese kingdom lasted until 1960, when elections brought in republican rule. The kingdom of Burundi lasted until 1966.

Somalia has a similar history of a Hamitic civilization imposing itself on Negro hunters and pastoralists. Another influence in the area were the Shirazi or Persians, whose mark remains in the principal mosque of Zanzibar and the Husuni Kubwa Palace site on Kilwa Island. These date from the 10th-12th Centuries AD. Little is known of how the Hamito-Semitic civilizations themselves grew up, or the circumstances in which they penetrated and colonized Africa.

*

Just as early European curiosity about East Africa was dogged by the legend of Prester John, the charismatic head of a doughty Christian community in the heart of darkest Africa, so European curiosity about the southern third of the continent is typified by stories about the kingdom of the Monomotapa. 'Prester John', presumably, was just a false view of Ethiopia or its King. The Monomotapa genuinely existed – although it is difficult to assess the real importance of his inland kingdom. There appear to have been more seamen's and traders' stories than fact, and when the domain was finally breached by the Portuguese, the travelers were disappointed. Nevertheless the Monomotapa ruled a considerable realm with some semblance of methodical administration, comparable to that of some contemporary monarchs in feudal and post-feudal Europe.

Barbosa, the Portuguese captain, writing of the Moçambique coast in 1517, said: 'Beyond this country, toward the West, lies the great kingdom of Benametapa, belonging to the heathen whom the Moors call Kaffirs: they are black men and go naked except from the waist.' Travelers from this kingdom reached the coast wearing tailed skins and bearing swords, bows, arrows and assegais with iron tips.

Relating what these warriors from the bush told him, Barbosa says: 'Two or three weeks' journey up-country is a

16

large town called Zimbaoche, in which are many houses of wood and straw. It belongs to the pagans, and the King of Benametapa often stays there; it is six days' march from there to Benametapa, which is on the route leading from Sofala to the Cape of Good Hope. In this town of Benametapa is the King's usual residence, in a very large building, and from there the traders carry the gold down to Sofala and give it, un-weighed, to the Moors for colored cloth and beads, which they prize greatly.'

Goës, writing a little later, says: 'In the middle of this country is a fortress built of large and heavy stones inside and out.' He calls the building 'curious and well-constructed . . . as according to what people say no lime to join the stones can be seen.' Goës talks of similar forts, commanded by the King's captains, elsewhere in the realm. He adds: 'The King of Benametapa keeps great state, and is served on bended knees with much reverence.'

The principal edifice, with – according to Barros, another Portuguese traveler who had never seen it – walls 'more than twenty-five spans in width', was presumably what is today called Great Zimbabwe, just off the Johannesburg–Salisbury road, in Rhodesia. Great Zimbabwe is probably over one thousand years in age. It has been frequently repaired and extended and the most modern ruins date from the 18th Century. The buildings are tall and massive, decorated with soapstone bird-gods. The doorways are ornamental. The buildings seem to be entirely African in style, with no trace-able foreign influences, although oriental porcelain, obviously bought on the coast, lies among the ruins of the decorations.

Modern Rhodesia and Zambia contain many lesser sites of this nature. The people who lived in this culture bought with copper crosses, such as still exist in Katanga, or with H-shaped copper ingots. The Phoenicians, who according to Herodotus circumnavigated Africa in the 7th Century, may have introduced the *handa,* an H ingot found in Phoenician vestiges in England. Alternatively the *handa* may have reached southern Africa from Phoenicia via Egypt and the Nile Valley. Either way, this distinctive 'coin' points to an early pattern of trans-continental or coastal trade, or to both.

There is evidence of several different cultures having

succeeded each other in the Zimbabwean settlements; that of the Mashona dates probably – according to one source – from the 12th Century (when they seem to have come South from the Zambezi) to about 1450, then again from around 1500 to 1700; about this time, the Rozwi, under their Mambo (King), overthrew the Monomotapa. The Rozwi are then thought to have refashioned and enlarged Great Zimbabwe. Later the Rozwi were displaced by the Nguni, coming from the South.

In 1835, the last Mambo of the Rozwi was flayed alive by the Swazi (whose present tribal homeland is a small country entirely surrounded by South Africa). The Swazi burned the Mambo's palace, *Thabas ka Mambo*. Three years later, the Zulu *impi* of Mzilikazi, who had broken away from the tyrannous Shaka, conquered the Swazi. Descendants of the Rozwi and Nguni are today a part of the Ndebele – in modern times, Matabele – while part of the Nguni are also the modern Zulu.

One important trace of the Monomotapa's kingdom was discovered in 1932, when a farmer called van Graan and his son and three friends climbed a tree-covered 'chimney' in a cliff at Mapungubwe, a South African village near the Limpopo River frontier with Rhodesia. At the top they found a royal burial ground thick with gold objects and other relics of a pre-European culture. A score of lesser sites were found in other parts of the Transvaal, with characteristic terracing, fortresses and considerable drystone dwellings.

The van Graan discovery and others show that the people in question buried their royalty flexed – standing. Cattle also got ceremonial burials. The skeletons suggest the people were Bushmen, Hottentots or a variation or combination of either or both. Later the dominant stock in the area was to be mostly Negro, but including strains from the Hottentot and other pre-Negro ethnes; researchers postulate that the original culture may have included a non-Negro ruling class. The goldsmiths of the culture are believed to have been a Negro people coming from the North. Reverence for cattle as symbols of wealth and prestige are common to many southern and eastern African peoples today.

The Iron Age began comparatively early in this part of

Africa. Adrisi, the Arab traveler-scholar, writing in 1154, reports on the export of iron from coastal settlements near the Limpopo mouth. In the 16th Century, the Portuguese established 'captaincies' in the Indian Ocean area. Sofala, the port for the Monomotapa's realm and the richest of the captaincies, was headed in the early 17th Century by Luiz de Figueiredo Falcão, formerly secretary to Felipe II, who gave him the post in 1607. In his three years – the usual period of tenure – Figueiredo reputedly made two hundred thousand *cruzados,* a tax-free sum equal to nearly a million dollars in modern money. This gives us some idea of the commercial development of the realm the Monomotapas ruled. As will be seen in the second part of this book, on pre-colonial Africa, the Portuguese ambition to link Angola and Moçambique dates from this early time.

Not much is known of African tribal government in the period, but it is clear that the Monomotapas, although strong and frequently tyrannous, were never absolute monarchs. Tribal custom and uncodified oral law guaranteed a measure of democracy – and presumably of anarchy. Most African populations on the eastern side of the continent had not reached the point of development where they could identify with an absolute sovereign – the simplistic, disciplined pattern whereby Euro-America's medieval ancestors achieved the beginnings of order, the forerunner of 'civilization'. The West African kingdoms were often, in this and other respects, to be more advanced than those of the East.

Materially, the Monomotapa's realm – or at least his court – enjoyed undoubted prosperity, hence the goldsmiths and artisans, the import of Chinese porcelain and silky Indian finery. The kingdom appears to have been amply self-sufficient in crops and game. As in medieval Europe, life was almost luxurious for a privileged few. Total illiteracy limited the creation of a true civilization, but travelers were impressed by the relative social dynamism, the willingness to try new ideas, the uninhibited copying of the Portuguese.

By the 19th Century, when the area was thoroughly penetrated for the first time in many decades, the original hopeful signs of pre-civilization noted by the early Portuguese explorers had disappeared. The hypotheses are numerous, but presumably internecine war and dynastic conflicts –

19   B

which had always been common, and in which the Portuguese often felt obliged to intervene on one side or the other – led to the extinction of the early culture.

In 1856, the explorer-missionary-doctor David Livingstone, on his way down the Zambezi to the coast, wrote that the 'only evidence of greatness possessed by his (the Monomotapa's) successor is his having about a hundred wives,' adding that 'when he dies, a disputed succession and much fighting are expected'.

The pacific or warlike characteristics of the tribes in South-Central Africa varied greatly. Livingstone, on the whole, found most tribes helpful. Henry Stanley, his explorer contemporary, had to fight for his life almost every mile of the way for long stretches of the Congo Valley. Dues, frequently exorbitant, were exacted by organized brigandage almost everywhere. But in most of southern Africa, actual violence to travelers appears to have been reasonably exceptional; sometimes these unaccountable white visitors were fed, nursed to health or helped by natives without apparent desire for gain.

*

West Africa was to achieve an advance on the East which has not been lost today; but the peoples of the West have their origins in the East and the North. According to legend, Kush was the son of Ham, the grandson of Noah. Kush's progeny fathered the Qaran, the Zaghawa, the Habeshar (Ethiopians), the Copts and the Berbers, the latter being the tribe that, well before Christ, had established itself to the North and West of the desert. The Hamitic legend gave birth in turn to many others, of which the Yoruba belief in a Nile Valley origin is one. Most West African peoples either came, or believe they came, from the East or North; science seems to agree with the tribal legends.

The earliest West African cultures known are those connected with Stone Age tools found near Jos, in Northern Nigeria; these are about forty thousand years old. In 1931, at Nok, in Zaria Province, terra cotta heads were discovered. This and later diggings in the area proved the existence of an early pre-civilization on the Nigerian plateaux. It appears to date from about 1000 BC to just after the death of Christ.

The Nok people had villages, and in addition to stone tools made decorations and jewelry.

To the Arabs, all countries South of the northern desert were *Bilad as-Sudan* – the 'Land of the Blacks'. Hence the languages of the area are known today as Sudanic or West Sudanic, and the desert, savannah and grassland area of West Africa is usually described as the Western Sudan. Before the Arabs, the Berbers called the land South of the desert *Akal 'n-Iguinawen*, from which first the Portuguese, then Europe in general, got the name Guinea, which now refers to the forest belt on or near the West African coast – the area south of the Western Sudan. It is not true that Guinea is a corruption of Ghana, or a misspelling of *gine*, the Susu word for woman – a theory based on the assumption that this was the first word seamen learned in foreign languages.

The worlds of the Mediterranean and the Western Sudan were in contact from ancient times. The size and extravagance of Lepcis Magna, the restored Roman city near Tripoli, suggests that it was the terminus of the Fezzan trade route across the desert. In the 5th Century BC, Herodotus says, the Garamantes (the Berbers of the Fezzan, the desert in the South of modern Libya) raided the 'Ethiopians' (that is, the 'Blacks') with light, horse-drawn chariots. Numerous rock-drawings bear evidence to the truth of Herodotus' account. The drawings are found along two routes, running respectively from the Fezzan and from southern Morocco to the Timbuktu loop of the Niger River.

The desert Berbers had probably had contact with the Negroes since the pluvial of the 5th–6th Century BC, when the Sahara was rippling grassland. Presumably, the two groups met frequently as they moved South and North into the prairie pastures. Later the desiccation of the desert was to divide these two pastoral worlds, making contact between them a matter of trade and war – and a test of endurance for both the warrior and the trader.

Given the perils of a voyage on the sand ocean, most trans-Saharan trade was inevitably in goods of a 'luxury' nature that carried a concomitant price. The exception was salt, carried southward from the desert and eastward from the Atlantic. From Guinea came gold, the principal origins being 'Wangara' and from mines in what later was called the Gold Coast. Other Guinean exports were kola nuts – one of the few stimulants permitted by Islam – and tusk ivory. Maghribi products, apart from salt, were horses, cattle, beads, trinkets and other metal goods, copper, cloth and cowries. The latter, used as currency, came from the Indian Ocean via Egypt.

Other currencies in use beside cowries included gold dust, blocks of salt, pieces of iron or copper or bolts of cloth. All these had roughly fixed values in terms of each other and of cowries, then the 'standard'. In addition to importing cloth and colored beads, the Sudanese countries also made their own, weaving lambs' wool and forging beads of glass such as are still produced in large quantities at Bida in Northern Nigeria. Slavery appears not to have been a feature of the Sudanese trade until the arrival of Islam in the western desert.

It seems likely that the changeover from tribal, 'clan' living to the notion of the elementary nation-state was the most important Guinean culture-import from North Africa. The North Africans possessed horses and camels before the Negroes, and this was yet another of the reasons why the dynamics of migration were from North to South. Territorial states emerged when the invaders appointed Governors on a territorial basis, rather than administrators for each ethnic group or tribe. The conquerors became absorbed, and 'states' were thus bequeathed to those who had once been the 'vassal' people. Modern colonialism, by giving reasonably viable states to every part of Africa, has carried the process further forward.

iii

Arab, Berber and Negro: the Almoravids

To FOLLOW THE VICISSITUDES of the Black African empires of the Western Sudan, it is necessary first to look briefly

North, to the Arab and Berber shore of the Mediterranean, the cradle of modern civilization.

African history, it has been said, springs to a considerable extent from the Sahara – which sprang, itself, from an only partly understood natural process of diminishing annual rainfalls. Geographically speaking, the whole Sahara transformation took place rapidly; the earlier notion that the Mediterranean coast of Africa was 'green' until the present era has been discounted. The rainfall on the coast appears to have changed very little over the past two thousand five hundred years at least. Yet Lepcis Magna had in its day at least sixty thousand inhabitants, and the water supply was sufficient for great cisterns and public baths. With about the same rainfall as now – seven or eight inches yearly, often less – the area was the granary of Rome and, agriculturally, must have resembled modern Kenya. In the days of Rome, and even more in the time of Carthage, elephants were common in the region, and substantial other roaming game.

As Bovill has proved, the whole human and agricultural achievement was the result of judicious catchment and irrigation. Cirta (Constantine) drew its water from twenty miles away, Caesarea from nineteen, Carthage from nearly ninety miles, by the use of enormous aqueducts. The water requirements of a Mediterranean Arab farmer are today put at one and a half gallons a day, or a fifth of the consumption of a farmer in tropical Africa. Assuming that these requirements were no heavier in ancient times, we can say that in Tripolitania, with an eight-inch rainfall, a catchment of one hundred and fifty square feet – an area just over twelve feet square – would provide this much. When Hadrian arrived in Africa, we are told, rain fell for the first time in five years – ample evidence that natural aridity was already well advanced, and that the desert coast blossomed thanks not to nature but to the work of Roman engineers.

In the Syrtis – now the central Libyan coast – desiccation reached its most relentless pace of growth; whenever cultivation ceased, with the collapse of Roman dams and massive cisterns, sands spread rapidly, and in a few decades the cities disappeared beneath them. Beside nature, other destroyers were the Beni Hilal – the Arabs of Egypt. Unlike the earlier Arab invaders of the 7th and 8th Centuries

23

AD, the Beni Hilal destroyed, or failed to preserve – and gave nothing in return.

The dry river beds or *wadis* which are such a distinctive feature of the Sahara are of course the work of nature. Most were rivers in the Quaternary, well before human times, when the rainfall was good. Some still flow for a short period each year. Large game survived until fairly recently. Lions, ostriches and hartebeest were seen in the Atlas well within present living memory, and leopards may still exist in these Moroccan fastnesses; but the elephant – smaller than that found today in tropical Africa – was eliminated by hunting in the early Christian era. The animal was sought for its use in war, its ivory, and the cartilage of its trunk, a stand-by of Roman cooks. As Bovill notes, huge quantities of fauna were massacred at the Roman games. Under Pompey, on one memorable afternoon, six hundred lions battled with the gladiators. Titus celebrated the inauguration of the Colosseum with games that cost the lives of nine thousand beasts, as well as thousands of gladiators. Trajan supposedly had 2,246 animals killed in a single day. But the main destroyer of game was the encroaching aridity, hastened by the destruction of the forests by encroaching man.

Residual desert fauna are the giraffe, the oryx, the sand monkey, Barbary sheep, desert foxes, lynxes, some gazelles and antelopes, and possibly a few lions and leopards. Many of these beasts can go without water for months or years, and some, including the desert sheep, goat and ass, do not drink from birth to death. The camel only drinks when worked – and even then some Red Sea camels drink sea-water.

The desert life that was hard or impossible for animals was difficult enough for man. Nomadic pastoralism was the only possibility. Toughness was a condition of survival, and the fight to preserve wells – or to capture those of others when one's own dried up – was naturally elemental and merciless. Today, the desert nomads live much as they have always lived, moving into the green country of sedentary peoples in the hot season, then moving back to a desolation in which man can only just survive for a short lifespan.

Historically, when desert pastures failed all the year round, and wells and boreholes dried up, the nomads might raid or even conquer the sedentary settlements. The courage, mobility and endurance of the desert pastoralists always made them a redoubtable foe for the sedentary cultivators. These battles resume much of the history of the Western Sudan, for there was for many centuries no real defense against the incursions. The twelfth dynasty of Pharaohs built a wall from Heliopolis to Pelusium to hold back nomads. The Assyrians created a barrier on the Euphrates against the Medes, and the Persians built a wall against the savage Huns. The Great Wall of China was to check the Mongols. No such remarkable defenses could be – or at any rate were – attempted on the western fringe of the Sahara. The best defense was a strong government and administration, able to call on extensive forces; such governments did eventually emerge.

Nomadic raiding has grown rarer in recent centuries, and is now quasi non-existent; but when strong government checked raiding it also often went too far and put an end to the previously peaceful seasonal migration of pastoralists – who were then obliged to fight among themselves for the little the desert, to which they were confined, had to offer. This was another characteristic cause of conflict in up-country West Africa. The desert's impoverished resources were strained to the limit, hastening the process of desiccation and reducing the number of oases.

In recent times, the crushing of slave-raiding in the Western Sudan also affected the oases. The desert pastoralists abhorred agriculture, and entrusted the cultivation of the oases to their Negro slaves. From the Nile to the Atlantic, in the dry season, the hardy Muslim peoples of the desert-fringe grasslands raided Negro 'Guinea' for slaves, selling the surplus into the desert itself. When British and French administration stopped slaving, the desert lords neglected the oases and the sands reclaimed many of them.

For mobility the desert tribes had a limited choice of animal transport. Loaded oxen need water twice a week, a camel three times a month. Both do about twenty miles a day, and carry a similar load – although the bullock takes a longer day to cover the distance. The riding camel, the *mehari,* is of course a much faster animal than the pack camel. Perhaps the basic desert animal is the donkey, which also does about twenty miles a day, carries about half as múch as a bullock or a camel, and needs no water. But the camel, introduced into Egypt by the Persians in the 6th Century BC (the quaternary camel was never tamed, and did not survive into historical times) is the desert animal *par excellence*.

The earliest peoples to cross the desert went, however, without any beasts of burden. In the time of Herodotus – who heard the story at second hand – five sons of Nasamonian chiefs of the Greater Syrtis set out West with water and provisions; finally, after weeks of march, they came to 'trees laden with fruit'. While they were gathering the fruits, they were surprised and captured by people they described later as 'black dwarfs'. Their captors took them across extensive swamps to a city by a great East-West river filled with crocodiles. Finally released, they made their way across the desert, home. Herodotus, like his informants, assumed they had found the upper reaches of the Nile; but it was presumably the Niger they saw.

The first great civilizing influence in Africa was Carthage. During their thousand years' occupation of the African Mediterranean, the Carthaginians' interest was principally commercial. They roved the western Mediterranean and went beyond the Pillars of Hercules – modern Gibraltar. Eventually, political and economic interests obliged the Carthaginians to acquire an empire in Africa, where the numerous natural harbors made ideal bases for a trading people. Carthage itself was a fine harbor, on a relatively easily defended promontory, close to the great trade routes. Their second city, Gades (Cadiz) helped guard the Straits of Gibraltar from the other side.

Treaties excluded the Romans from the Carthaginian trading empire. A Roman ship, forced to seek shelter in a Punic port, had to leave once weather and repairs made this possible. The Carthaginian alone could penetrate the Straits, since beyond these lay the secret source of Carthaginian tin – Brittany and Cornwall. The Roman writer Strabo recalls how a Gades captain bound for Cornwall, finding himself shadowed by a Roman galley, ran his ship aground, losing both vessel and cargo – but taking his pursuer with him. All the North African coast west of Cyrenaica (modern eastern Libya) was Punic 'territory'.

The main products of Carthaginian enterprise were carbuncles, (European) slaves, gold, tusk ivory and ostrich feathers. The last two came from North Africa itself. The Fezzan route was principally used for gold. The Carthaginians slaved mainly to the North – both for themselves and for sale. An important source for this commodity was the Balearic group, where the lusty islanders would sell three or four men for one woman.

Negro slaves were not a prominent feature of the Carthaginian domains, although there were Negro Carthaginians, both slave and free – and Negroes in the Carthaginian army which invaded Sicily in the 5th Century BC, as skulls in Punic cemeteries reveal. Frontinus records that as prisoners of war they were paraded naked before the Greeks to instil contempt for Carthage in the soldiery. Most of Carthage's slaves were either bought or seized in war; there was relatively little raiding, but Carthage's own peasants, and the Berbers of the neighboring desert, were probably enslaved when demand surpassed supply. The few Negro slaves of Carthage must have come from the Fezzan – the southern Libyan desert. The Garamantes, who hunted the Negro troglodytes, must have sold the fruit of the hunt, and Carthage was the best customer of the Garamantes.

Gold also reached Carthage by the Garamantes road, from the Fezzan to Lepcis Magna. Another gold trail was the Taghaza route from the Niger at Timbuktu to Sijilmasa in Morocco. The origins of the gold were still a secret for the Mediterranean trading peoples – a secret closely guarded for another two millennia.

Herodotus recounts that it was known that there were two sources – 'a country in Libya, and another beyond the Pillars of Hercules'. Without knowing where 'Wangara' and the gold-producing country 'beyond the Pillars' really were, he explains how when traders came to the coastal country (modern Ghana) that handled the production of the second source, the visitors would lay their wares out on the beach, return to their ships and then contrive a smoke signal. The natives would emerge from the bush and leave gold beside the goods. They would then withdraw. The Carthaginians would return to the shore and see how much gold had been offered. If it was enough, they would take their price and

27

go. If not, they would return to their ship and wait. The natives would come and add more gold dust. This would go on until both sides were satisfied. The intense suspicion which this method of trading shows may have been provoked by the fear of slave-raiding.

It was probably in the 5th Century BC that the Carthaginians sent their famous convey of sixty galleys with several thousand men and women to found Colonies on the West African coast. The expedition was led by the Suffete Hanno. Two days from Gibraltar, Hanno founded Thymiaterium – modern Mehedia at the mouth of the Wadi Sebu. Farther down the coast the pioneers built a shrine to Poseidon, then continued southward to plant five more Colonies. Collecting interpreters among the Lixitae, they pushed their voyage further. The next outpost settled was probably modern Arguin, off the Atlas coast. Further on they found a river filled with crocodiles and hippopotami – presumably the Senegal at modern Saint-Louis. This river, if they had known, led to some of the goldfields of 'Wangara'. Another river mouth which they charted was presumably the Gambia, and the journey southward from there includes a description of a great volcanic eruption – almost certainly Mount Kamerun.

They found a gulf which they called the Southern Horn, and which may have been the Ogowe, and here they came upon an island full of savage, hairy people, mostly women, whom the Lixitae were convinced were gorillas. Efforts to catch the men failed, but three women were taken. These bit and scratched so much they had to be put to death. Their skins were taken back to Carthage. Modern science believes the victims were a hirsute breed of pygmies.

As the voyagers were running out of supplies, they turned North, and the ships finally found their way back to Carthage. Presumably the southern part of the trip, beyond the area of the 'Colony', was a search for gold. Lack of mention of any reason for the journey's second phase suggests this was the case.

The first Europeans to explore the coast were the Portuguese in the days of Prince Henry the Navigator. They also sought the origins of the gold dust trade. They may have been encouraged to press further South, to the Cape itself, by the unsubstantiated legend that the Phoenicians, under Pharaoh Necho (609-588 BC) had circumnavigated the continent.

*

When Rome defeated Carthage, it inherited Carthage's far-flung imperial responsibilities. Apart from the Provincia Africa around Carthage city, the Romans decided to leave the rest to the native rulers. They thus set the precedent for indirect rule, and gave a name to the continent. The association of the name Africa with Carthage city is recalled in the treaty between the Bey of Tunis, Husaïn Pasha, and France in 1830: his realm is called the *Royaume d'Afrique*. By the time of the Emperors, all the Maghribi coast, from Lepcis to the Pillars, was part of the Provincia.

Like all other colonizing peoples, the Romans found that their responsibilities grew year by year. Incursions from the nomads made even the coastal fringe of Africa hard to hold. Perhaps not appreciating the seasonal nature of the moves – and the economic necessity for the nomads, in the dry season, to seek pasture for their beasts in sedentary territory – the Romans resolved to keep the nomads, peaceful or warrior, within the desert permanently. Roman efforts to keep the Berbers permanently at bay made all the nomads the sworn enemies of Rome. Their tents and oases became a meeting ground for the rebels of the sprawling Empire. The Romans responded by trying to garrison the northernmost oases.

From the three towns of the Emporia – Lepcis, Oea and Sabratha, from which Tripolitania got its name – the Romans resumed the trade which the Carthaginians had had with the warrior Garamantes; but the enmity between the desert and Rome soon made itself felt in this area too.

Herodotus describes the Garamantes as 'very powerful'; Tacitus calls them 'invincible'. In the Fezzan – then referred to as Phazania – they lived in a series of oases, with their capital at Garama, modern Germa. Their whole territory extended eastward to the Nile and northward to the Syrtis coast of the Mediterranean. An originally Caucasian (Tebu) people who had interbred with their Negro slaves, the Garamantes practised a local form of the Egyptian faith. Their modern descendants are the Qaran. It seems likely that, like the other nomads, they had preferred the mercantile Carthaginians as coastal trading partners to the military Romans; friction with Rome was constant.

A few decades BC, the Romans took the perilous decision to send an army into the Fezzan to subdue the troublesome Berber-speaking tribe, who had recently helped the rebellious Gaetuli against the colonizers. In view of the temerity of putting legions into the desert, we may assume the Romans acted after prolonged provocation. The desert legions were placed under the command of a Spaniard, Lucius Cornelius Balbus. His campaign was successful, and Balbus became the first foreigner to be accorded a 'triumph' on his return to Rome.

The conquest was to remain unchallenged for nearly a century. Then, in AD 69, Lepcis went to war with Oea, which successfully called for help on the Garamantes. The Legate of Numidia, Valerius Festus, hurried to the aid of Lepcis. He defeated Oea and their allies, the Garamantes, and would have pursued the latter far into the desert if they had not filled in their precious wells as they retreated. At this point, the Romans and the Garamantes came to a warriors' peace; in the years that followed, the desert tribe helped the Romans make two long, camel-borne trans-Sahara expeditions, reaching the Tibesti in modern Niger.

The camel was then a new feature of desert transport. It was at Thapsus, in 46 BC, that the Romans had first seen tamed camels, when they captured twentytwo of them from Berber irregulars. The camel was probably brought into the Western desert by the Zenata Berbers, (who produced the dynasties of the Merinids of Fez and the Abd al-Wadites of Tlemcen). The Zenata appear to have originated East of Cyrenaïca, in modern western Egypt. With their camels they reached and settled as far as the Atlas mountains of Morocco.

Roman use of the camel, as a military 'transport', probably came some time after the incident at Thapsus. The camel was to be to desert warriors, for nearly two thousand years, what the air force has been to modern arms. The camel gave rapidity, mobility and a range of action never dreamed of. It brought an end to the age of clan feuds, and a beginning of the age of large-scale African warfare. It also brought the great ports, like Lepcis, within the reach of every trading community in the western desert.

It was under Septimus Severus, who became Emperor in 193, that Lepcis reached its *apogée*. This Lepcis-born Carthaginian, who was to die at York in 211, made the terminus of the gold and carbuncles trail one of the great ports of the Mediterranean. He strengthened the defenses of the Limes Tripolitanus, and generally sought to build up his native state, installing oil presses and planting thousands of olive trees – some of which are still alive today.

Much of the desert's history remains incomplete and always will. In the remote Hoggar of the central Sahara, near the oasis of Abalessa, there stand the ruins of a large fortified house in a style still practised by the Tebu of Tibesti but not by the modern Twareg. Tradition always said it was the home of a Queen, Tin Hinan, who arrived from Tafilelt in southern Morocco on a white camel, and from whom the ruling clan of the local Twareg claim descent. Then, excavation revealed a tomb – and the tomb contained the bones of a woman of the Pharaonic, royal type. On the arms of the skeleton were silver and gold bracelets; on the breast a gold pendant, and chalcedony and other beads; the tomb also contained aggrey beads, a fertility charm, herbs, dates, grain, Roman milk-bowls, Constantinian coin and other gifts. Where Tin Hinan came from and why – and how and why she became the ruler of such a remote wilderness – has never been explained.

•

Of all the white desert peoples whom the Romans called the Libyans – and whom the Arabs called the Berbers – the most important in ancient times were indisputably the Twareg (sing., Targwi). These people, since some time before AD 1000, have worn a *litham* or veil across their features – presumably for remote religious reasons which have now been lost – and are therefore known in modern Arabic as *Muleth 'themin,* the Veiled People. The Twareg subdivide into clans, the most historically significant being the Sanhaja clan.

There are two castes, the ruling Imajeghan and the Imghad serfs. Their Temajegh tongue is written in T'ifinagh script, partly derived from ancient Libyan calligraphy. Although Muslims, the Twareg – as Bovill points out – appear to have been partly followers of Mithras at some time in their past, and there are Christians traditions too. They are, for instance, monogamous, and their favorite ornamental *motif* is the cross. They wear it in jewelry and on their shields, where it is depicted rising out of an heraldic sea of glory; their swords are cross-hilted, the great pommels of their camel saddles are formed in a cross, and many other articles of daily Targwi life are also cruciform. Further possible evidence of a Christian influence in their past is the association of angels (*andjelous*) with their conception of God, and the use of Samuel, David and Saul as names.

Twareg camel-drivers controlled the Ghadames–Ghat road (to the Hausa country), the Lepcis (or Tripoli)–Fezzan– Kawar road (the Garamantian road to Bornu, the kingdom around Lake Chad), and the Cyrenaïca–Kufra–Wadaï road. They shared the Sijilmasa–Walata road with the Berabish – Berberized Arabs. Broadly speaking, the Twareg shared the whole desert and the northern fringes of what we today call the Western Sudan with migratory Arabs and Jews. These other peoples preserved, to a large degree, a separate identity from the Berbers in the desert, but were absorbed into the populations in the more thickly inhabited Negro countries of the Sudan.

The two main Jewish migrations appear to have met in the Futa chain of modern central and northern Guinea; the cattle Fulani who spread from there across up-country West Africa, and particularly across Northern Nigeria, are strongly infused with a Jewish strain – although today, like almost all the peoples of the West Sudan, they are Islamized.

From the 4th–7th Centuries, North Africa was wracked by religious persecutions, rebellions and feudal wars. The Caesars' law, the *pax romana*, degenerated into chaos. The first advance of the Arabs West from Egypt began in 642. Religious zeal was already partly spent by then, and lust for conquest of a new province – the Maghreb (West) – was the true motive. In 678, the assault was renewed, and under Oqba ibn Nafi they swept triumphantly to the Atlantic – where Oqba spurred his horse into the ocean to mark his triumph. His great military achievement was to prove short-lived. Everywhere the Berbers rose; under one of their kings, Qoceïla, and with aid from the Greeks – who were disturbed by the spread of the Arabs -- the desert warriors killed Oqba and massacred his forces near Biskra in 683. They razed Kairwan and pursued the remnants of the invaders all the way to Egyptian soil.

A few years later, Hassan, the Arabs' Governor of Egypt, set out on a renewed attempt to subdue the Maghreb. He rebuilt Kairwan and razed the great trading site of Carthage. Again the Berbers rallied, under a shrill Zenata prophetess named Kahenah. The Arabs were held at bay until 703, when Kahenah went down to defeat. Again the victory was short-lived and it was only five years later that the Arabs, under Musa ibn Noseïr, finally returned to the Atlantic shore.

Thousands of Berbers converted to Islam, and with the aid of these new warriors the horsemen pushed on into Spain in 711. In contrast to their negative record in politics and culture in North Africa, in Spain the Arabs were to render of their best; modern Spanish and Portuguese culture owes much to them.

The occupation of the Maghreb was constantly challenged; for three centuries, war was commoner than peace. Finally, in the 11th Century, the Berbers drove the Arabs back once more against the Nile. A few decades later the nomadic Beni Hilal and Beni Soleïm, driven from their native Arabia, challenged the Berber stronghold – urged on by the Fatimite Qalif of Cairo, who was anxious to be rid of them. The two hundred thousand Bedawin were of the same 'invincible' warrior stripe as the Twareg. The Beni Soleïm remained in Cyrenaïca; the Beni Hilal pushed on West, sowing a bitter trail of blood. The great Arab historian ibn Khaldun compared them to a swarm of locusts. They desiccated the oases, swiftly used up the remaining forests and instilled a culture that never rose intellectually above the sword.

The Berbers, among the most zealous racial purists known to history, withdrew into the mountain areas of South Morocco and the central desert associated with them today. Bovill writes:

'The persistence with which the Berbers have maintained their purity of race has constantly astonished the ethnologists. In spite of the introduction into their country of Phoenician,

Roman, Vandal, Jewish and Arab blood, they show few traces of alien stock. Particularly striking is the way in which Berbers and Arabs have failed to amalgamate. Although they have lived in the closest proximity for over a thousand years, during which the Arab has imposed his religion, language. dress and many of his customs on a large part of the Berber population, the latter have preserved their distinct racial type. In the Aures mountains, for example, only about 25 per cent of the population have dark eyes. The Arab remains primarily a herdsman, dwelling in tents, fanatical and deeply superstitious, with a feudal tribal organization. The Berber, on the other hand, is a highlander, a tiller of the soil, and a dweller in towns and villages; he is essentially democratic; although capable of fanatical outbursts, he is rarely moved by religious enthusiasms.'

The Berbers, like the Jews, intermarried when they found themselves among Negro peoples, but kept their distance from Arab neighbors.

One positive result of the Arab occupation of the Western desert was the interest it drew, to this part of the world, of Arabic scholars – who often accompanied, by camel or ship, the trading expeditions. For our knowledge of the history of the Western Sudan, we owe everything today to such writers as al-Bakri, al-Adrisi, ibn Battuta, ibn Khaldun, ibn Haukal, al-Omari, Yaqut and indirectly Masudi.

Masudi, a 10th Century Baghdad scholar, was the master of many of them. Although his area of travel was the Indian Ocean – China and Madagascar – he influenced many Arab students of the Sudan. Ibn Haukal, also of Baghdad, was the Western Sudan's first explorer. He visited Audoghast, the Targwi capital, and the unidentified capital of 'Ghana', where he saw the Niger flowing to the East and mistook it for the Nile.

Abu Obeïd al-Bakri, an 11th Century Spanish-born Arab of patrician stock, was the first great geographer of North Africa, including parts of the West Sudan. Al-Adrisi, who belongs in the following century, was also an Iberian Arab. Although his grandfather had been Emir of Malaga, he served in the household of the 'infidel' Roger II, the Norman geographer-King of Sicily. Adrisi was born in Ceúta, now a Spanish enclave in Morocco, in about 1100.

34

Yaqut was an 11th Century Greek who was kidnapped and sold – in his native Baghdad, as a child – to an Arab who educated him and encouraged him in his studies of geography. Al-Omari was a 14th Century Damascene who served in the household of the Sultan of Egypt.

Ibn Battuta was a 14th Century Tangerine Berber of urbanized stock. Raised in theology, he made the pilgrimage to Mecca at twentyone and got the taste for travel. From Mecca he trekked to India, where the Sultan of Delhi was noted for his patronage of scholars. The Sultan was impressed and made him the Malikite *Qadi* of the city.

After seven years with the Sultan, ibn Battuta was sent to China by him on a mission. Ambushed and robbed on the trail, he escaped and set off South, reaching the Malabar coast and the Maldives, where the ruler also made him *Qadi*. His severity in court was so great that he was soon obliged to sail away, in fear of the vengeance of his victims. He went to Ceylon and Assam and journeyed across Asia to Peking, where the Mogul Emperor declined to grant the unusual visitor an audience.

By Sumatra, Malabar and Syria he finally returned home to Africa and reached Tangiers in 1349, after twentyfour years of travel. Shortly after, he set out for the only Muslim country of importance he had never seen, Bilad as-Sudan. His account of his travels is the most precious Black African record of medieval times. He returned to Fez to die in 1368 or 1369, having sailed, ridden and walked about seventyfive thousand miles in an extraordinary lifetime.

Ibn Khaldun, ibn Battuta's contemporary, was a Spanish Arab, whose family had fled from Spain at the time of the Almoravids. He was born in Tunis in 1332. He served at the court of the Sultan there, and later at the court of Fez. Jailed for a political offence, he was obliged to leave the sultanate; he lived for some time on the glibness of his tongue in the courts of Granada, Bugi, Biskra and Tlemcen. It was on his return to Tunis that he probably began his standard history of the Berbers and Arabs.

He moved on to Cairo, where scholars were appreciated, and was made Malikite Mufti there. In 1387, he retired to a remote village to sift his voluminous notes and compose his work. He took fourteen years. Recalled to Cairo as Mufti, the zeal with which he dispensed Quranic punishment, like that of ibn Battuta in the Maldives, made him intolerable to the populace. In 1400, he accompanied the Sultan on his unsuccessful attempt to save Damascus from the Tartar Tamerlane, whose captive he became. He died in Cairo in 1406, recognized as the greatest scholar of his day.

One black Arab scholar was Abderrahman es-Saadi, a 17th Century Timbuktu native of the ruling caste, who wrote a history of the Sudan up to 1655. A copy of the book, *Tarikh es-Sudan,* was discovered by the great German explorer Barth, at Gwandu in Northern Nigeria, in 1853. Two other copies have since been found.

*

At the Western Sudanic end of the desert trail from the Maghreb lay an iron-working kingdom or kingdoms, generically referred to by Arab and Berber chroniclers as 'Ghana'. The northern end of this trail was at Sijilmasa, lying in the Tafilelt oasis of South Morocco. Al-Bakri speaks well of this latter city, its buildings, its Twareg people, its cool highland climate, its wealth derived from the gold trade with 'Wangara' and the salt trade with Taghaza, twenty days' march away. Toward the middle of the 8th Century, the Arabs, who held Morocco at the time, sent an army off through Sijilmasa to attack 'Ghana'; it returned with considerable gold. The troops damaged a capital which has never been identified in modern terms. The accounts of this attack in al-Bakri, ibn Haukal and the *Tarikh al-Fettach* appear to be the only mentions of a city or state called Ghana in medieval written records.

Es-Saadi, describing a state whose identity is still not clear to historians, says Ghana had twentytwo kings from the beginning of the Muslim era to the end. (Al-Bakri tells us 'Ghana' was the title of the King, but it is obvious from many mentions in narratives that it also describes the country. The word seems, at all costs, to have been used by Arabs and Berbers only.) The ruling caste of the 'Ghana' in es-Saadi – who wrote from late travelers' hearsay, and oral 'records' – had been for many dynasties white, but the major group of the people were black Mandingos. The Soninke branch of the Mandingos, es-Saadi says, had finally put a member of their own group on the throne, and it had been under black rule that this kingdom had reputedly reached its greatest peak, in the 9th Century. The probable frontiers of the kingdom or kingdoms covered by the Arabized Berber name were the Niger in the East, the Senegal and the Baule in the West and South, the desert to the North.

A Targwi federation under Tilutane, chief of the Lemtuna tribe, had pushed into 'Ghana' – that is, the Western Sudan – with (reputedly) one hundred thousand camel-borne cavalry in the 8th Century. The trip was not long, by desert standards, since Audoghast (now Tegdaoust), the Lemtuna fief, was only two weeks from 'Ghana's' capital, to which it was twice as close as it was to the coast of Mauritania. Audoghast was a Berber town with large buildings, date groves, an Arab trading community and vast numbers of Negro slaves. Rich on trade, Audoghast was then famous throughout the desert for its scholars and cooks and the beauty of its white women, on whom al-Bakri dwells at length.

In the 11th Century, the Paramount of the Sanhaja Berber, Yahia ibn Ibrahim, stopping off in Kairwan on his return from the *Haj* to Mecca, was impressed by the devout Islamic scholar Abu Amran, who was equally astonished by the ignorance of the desert chief. Yahia, shamed, asked the holy man to send his people a *fqih* or instructor, and Abu provided Abdullah ibn Yasin (or Yasim). The peace of two continents was finally to be disturbed by this austere fanatic.

Yahia's own Jedah tribesmen found the asceticism which Abdullah preached so bitterly intolerable that, before he had been with them long, they burned his house and drove him into the western desert. With two Lemtuna disciples, he trekked on down to the Senegal, where he probably settled on an island in the river; alternatively, he may have made his home on Cabo Verde, site of modern Dakar. Here, in a 'fortress convent', he withdrew from the world, absorbed in deep devotions. This attracted attention, and a colony of disciples formed. When he had about a thousand followers, Abdullah called them together and urged them to go out and preach the true faith. He called the body Al Morabethin ('Those of the fortress'), from which most European tongues have drawn the word Almoravids and the French the term *marabouts*. (The local word today is *marabti*.) In 1042,

37

Abdullah led the Almoravids against the Jedala and the Lemtuna; the ascetics soon defeated the luxury-loving, slave-owning traders. Prisoners were given a choice between death or conversion to the Almoravid sect, whose numbers consequently grew rapidly.

But Abdullah imposed such sharp restraints on the now enlarged legion of his followers – including forbidding the loot and rape which were the traditional fruits of military victory, even for the devout – that before long the exasperated Almoravids repudiated their general, who returned to his origins at Sijilmasa, and his own original instructor. Wagag, the instructor, deeply impressed by his former pupil's aura of *barak'a,* raised troops for him: in 1048, he sent these forces into the desert saying that all who would not do Abdullah's bidding would be cut from the corporate body of Islam; all who opposed Abdullah's march should be put to death. In a few years, the western desert had rallied to the Almoravids.

Professor Vincent Monteil gives an economic explanation for Abdullah's second campaign: 'The veiled Sanhaja, camel and caravan men, found themselves blocked from all directions: the summer pastures, to the North, were closed to them by the Zenata who levied tolls on the caravans, held the Wadi Dra'a and cut the migratory pastor's trail to the Middle Atlas; the passes of the Western High Atlas were barred by the Berbers, the Masmuda; at the same time, to the South, the road to Sahelian pastures was closed to them by the Blacks. Understandably, the desert "seemed too small" to them' (the Sanhaja). In addition, Monteil notes two temporary factors adding to the provocation in 1048: the Egyptian caravan route was abandoned in favor of the Moroccan one, because of insecurity and sandstorms; and there was an exceptional drought.

*

By 1051, Abdullah ibn Yasin controlled an army of thirty thousand men, most of whom were fanatically prepared to die for their testing faith; after mopping up a few areas of resistance, Abdullah swung this magnificently disciplined force North, captured his own city of Sijilmasa in 1053 and slew the Emir there. He next took Audoghast, which had fallen under the tutelage of 'Ghana' and was divided against itself. The Arab and Berber trading castes hated each other and both hated the tyrannous Soninke rulers.

It was 1054, and the area between the Sudan and the Maghreb – and including large parts of both – was now effectively Almoravid. Abdullah turned on Morocco itself, the *Maghreb el aqsa* (Furthest West) of the Arab world, but after a long and indecisive campaign was killed in battle three years later. His successor died shortly after, and the Emir of the Almoravids, Abu Bakr, assumed both spiritual and temporal power; he strove to keep the traditionally suspicious Berber clans together – a difficult task now that Abdullah was no longer there to be loved and feared. Eventually, serious revolt began in the desert South.

Handing over the rest of his force to his cousin, Yusuf ibn Tashfin, Abu Bakr set his face to the Sahara, conquered the troublesome tribes and inflicted a defeat on the Soninke warriors as well. When he returned to the Maghreb, he found Yusuf exalted by a series of military victories, and unprepared to give the Emir back his other armies. Yusuf was to prove a doughty successor to Abdullah himself.

Skinny and sunburned, with a straggly beard and kinky hair, low heavy brows and an aquiline nose, Yusuf lived mostly off barley and camel's milk. His voice was soft but brooked no word of contradiction. This fanatical ascetic thrust his way into the Maghreb, founding Marrakesh (from which comes the modern word Morocco) in 1062. He entered Fez the following year, then Tlemcen, then Algiers. Soon, Mu'tadid, the Arab ruler of Seville, had lost all his African regions to the Almoravid Berbers except the heavily defended ports of Ceúta and Tangiers. Mu'tadid decided to seek an alliance with Yusuf, who was asked to help the Spanish Muslims against the encroaching Christian kingdoms.

Yusuf barely acknowledged the message and, scenting fear in Seville, sailed his troops across the Straits and entered Algeciras, which he built into a base for a war on Spain. The desert nomads were greeted with at least an appearance of welcome in the poor Muslim villages; Yusuf finally allied himself with Mu'tadid and marched on the Christian hordes. Despite the vastly greater numbers on the European side, Yusuf out-generalled and defeated the *kafiri* force at Zallaga,

where the leading *kafir*, King Alfonso of Castile, was
wounded. The conqueror married a Christian maiden of
Ceúta. Then, apparently moved by a new religious motive,
Yusuf abandoned the Spanish War as suddenly as he had
started it. Leaving three thousand Berber guardsmen at
Mu'tadid's disposal, he took the main body of his army back
into Africa.

The Castilians then returned to the attack on Muslim
Spain, so Yusuf retraced his steps. A true ascetic Almoravid,
in contrast to the exacting and debauched Emirs, he was
greeted, on his return, by the ordinary Muslim people of
Southern Spain, as a sort of Messiah. Still a man of austere
simplicity, imposing rigorous controls on his troops, and
incorruptible, Yusuf forbade all taxes not permitted by the
Quran. He soon had every man, woman and child prepared
to fight for him. He began by the conquest of his former
allies, the corrupt Arab ruling class. He took Granada and
Seville from them and headed north. By 1102, Yusuf and
the Almoravids ruled from the Senegal to the Ebro. He
survived only four years, and his simple tomb at Marrakesh
was said by his contemporaries to have been in keeping
with the man.

Yusuf's achievements died with him. His successor, a
twentythree-year-old son called Ali ibn Yusuf, had never
known the austere life of the desert camps. The old Berber
chiefs could not respect this youth in the way they had
adored his rugged, stubborn father. Soon, he was dependent
for his uneasy power on the Christian slave militias. The
virtues of Yusuf's devout rule disappeared and Ali became
a frightened oppressor. Finally, the Andalusian Arabs rose
against the Berber overlords; in the Maghreb a new devout
Berber sect, the Almohads (in Berber: Muwahhadi), overthrew Almoravid rule there as well.

The Almohads were tough mountain-dwellers of the Atlas
in origin, and their first leader was a literate, self-chosen
Messiah called ibn Tonmart, nicknamed by his followers
Asafu, 'the torch'. He had the Quran translated into Berber,
which he wrote himself in Arabic script. He forbade the
men's veil, alcohol, wedding celebrations, and much else. To
war on the Almoravids, he instituted a parliamentary Berber
State, which he rigorously and ruthlessly purged from time

to time. But most of the conquest of Almoravid Morocco was accomplished by his disciple and successor, Abd al-Mu'men, the builder of the Qutubiyya of Marrakesh. Under Abd al-Mu'men, the Almohads established a fairly prosperous kingdom stretching from the Atlantic to the Syrtis coast.

From the collapse of the Almohads a century later emerged the Zenata dynasties of the Hafsids of Tunis, the Abd al-Wadites of Tlemcen and the Merinids of Fez.

The old Western Sudanic kingdoms

IT IS AGAINST THE BACKGROUND of these centuries of battles, scholarship, piety and massacre in North Africa that the emergence of black kingdoms among the southerly trading partners of the Arabs and Berbers must be seen. A great part of Black Africa's history – that is, the history of the Bilad as-Sudan – begins in white North Africa; this area united on only rare occasions, but was for many centuries united in its enmity for the great, prosperous, Negro-governed kingdom or kingdoms of 'Ghana'. As well as by covetousness, the Arabo-Berber attitude was conditioned by the treatment of Arabs and Berbers under many of the Negro kings – a tit-for-tat for the Muslim custom of looking on the Negro world as a source of slaves; and the Northerners, bred in the shadow of the mosque, were incensed that so much wealth should be controlled by 'pagans'.

Merchants of the Barbary Coast are the sources for the best description we have of the capital of Ghana, or the best-known 'Ghana' of the time, in al-Bakri. Kumbi, or Kumbi Saleh, one possible site, was unearthed in 1914 by the French administrator Bonnel de Mezières. Funds to pursue the digging did not become available until 1939, and excavations ceased with the outbreak of World War II. They were resumed in 1949. Kumbi is on the Mali-Mauritania border. It is divided into two cities, six miles apart. In the original city of Ghana described by al-Bakri (which may or may not have been at Kumbi), the Muslim city had about ten mosques and attracted Islamic scholars; the pagan city, which was then the seat of the court, was called al-Ghaba, the Grove. The dwellings were of thatched adobe, with a few in stone.

Al-Ghaba's name came from the sacred thickets, possibly of thorn, which surrounded the pagan area: in these coppices, the fetish priests carried out their hoary rites, sacrificed royal prisoners, and buried kings. Elaborate ceremony typified the court, al-Bakri records. On ceremonial occasions, the King wore a gold head-dress and jewelry. Behind him, according to the mercantile informers of the Spanish Arab historian, ten pages held shields and gold-hilted swords. To the right stood the hostage sons of vassal chiefs, with ornaments about their hair. The viziers sat in front of the monarch; the Governor of the City squatted at his feet. Around the pavilion stood ten horses with gold trappings, and hounds with gold and silver belled collars mounted guard.

This canine presence at the court is curious, for few if any modern African nations train or nourish dogs; these are usually regarded as mere hygienic carrion, like hawks and vultures, although in a few places they are used as aids in hunting. The breeding of house animals and birds is a recurring characteristic of the great civilizations of the Occident and Orient. Black Africa's abandonment of this refinement may have been due to the later influence of Islam, with its dietary superstitions and animal exclusives.

Already, in al-Bakri's day, there were many Muslims among the court dignitaries; the treasurer, most of the viziers and the interpreter were usually chosen from this community – much as today men for positions of trust in certain fields are very often chosen from the European community. Ceremonies were announced by the beating of the drums, the *deba* (royal Soninke drums are still called *daba* or *taba*). The audience knelt, the Muslims applauding the King's approach and the pagans pouring dirt on their bowed heads. The royal treasure included a gold nugget said by Adrisi to weigh thirty pounds and to serve as a tethering block for the royal mount. A nugget of sixty pounds has been found in recent times, so Adrisi's version is probably accurate enough. Rumor in the trading centers of the Mediterranean raised the great nugget's size, and when it was sold, much later, by a Soninke King to the Egyptians, ibn Khaldun reported that it weighed a ton.

When the King of al-Bakri's 'Ghana' died, his comfort in the after-world ordained the nature of his rites: his body was stretched on rugs and cushions and laid in a great wooden shell. Robes, food and drink were arranged close by, and the royal cooks were buried with their departed master. Mats were hurled over the timber mausoleum, and then the populace built a mound of earth on top, surrounding this with a shallow moat.

The trader-travelers were principally interested in commerce and the signs of wealth; their accounts, as reproduced by al-Bakri back in Spain, tell us little of the folk themselves. We know that they grew a form of millet, perhaps sorghum, fished the Niger and raided neighboring tribes for slaves. Al-Bakri says the Ghana of his time could raise an army of two hundred thousand for this purpose, including forty thousand bowmen.

Al-Adrisi describes Ghana's capital as the main market of the West Sudan. So great was its gold *entrepôt* trade that it imposed controls on the amount of the metal marketed. Nuggets were Crown property, and only gold dust could be exported. To the North, in coral-ringed Ceúta, beads were made for the Negro trade. Merchants set out from Sijilmasa, Dra'a and similar places with these beads and other jewelry; passing through Taghaza, they acquired salt. At the city of 'Ghana' they traded beads and salt and picked up native agents who went with them twenty days further into the black country, down to the Senegal, where trading closely resembled that found by the Carthaginians and described by Herodotus. When the caravan reached the river, the traders beat drums to encourage the naked natives to emerge from the holes in the ground in which they lived. The troglodytes, however, did not appear until the merchants had withdrawn, having spread out their trade goods beside the river. Gold dust was put beside the piles of goods, and after various goings and comings and increases in the amount of gold the merchants took their price and withdrew, leaving the goods and beating drums to signify that the deal was done.

Naturally the sophisticated travelers sought the source of the gold itself, but when a Negro was once captured he pined to death without incurring the wrath of his gods by giving away the tribal secret. The Negroes then stopped the trade for three years, and apparently revived it only when Soninke craving for salt became too great.

Cà da Mosto, writing in the fifteenth century, reports Arab and Sanhaja Berber traders in Sijilmasa as saying that 'silent barter' was still the custom among some of the West Sudanic tribes. There is evidence of 'dumb trade' in various parts of 'Wangara' much later. (History offers similarities; the Romans bought silk from the Chinese in Parthia this way. The fifth century Chinese traveler Fa-Hein observed dumb barter in Ceylon. In pre-Christian Ethiopia, gold was sold in this manner. Congolese pygmies practised this custom at the outset of colonization less than a century ago, and it is not impossible that some pygmy groups still use it.)

*

A 20th-Century historian says of 'Ghana': 'The empire's origins seem to lie, around the 3rd and 4th Century AD, in the settlement in Aukar, at that time inhabited by Mande-speaking Negroes, principally Soninke, of a group of immigrants from North Africa. . . . The identity of these settlers is not certain. They may have been simply Berber pastoralists, but there is some reason to believe that if not actually Jews, they were Berbers who had come under Jewish influence and who may have possessed some Jewish strain. At some time about the 4th Century, the immigrants seem to have established their rule over the Negroes among whom they were living, and founded a dynasty (traditionally of fortyfour kings) which ruled over Aukar and Hodh until the end of the 8th Century. In about 770, this dynasty was overthrown by a Negro Soninke dynasty, which then ruled in Ghana until at least the time of the Almoravid conquest.' The former white ruling caste became, it is theorized, by intermarriage, part of today's Fulani tribe, whose language is related to those of the Tukolor, Wolof and Serer of Senegal.

44

Other historians point out that there must have been more than one Ghana, since the name seems to apply to so many places at different epochs. The term, as mentioned, meant both the country, (sometimes) the city, and the King. The word appears to come from the Berber *agan*, meaning 'the bush' – in loose modern parlance, the 'sticks'. The Mauritanian Arab version of *agan* is *gana*, which is probably a more phonetic spelling for the old kingdom or kingdoms.

'Ghana' was legendary among Arabs and Berbers for its gold; but it was also a slave-trading kingdom (or kingdoms), and Arab records say the Ghana slave market was famous for having wares at all seasons. To the west of Ghana, the kingdom of Tekrur, which was founded by the Tukolors, also dealt in slaves and gold. The Tukolors are found in modern Senegal and more numerously in the Futa of eastern Guinea, where they are called Tekarir. The overthrow of 'Ghana' and its neighbors became a religious and commercial imperative of Islamic Maghreb politics.

The division of privileges in the ancient Ghana pictured by al-Bakri was not unlike that of white South Africa today, where the 'English' have a quasi-monopoly of finance, mining, industry and wealth, while the cruder, less developed group, the Afrikaners, have a stranglehold on power based on numbers. In 'Ghana', many Soninke, particularly the moneyed class, were Muslim, but contemporary observations indicate that by the time of the Negro ascendancy of the throne both the power and the population-majority were pagan; the Maghribi traders and the ascetic, evangelizing Almoravid movement were of one mind on the need to conquer pagan Ghana.

Abu Bakr's defeat of the Soninke in a battle in 1062 may well have been part of a plan to vanquish the black Ghana of the day. When Yusuf insisted on keeping the van of the army of the Almoravids, the Emir returned across the desert and set about establishing his own Almoravid empire in the Negro or partly-Negro South; in 1076 he finally captured what was described as the capital of Ghana, put the pagans to the sword and brought the country and its gold trade under Almoravid control.

Here, too, Almoravid rule was short-lived. In victory, the Berber tribes feuded, and in just over a decade the Soninke had recovered their independence from the Caucasian-led invaders. Then, the victorious Soninke also quarreled, and internecine warfare sapped the authority of a state torn by crisis and the contradictions inherent in historical maturity. Collapse was near. In 1203, the Susu (now the predominant people of Western Guinea, including Konakri) took the capital of 'Ghana' for itself after the Susu leader, Sumanguru, had annexed the strategic citadel of Jara.

Rejecting the barbarity of Susu rule, the Arab and Berber merchants and the wealthier Soninke traders abandoned the capital – which may have been Kumbi – and went North into the desert for about a hundred miles; there they founded a new city at the caravanserai oasis of Walata, whose trading wealth soon exceeded the fortune of their former city which became a ghost town. But continual mentions of 'Ghana' even as late as the 18th Century make it clear that either the 'empire' only shifted its cartographical position, or – more probably – that there was more than one Ghana in history, and possibly that some of the Ghanas or Ganas co-existed.

Some historians referring to a later 'Ghana' may be referring to Walata. Because the name Ghana could, like Mali, be applied to almost any West Sudanic kingdom, its use continued to occur in travelers' tales. In the 14th Century – well after the fall of Soninke and the rise of 'Mali' – ibn Khaldun reports a conversation in Cairo with a certain Sheikh Othman, described as being a 'fqih in Ghana'.

*

The Susu or Sosso were members of the So clan of the Fulani of Tekrur. They called their empire Kanyaga. Made over-ambitious by their conquest of decadent Soninke Ghana, Sumanguru and his Susu now turned South and challenged the Mandingo realm, Kangaba – better known as Mali. As the Susu warlords read the political situation, the Mandingos, an Islamic tribe, were the only threat to their power in the Western Sudan.

To weaken Mali, the Susu contrived the deaths of eleven brothers who were heirs apparent to the kingdom. A twelfth brother, Sun Jata (Sun is an abbreviated form of his mother's name; Jata simply means he was her eldest son) was spared – probably because he was, in childhood, weak and sick. Under

46

the assumed name Mari Jata, he was to emerge as the Mandingo nation's hero-figure; his praises are still sung today.

In 1235 (some sources say 1240), Mari Jata, who had
reputedly converted to Islam by then, destroyed the Susu
army at Kirina and pushed his own forces northward into
the desert fringe. He moved the capital to Niani – also known
as Mali or Mande. In ensuing years, his officers moved troops
as far as the Gambia River and Tekrur – where the defeated
Susu clan had fled, and where they managed to resist, retaining the monarchy of Tekrur for a century. They were finally
overthrown, in about 1350, by the Wolofs.

The tribes of the 'Wangara' goldfields also resisted Mari
Jata's attempts to convert them to Islam, but they accepted
his overlordship. Wealthy and extensive, the fame of Mali
spread to Europe. Mari Jata's grandson, Mansa (King) Musa,
when he took the throne, further increased the fame of the
Empire by his famous pilgrimage to Mecca.

Mansa Musa came to the throne in 1307; he performed
his memorable *Haj* in 1324. At Walata, and in Libya and
Egypt, he startled natives and foreign traders with the
immensity of his wealth. Mounted on an Arab steed, the
monarch was preceded by a clutch of half a thousand slaves,
each bearing a gold staff weighing about forty pounds. In
Cairo, he left his mark by his piety, generosity and arrogance.
He refused to kiss the earth before the Mameluke Sultan –
who nevertheless seems to have afforded him the hospitality
due to his royal rank.

The copper-complexioned Sudanic King brought with
him nearly one hundred camels, each bearing about three
hundred pounds of gold for purchases and gifts. Al-Omari,
who visited Cairo twelve years later, found the people still
remembering how good the visit had been for trade; Mansa
Musa's followers had readily paid high prices for all they
bought, and particularly for fine cloth and light skinned
women slaves. In the holy places, Mansa Musa's generosity
had been so great that the market value of gold dust had
plummeted; it took a decade to recover.

On his way home, Mansa Musa received a messenger who
brought him news of the fall of Gao, capital of Mali's powerful Niger-side neighbor, Song'hai. This spectacular addition
to the Empire made the King of Mali change route and visit

Gao, where he received the submission of the defeated monarch and took his two sons hostage. Then Mansa Musa ordered his Andalusian architect-poet, known as es-Saheli – whom he had taken on in Mecca – to build a new mosque in Gao. It was to be the first building in the Western Sudan made of fired bricks; its foundations still exist today.

The fall of Gao brought Mali the other great city of Song'hai – Timbuktu, which had inherited the trade and cultural life of Walata, and attracted to it the once primitive, now scholarly, mercantile desert tribe of Walata, the Jedala. Mansa Musa developed Timbuktu, and es-Saheli embellished it with a new mosque and other buildings. The Jedala scholars of the new Sankore mosque attracted, in their turn, cultural pilgrims from far away. These Jedala scholars, believed to have originated from regular intermarriage between Portuguese Jews and Arabs, 'survive' today in the Portuguese name Guedella or Guedalla.

If the portrait of Mansa Musa which accompanies the Catalan map of Charles V is accurate, the ruler of all this was a man of medium height with a full beard and a pot belly. He dressed simply in white but wore a fine gold crown apparently modeled on those of Western Europe. Middle Eastern contemporaries of his *Haj* were surprised by his brown complexion: he had been reputed – like everyone connected with the mysterious Bilad as-Sudan – to be black.

Mansa Musa died in 1332. He had created the biggest of all sub-Saharan African Empires, and probably the best-governed. It had attracted many Egyptian, Moroccan and other settlers, known collectively as *Ture* – stranger(s). On European maps of Africa at the time, the importance of the Empire of Mali was one of the most clearly depicted features. (The name 'Mali' means 'where the king lives' and could thus be the name given to any Mandingo capital. Mande is a variant of Mali. People subject to a Mali, or Mansa Seat – King's Seat – were called Mandinka, Mandingo or Malinke. The name Malinke has survived as the name of a tribe, of which modern Guinea's first President, Sékou Touré – Ture – is a member. The modern Mandingo are a Gambia riverain tribe. The Hausa name for Mandingo or Malinke is Wangara.)

After Mansa Musa, it was the usual story: his son Maghan lost much of the Empire in four short years. First his garrison in Timbuktu was routed by the Mossi warriors from Yatenga. Then the two hostage sons of the King of Song'hai, Ali Kolen and Sulayman Narh, escaped to Gao and raised a rebellion which gave the throne there to Ali Kolen. Maghan was succeeded by his uncle Sulayman, who recovered some of the lost terrain, but not Gao or Timbuktu. It was during Sulayman's reign that Mali was visited by the Tangerine historian ibn Battuta. By then there were probably many 'Malis', but one more important than the others.

The Berber writer set out from Morocco in 1352, passing through Sijilmasa and the salt market of Taghaza. At Tasarahla, he records, an almost blind Mesufa *takshif* was sent in front. The *takshif's* job was to go at all speed, alone, to Walata and ensure that water was sent out to meet the advancing caravan. If he himself did not arrive, the caravan might well perish. Blind or nearly blind messengers were popular, as they apparently found their way better in the desert than most people, depending strongly on their sense of smell and recognition of terrain by touch.

Ibn Battuta reached Walata two months after Sijilmasa. The town was then an outpost of Mali. The writer was surprised by the beauty of the women and by their un-Islamic independence, as well as by the local custom of uterine descent. Women of the royal clans (Keïta, Konate, Kulibali, etc.,) wielded considerable power. The country was so peaceful he proceeded to Niani, the capital, with only three companions. They carried no food with them for the twenty-four day march, bartering instead for their substenance with salt, beads and aromatics. He crossed the Niger – mistaking it for the Nile.

After recovering from a sickness in Niani, ibn Battuta visited the court, where customs seem to have been similar to those of al-Bakri's Ghana. Audience-seekers wore rags and poured dust on their shaven heads. Men twanged their bowstrings as a sign of applause. Two tethered goats were there to ward off the evil eye. Ibn Battuta saw the King give some cannibal visitors a woman – whom they killed and ate, smearing her blood on their cheeks and ears.

The sophisticated visitor also found points to admire. His narrative reflects the usual Arab and Berber disdain for the Black African, but he admits to finding the Sudanics just in

49

their business dealings, law-abiding, commendably pious. He was impressed with the volume of trade, and reports camel-trains of twelve thousand beasts reaching Walata from the Mediterranean. He was however shocked by the habit of eating carrion, dogs and asses, and by the nakedness of women, a habit which he found even among those of the royal court. The thin veneer of Islam sat lightly on the country: the people, although devout, still branded themselves on the face to show their clans, and followed tribal rites. The powerful goldsmiths' clan, in particular, remained pagan.

The writer spent eight months in Niani, returning home on camelback by way of Timbuktu, whence he canoed down the Niger through Song'hai. He was given a Song'hai boy as a slave. He spent a month in Gao, then joined a cara-van for Takedda bringing six hundred women slaves for Sijilmasa and Fez, passing through the great desert of Aïr. His observations reflect the considerable trans-Sahara com-merce of the period, and the links between Maghribi and Sudanic traders. He saw Mali, not at its height under Mansa Musa, but in a relatively prosperous aftermath. Fifty years later, it had become a small, ruined kingdom.

Song'hai, having recovered some of its former glory under Ali Kolen, was more fortunate. The capital at Gao, like the capital of al-Bakri's Ghana, had its pagan and Muslim halves, but most of the people were still pagans. In 1468, under Sonni Ali, the Song'hai army marched North to the other great city of the Niger River in the Sudan – Timbuktu – and captured it. Es-Saadi recalls that Sonni Ali's exactions were harsh and bloody.

The people of Timbuktu were dark-skinned but had partly Berber ancestry. They scorned the Song'hai, although the ruling house of Gao was also of Berber origin, and they particularly hated Sonni Ali, whom es-Saadi describes as a tyrant, a libertine and a crook, one who revelled in the death of the intellectual and pious. Insanely sadistic, he once obliged a woman to pound her living baby to pulp in a mortar, and feed it to dogs. On more than one occasion, he had victims burned to death before him; others were walled up. He had an unfaithful concubine's belly ripped, and himself snatched out the foetus. Qati says he could 'never see a Fulani without killing him'.

The King of Song'hai pushed on to Jenne, which according to legend had withstood ninetynine assaults by the Kings of Mali. The city, with its great salt market, fell to Sonni Ali only after several years of siege. The final victory probably came in 1473.

The Mossi, disturbed at Sonni Ali's success, drove northwest and captured Walata, withdrawing after sacking the city. Sonni Ali decided to take this Malian market-site himself, and even started to build what was intended to be a two hundred mile canal from Lake Fagbine to Walata, to afford him the mobility of transport vessels. But fresh attacks from the Mossi caused the tyrant to abandon this ambitious project. To the great relief of the people of Timbuktu, he died in 1492. In twentysix years, he had transformed a petty kingdom into the largest Empire in the region at the time.

Sonni Ali was succeeded by his son; but the throne was soon usurped by one of his father's comrades-in-arms, Muhammad Ture, who took the title Askia and called himself Askia Muhammad I. He was as great an organizer as Sonni Ali, and had more respect for religion and for scholarship. He fathered an Islamic revival; the intellectuals, who had suffered under Sonni Ali, became the favored children of the régime. Under the first Askia, Gao and Timbuktu prospered.

Askia Muhammad made a pilgrimage to Mecca soon after his accession, taking with him five hundred cavalry, a thousand infantry and three hundred pieces of gold, of which one third was for philanthropy in the holy cities.

Muhammad consolidated the rule of Song'hai and spread it further. His main conquest was probably that of the Hausa states – fertile country between the Niger and Lake Chad. The Hausa were noted farmers, weavers, dyers, tanners and smiths who lived in walled towns, some of which – Gobir, Katsina, Zaria and Kano – attracted resident Arab merchants. The Hausa were not, however, a military people and – except at Kano – offered little resistance to the Askia. His domains now extended to the frontiers of Song'hai's traditional enemies, the Twareg, who were provoked by the occupation of the Hausa country – seasonal pasture for the nomads. The Askia, to secure his far-stretched frontiers, occupied the Aïr and drove the Twareg further into the desert. Bovill comments: 'But, like the French in the early 20th Century, the Askia had yet to learn that the surest way to lay up trouble for the future is to deprive nomads of their . . . grazing grounds.'

In addition to seeking a head-on collision with the Twareg, the Askia soon faced a defection closer to home. Kanta, King of Kebbi, who had warred at the Askia's side in Hausa and Aïr, suddenly rebelled against the vassal status of his small domain, and declared Kebbi independent. Legend says he was dissatisfied with his share of the spoils of victory in the Askia's campaigns. Backed by a peculiarly stubborn and determined people, surrounded by a protective wall of swamp and marsh, Kanta successfully held his capital Surame against the Askia's attacks.

Kanta's principal problem lay for a while less from the Song'hai, who had the swamps to cross in their march from the West, but rather to the East of Kebbi, where *Maï* Ali of Bornu viewed with concern the rise of a neighbor capable of defying Song'hai. The Kebbawa threw back *Maï* Ali's attack – in many ways a greater military feat than their defiance of the Song'hai legions. Kebbawa legend says Kanta's gilded canoe still lies in the marshes below Birnin Kebbi. The tribe's warrior achievements continued into modern times: after the British conquered Sokoto and Gwandu they found that the Sarkin Kebbi Samma Ismaila of Argungu, only a few miles away, had been successfully holding off attacks, for decades, from the two powerful Fulani capitals.

Today the Song'hai people are dispersed, and little remains of the glory that the Askias built; but, interestingly enough, the formerly Targwi city of Agades in the Aïr is still peopled by folk of predominantly Song'hai 'blood', and the city is Song'hai-speaking. The Twareg are there, but they have never retaken political control of the town.

The first Askia's victories had turned sour even before he died. Three of his sons, led by the eldest, Musa, rebelled against him. The Askia called on his brother Yahia for aid, but the sons killed their uncle, marched into Gao and forced the Askia to abdicate in favor of Musa. This was in 1528.

Musa, a tyrant, was later assassinated. He was succeeded by Askia Bengan Korei, the leader of the unsuccessful assault on Kebbi, who banished the old Askia to an island in the Niger, where he died in squalor.

*

In the 16th Century, knowledge of the Sudan was greatly enriched by the writings of Leo Africanus, a young Moor born in Granada and taught by a *fqih* in Fez; the youth was among the prisoners who were taken when an Arab galley was captured by Christian corsairs, off the Tunisian island of Djerba, in 1518. In view of his erudition, the pirates presented him to Pope Leo X, a Medici and an arts patron, who freed and converted him, changed his names from al-Hassan ibn Wezaz to Giovanni Leone (the Pope's own names), and encouraged him to complete, in Italian, a work the young man had already begun in Arabic, based on his travels: *The History and Description of Africa and the Notable Things therein Contained*. It appeared in 1526, three years after the Pope's demise.

Leo Africanus stressed the importance of the Sudan in Maghribi commerce. A gift bestowed by the Sultan of Fez on a fellow-Moroccan, for instance, is described as being almost entirely composed of Sudanic produce: fifty slaves of each sex, ten eunuchs, twelve camels, one giraffe, sixteen civet-cats, a pound of civet, a pound of ambergris and six hundred gazelle skins.

In about 1510, Leo was part of a mission sent by the Sharif of Fez, Mulaï Muhammad al-Qaïm, the founder of the Sa'adian Dynasty, to Song'hai, the young writer, then less than twenty, traveled in the wake of the Askia's victorious armies. At Timbuktu he recorded the presence of water conduits in the flood season, and was impressed by the abundance of corn, cattle, milk and butter. Salt was brought five hundred miles from Taghaza, and a camel-load of salt was worth more than the beast itself. Leo Africanus found the inhabitants of the city 'people of a gentle, very cheerful disposition.' They 'spend a great part of the night in singing and dancing through all the streets of the city: they keep great store of men and women slaves, and their town is much in danger of fire: at my second visit, almost half the town was

53

burned in five hours. Outside the suburbs, there are no gardens or orchards at all.'

He describes the Askia's court: 'The rich King of Timbuktu hath many plates and scepters of gold, some whereof weigh thirteen hundred pounds: and he keeps a magnificent and well furnished court. When he traveleth any whither he rideth upon a camel which is led by some of his noblemen; and so he doth likewise when he goeth to warfare, and all his soldiers ride on horses. Whosoever will speak unto the King must first fall down before his feet, and then taking up earth must sprinkle it upon his own head and shoulders: which custom is ordinarily observed by them that never saluted the King before, or come as ambassadors from other princes.

'He hath always three thousand horsemen, and a great number of footmen that shoot poisoned arrows, attending him. They have often skirmishes with those that refuse to pay tribute, and so many as they take they sell unto the merchants of Timbuktu. Here are very few horses bred; the merchants and courtiers keep certain little nags which they use to travel on: but their best horses are brought out of Barbary. And the King, so soon as he heareth that any merchants are come to town with horses, commandeth a certain number to be brought before him; and, choosing the best horse for himself, he payeth a most liberal price.

'Here are great store of doctors, judges, priests and other learned men, that are bountifully maintained at the King's cost and charges. And hither are brought divers manuscripts or written books out of Barbary, which are sold for more money than any other merchandise. The coin of Timbuktu is of gold without any stamp or superscription: but in matters of small value they use certain shells brought hither out of the Kingdom of Persia.'

Leo Africanus gives the value of cowrie shells as being, then, four hundred to the ducat, his name for the local gold coin; he says six and two-thirds of these coins weighed an ounce. The Moorish writer appears to have seen Timbuktu at its best, thanks to the presence of the Askia and his extensive court.

He also visited Jenne and Niani (Mali). He found Jenne rich in food and cotton, which they bartered for armor and golden pitchers. In Mali, where they were recovering from the attacks of the Askia, he also found cattle, grain and

54

cotton in abundance. The people were hospitable and prosperous, and there were learned Muslims in the city mosques. Leo Africanus added: 'The people of this region excel all other Blacks in intelligence, civility and industry.'

The Askia's capital, Gao, was an unwalled city of uneasy contrasts. 'The houses thereof are but mean, except those wherein the King and his courtiers remain. Here are exceeding rich merchants: and hither continually resort great store of Blacks which buy cloth here brought out of Barbary and Europe.' Of the slave market, he says: 'A young slave of fifteen years of age is sold for six ducats, and so are children sold also. The King of this region hath a certain private palace wherein he maintaineth a great number of concubines and slaves, which are kept by eunuchs.'

The King had a guard of horse and foot. The market of the town was brisk. 'Horses bought in Europe for ten ducats are sold again for forty ducats, sometimes fifty. There is not any cloth of Europe so coarse which will not here be sold for four ducats an ell.' Fine cloth sold for as much as thirty golden ducats. Swords, saddlery and spices got high prices, and Leo Africanus found salt 'most extremely dear'. There were abundant supplies of gold.

He went to Hausa, another recent Askia conquest, and admired the weavers, metalworkers and shoesmiths of Gobir. Other Hausa kingdoms which he describes are Zamfara, Katsina, Kano and Zaria, all desolated by the recent war with Song'hai, and crushed by the burden of paying tribute.

He pushed on out of the Askia's Empire, into Bornu, where gold was so plentiful that hunting dogs wore gold collars. But success in war had assured Bornu of an even greater glut in slaves and they sought to use these alone as currency in their barter with Barbary. They paid, Leo Africanus records, up to twenty slaves for a good horse. Leo then turned North to home, probably through Agades. While in Hausa, he had seen rice-paddies in the flood-waters of the Niger, and as a consequence map-makers began to record a lake (the Lago de Guber on Giacomo di Gastaldi's 1564 chart) as lying above Timbuktu – the Niger being confused with the West-flowing Senegal. This fictitious lake persisted on maps until the end of the 18th Century.

*

The Askia's conquests made Song'hai a rich medieval empire, which naturally excited the covetousness of Barbary, its trading partner. In its heyday, Song'hai extended from the Sahara to the rain-forest, from the Atlantic almost to Lake Chad. The Empire was largely fertile and well-watered, abounding in animals and fish, rich in crops. Its artisans and miners provided gold, iron, copper, leather or goods in these materials with which to purchase imports, and there was a permanent surplus of gold and slaves: Song'hai's principal economic problem was how to stimulate to the maximum the Mediterranean demand for these two major sub-Saharan African exports.

To challenge this Empire could only be the task of a major power. In 1578, Portugal was defeated by the Moors at the battle of al-Qsar al-Qebir, leaving twentysix thousand dead on the field and barely one hundred survivors. The dead included Portugal's King Sebastião and the Moorish commander Abd al-Malek, who had named as his successor his twentynine-year-old brother Mulaï Ahmed, son of a Negro concubine. The new Sharif added to his name 'al-Mansur' – the Victorious.

By this time, power in Marrakesh had passed from the Almohad and Merinid dynasties to the Sa'adi clan, claiming to come from the Hedjaz and to descend from the Prophet. Flushed by their victory over the Portuguese, the Moors began to look further afield. There was a Papal ban on selling war material to the Muslims, but England's Queen Elizabeth provided al-Mansur with cannon-balls, ship's timber, oars and the services of English shipwrights in exchange for Moorish saltpeter – which was needed to make gunpowder. Philip of Spain protested, but the true aim of Moorish military ambitions did not lie in Europe: a closely guarded secret, al-Mansur's plans were to conquer Song'hai and seize its goldfields.

The first objective was originally to be Taghaza, where the Negro slaves of the Mesufa Twareg mined the salt which was exchanged for gold in the Western Sudan, by the traditional dumb barter. Ibn Battuta had described Taghaza as 'an ugly village, with . . . houses and mosques built of saltblocks, roofed with camel skins. There are no trees.' The slave diggers lived on dates brought from Dra'a and Sijilmasa, camel meat, and fonio from the South. Ibn Battuta said that at the time of his visit a camel load of salt was worth about an ounce of gold, at Walata. In Mali it was worth up to four times as much. Smaller hunks of salt were used as currency by the slaves. Leo Africanus described the salt as 'whiter than any marble'.

The sources of the miners' food were twenty days' march away, so that life itself depended on the continuance of the trade. Food was frequently scarce, and there were cases of starvation. Leo Africanus, when there, had to drink brackish water from wells near the salt pits, when fresh water supplies from the oases failed to arrive on time.

Before al-Mansur despatched his expedition, however, he decided against seizing Taghaza, probably for fear of provoking retaliatory raids on Morocco by the Twareg. Instead, a more circuitous route to Song'hai was chosen, and the initial force – reportedly twenty thousand men, but probably less – perished to a man, in the desert. Al-Mansur then decided to take Taghaza, which he did with a force of two hundred crack warriors. But the Negroes fled and Askia Daüd forbade them to return. The mines being unworkable without the slaves, the Moors abandoned Taghaza.

Then began the most remarkable military campaign fought in Africa until recent times, one which still has 20th Century echoes in Morocco's 'claim' to Mauritania.

We are in 1589. Al-Mansur, in Fez, received a courier from Marrakesh. The letter he carried was from a Negro called uld Kirinfil, whom the new Askia, Ishak II, had banished to Taghaza, whence he had escaped and come to Marrakesh. The writer claimed to be Ishak's elder brother and proclaimed Ishak an usurper. Actually, uld Kirinfil was an impostor, but his case gave al-Mansur the pretext he needed to invade the desert. (One source says al-Mansur first sought to negotiate with the Askia, who responded by simply sending the Sultan 'javelins and spears'.)

The Moors habitually relied on numbers for victory. The Song'hai campaign clearly needed different tactics, since only by limiting numbers was there any hope of getting an army across the parched Sahara. The Moors had firearms, which would give them an obvious advantage over the vastly greater numbers of the Song'hai; but they also needed picked troops and a good commander. Al-Mansur chose a blue-eyed Spanish slave from Las Cuevas in Granada, Judar, who was at once promoted Pasha. Under this eunuch were ten *qaïds*, four of them also European apostates. The army was to be four thousand strong, half of them Europeans, half Spanish Moors. The cavalry which composed half the force was three-quarters Moor, one-quarter European. Only the Europeans carried firearms; the Moorish horsemen were to charge the foe with lances.

Some of the Europeans in the force were neither slaves or apostates but free renegade Christians, many of them French. This apostate and mercenary *élite* had all the artillery, including six large cannon. Some of the musketeers were Portuguese survivors of al-Qsar. The language of the army was Spanish. The cavalry horses, the one thousand pack-horses and the eight thousand camels were almost equally carefully chosen, and a thousand camel-drivers were attached to the expedition. The huge transport animal force is explicable by the fact that for long stretches of the fifteen hundred-mile march the army and its horses would rely on the food and water carried in the rear. Other stocks included one hundred and eighty tents, thirtyone thousand pounds of gunpowder, hundreds of bullock-skins for drinking-water, plus lead, shot, tow, pitch, rosin, ropes, spades and picks. Food included grain and pressed dates.

On October 16, 1590 (some sources say 1591), the expedition marched out of Marrakesh. It was months before news of the army filtered back to Morocco – and then it came with almost humorous indirectness. A camel-owner from Arawan, a few days' march North of Timbuktu, appeared at the Sharif's court to complain that he had been peacefully grazing his beasts one day when Judar's army had emerged from the dunes and seized the sleepy herd. The man's complaint proved that the force had crossed the desert – and perhaps that Judar had found an original way of getting the news back to Marrakesh.

According to Mahmud Qati's account in the *Tarikh al-Fettach*, only one quarter of the four thousand men survived to face the first encounter with the Song'hai. Water must have been the principal handicap, and the route taken had to be determined by water-holes. Leo Africanus recounts that in the Azaoad desert there were two marble monuments, one to a rich merchant, the other to a trader who had sold him a cup of water for ten thousand ducats; both parties in this vain barter died of thirst.

Ishak, when he learned of the approach of the desert army, sent out fleet messengers with orders to the outposts to fill in the wells. The messengers were captured by Twareg, who were later fallen on by Judar's warriors on the march to Gao. Ishak had also ordered his fighting men to rally; but in the villages people believed it impossible that anything more than nomad irregulars could march upon them from the North, and it was only relatively late that a Song'hai force began to gather. The first engagement was at Tondibi, about thirtyfive miles from Gao.

Qati estimates the Song'hai force at eighteen thousand cavalry and nine thousand seven hundred foot. Although nominal Muslims, they were accompanied by scores of witchdoctors and countless talismen and charms. Qati says the thousand survivors from Marrakesh were all cavalry, about half European and half Moor. The Negro troops began the action by driving a herd of cattle at the enemy, but the Moors opened their serried ranks and let them through.

Judar's forces then charged from both the flanks; the defending forces disintegrated, save for a royal bodyguard of 'suicide' bowmen who knelt their shins lashed to their thighs so that they could not move – firing arrows until they were overrun and massacred. The Moors took gold loot from the battlefield: but when Judar and his men entered Gao itself they were disappointed at the squalor of the city. The citizens had fled, taking everything they had: neither gold nor any other signs of wealth remained.

But Askia Ishak's will to resist had gone. He made peace offers to the young Spanish Pasha. He would swear allegiance to the Sharif of Fez, and give the Moors the right to import salt and cowries into Song'hai. He would pay tribute of one hundred thousand miqtal (twelve thousand five hundred ounces of gold) and one thousand slaves. His principal aim seems to have been to avoid a long military occupation that might give Morocco permanent rights in the conquered country.

Judar would certainly have liked to accept the terms. His army, retainers and pack beasts were decimated, and he was disappointed in the miserable, undeveloped state of the country. But he had no plenipotentiary powers, and had to send off despatches to the Sharif for instructions. In his report he stressed the army's feeble plight, the state of the country. Four hundred of his men had died in the first two weeks and, on Ishak's advice, he had moved to healthier Timbuktu, a march of twentynine days up the river bank. There, he received the Sharif's reply. Al-Mansur was far from satisfied. Judar, he said, should have left a garrison in Gao; he should have taken hostages.

Back in Fez, the mulatto Sultan issued a proclamation heralding the great victory of Tondibi, and talking of a land of surpassing wealth. No explanation, Bovill notes, was given for the levying of further troops, or the sending out of a new, more ruthless general. Al-Mansur sought only to give his people and the envoys at the Sharifian court an impression of unmitigated victory; to make it sound more complete, he showed the Ottoman ambassador a severed hand and claimed that is was Ishak's.

The Barbary merchants were less enthusiastic than the Sharif about his desire to seize the Sudanic goldfields. The traders were, on the whole, satisfied with the traditional dumb barter system, and feared that the Negroes might refuse to work the alluvial deposits if Song'hai was oppressed by an occupation. They also knew the goldfields were much further south than Gao – although they did not know where they were – and they doubted if the Moorish army would ever reach them.

Judar's successor was to be another European eunuch, Mahmud ben Zergun; probably a Spaniard or a Portuguese, he was *qaïd* of all the renegades in al-Mansur's kingdom. Although the desert wind was blowing and it was the worst time of the year to make the Sahara crossing, he was ordered to set off at once with forty other Europeans and to travel only in the cool of the desert night. All the party reached Timbuktu safely in the short time of seven weeks.

There Mahmud cut down all the trees that he could find, and pulled the wooden doors off all houses that possessed this bourgeois luxury, and made two boats. Leaving a small garrison in Timbuktu, he set off down the Niger, destroyed the Song'hai army at Bamba, and caused such confusion in the ranks that Ishak was cut off from his forces and killed by marauders – probably Twareg. Thousands of the Song'hai deserted to the Moors, and the new Askia surrendered.

Provision troubles remained, for there was a famine. The Moors ate their camels and horses, and appealed to the beaten Askia to send them food. Although Song'hai was suffering also, the new Askia was glad to be able to show his good faith and he sent provisions. He was then summoned to the Moorish camp to swear allegiance to al-Mansur. When he and his court arrived, they were treacherously murdered. Mahmud appointed a puppet Askia in Timbuktu; but this man got little obedience, and the undefeated Song'hai to the South appointed a separate Askia of their own. He was soon succeeded by a much stronger leader, Askia Nuh, who raised an army that was to bedevil the Moors for nearly four more years.

Since the advantage of the Moors was firing power and the advantage of the Song'hai was numbers, Nuh soon learned to avoid open combat and to prefer what we should today call guerilla tactics. He retreated into Borgu, a country of forests and swamp, leading the Moors after him into this natural trap. Supported by the local populations, Nuh constantly harried the white troops, who succumbed to the damp heat, strange food and diseased river-water. Their animals fell an easy prey to the tsetse fly.

Mahmud sent a long despatch to the Sharif declaring a permanent military conquest impossible. By this time, al-Mansur appears to have realized that Judar had been right in his initial assessment of the problems. To support Mahmud in his withdrawal, and negotiations with the Song'hai, he sent him fifteen hundred fresh cavalry, a like number of foot soldiers and five hundred spare horses. Later, four hundred more men were sent in a separate desert convoy. By the time the survivors of these expeditions arrived, in 1594, Mahmud had wisely withdrawn up the Niger to Timbuktu, leaving a small garrison in Gao.

Reviewing the Moorish campaign in the Western Sudan, it is clear they did not use all the advantages that their firearms gave them. They failed to exploit the countless tribal rivalries, and instead antagonized each and every population group by their cruelty and treachery. Historically, the result of their campaign was a general breakdown of order throughout the region. Twareg raids became bolder and more incessant, and warfare and plunder of all sorts became the order of the day.

While Mahmud had been down-river, the Twareg had already attacked Timbuktu, and the Moorish garrison had only been saved by reinforcements of three hundred men rushed up the Niger. This relieving force was led by the only officer of the Moorish army to have left behind a constructive record, a European named *Qaïd* Mami ben Barun. Although he had permission to slay all the townspeople of Timbuktu, who had themselves risen up against the Moors, he showed great moderation, paid for all his troops' supplies – and killed, with his own hand, a Moorish soldier who had robbed a Negro. He apologized to the religious leader of the city, the aged Abu Hafs Omar, for the excesses of the Moorish garrison.

To quote an authority on the period, 'Public confidence was restored, the people swore allegiance to the Sharif (of Fez), the fugitives returned from the desert, the trade routes were re-opened, and life in the city again became normal.' Encouraged by Mami's magnanimity, the scholars and merchants of Jenne hastened to make their submission and pay a tribute of sixty thousand *miqtal.*

Mami also showed himself ruthless when the situation justified it: he turned on the permanent trouble-makers, the outlying Twareg, killing every man he found and selling the women and children of the nomads into bondage. This so flooded the slave market that slaves were changing hands for the equivalent of a few cents each for several months. The Sanhaja Twareg retaliated, massacring a Moorish outpost; but when Mami's commander Mahmud returned from the South, his troops, plus two thousand timely reinforcements from Morocco, massacred the Sanhaja.

Mahmud then put into action a skilfully treacherous plan to plunder the city of Timbuktu. First he sent a crier through the streets saying that on the morrow there would be a house-to-house search for arms – but that houses of descendants of the saintly Sidi Mahmud, a former *qadi,* would not be searched. The rich hastened to deposit their wealth in the houses of the privileged clan, for it was known that the Moors would steal everything they found.

The citizens were then summoned to the Sankore mosque to swear allegiance to al-Mansur, and then dismissed. The descendants of the holy man were then convoked. The doors of the mosque were locked on them, and their 'exempted' houses, regorging with the long-accumulated wealth of Timbuktu, were systematically plundered from roof to cellar. Many prisoners in the mosque were also put to death; one hundred thousand *miqtal* of the loot was set aside for the Sharif in Fez; the commander and his followers shared the rest.

Even before the pillage, the despairing citizens of Timbuktu had, through Abu Hafs Omar, sent envoys to Marrakesh in 1592 to plead with the Sharif for better treatment. Al-Mansur professed dismay at their plight and sent them back with promises of redress and reform, and an escort of warriors under bu-Ikhtiyar, the renegade son of an unidentified Christian prince, who carried orders for more humane treatment for Timbuktu.

When the party reached Taghaza, it learned that it had been deceived. A desert messenger had been sent ahead with different orders. Omar and the scholars of Timbuktu were in chains already. Some months later, enfeebled by imprisonment, all were ordered to take the desert trail to Marrakesh. Among those who survived this ordeal were the aged Omar and the local historian Ahmed Baba.

When Omar and the literati were arrested, a European *qaïd*, Ahmed ben al-Haddad, assuming the measure to be part of Mahmud's personal excesses, slipped away across the desert himself to report to the Sharif the treatment of the people of Timbuktu. This time, al-Mansur apparently was genuinely impressed by the rapacity of his pro-consul, and particularly incensed to learn of his favorite expression: 'My sword is my sultan.'

When, shortly after, Omar and the other scholars reached his court he learned that the rapacious Mahmud had reserved for the royal purse only one hundred thousand *miqtal* of the plunder of Timbuktu. This incensed the Sharif as nothing else before had done, and he ordered another European *qaïd*, Mansur ben Abderrahman, to Timbuktu, with instructions to take over power from Mahmud and to put the desert general to an ignominious death.

Meanwhile, Mahmud was still conducting the difficult war against Nuh. He had established Moorish control of the river from Jenne to Gao, where the first desert commander, Judar, was in charge of the garrison. In the field, Mahmud received a friendly warning sent by the Sharif's son, Mulaï (prince) Abu Fares, of the fate that now awaited him. He at once launched a reckless attack on Nuh's forces, and sought and found death in battle. Nuh himself was killed in an encounter with the new Pasha, Mansur, shortly after.

The new commander saw that the situation was desperate. The Moors controlled the river, but not the back country. They had imposed neither order nor administration. They had not found the goldfields. They were permanently at war. Moreover, in Gao, the veteran campaigner Judar was unwilling to hand over to yet another newcomer from Marrakesh.

Mansur died shortly after, and it was assumed by commentators at the time that Judar had poisoned him. A fresh qaïd was despatched from Morocco, and Judar apparently poisoned him too. At this point, the only challenger to the Spanish eunuch's authority was Qaïd al-Mustafa, the incompetent, cruel Governor of Timbuktu: Judar strangled him with his own hands. Back in Marrakesh, al-Mansur got the point that, if he wanted someone to command his army, Judar it would have to be.

Fearing that the desert general would now declare himself independent, as the ruler of Song'hai, the Sharif hastened to assure Judar of his favor; he asked him to return to Morocco to quell a local rising. Judar replied that he would not come home until a competent Governor was sent to take his place. The Sharif sent two civilians, one a Portuguese; but Judar said the Mandingos of Mali were getting ready to attack, and civilians would be incapable of leading the defense against them. The Sharif then sent Ammar Pasha, who had previously led reinforcements out to the Sudan. A Portuguese eunuch, Ammar divided his one thousand men into two columns, one of which arrived, while the other perished to a man in the Sahara. Judar agreed to hand over to him.

Jasper Thomson, an English merchant living in Marrakesh, wrote a letter to a friend in London on July 4, 1599, recounting the return of the desert hero:

'Six days past, arrived here a nobleman from Gao called

64

Judar Pasha, who was sent by this King ten years past to conquer the said country, wherein many people of this country have lost their lives. He brought with him thirty camels laden with tibar, which is unrefined gold, yet the difference is but six shillings in an ounce weight between it and ducatees; also great store of pepper, unicorn's' (presumably rhino) 'horns and a certain kind of wood for dyers, to some 120 camel-loads; all which he presented unto the king, with fifty horse, and great quantity of eunuchs, dwarfs, and women and men slaves, beside fifteen virgins, the King's daughters of Gao, which he sendeth to be the King's concubines. You must note all these be of the coal black hair, for that country yieldeth no other.'

The writer valued the thirty camel-loads of gold at £604,800 – about eight million dollars in modern money.

As Judar had expected, the Mandingos rose after his departure and there were several smaller tribal disturbances. Ammar put them down, but with difficulty; he was replaced by Sulayman Pasha, who turned out to be both a good general and an able and relatively humane administrator. He moved the troublesome Timbuktu garrison to a camp outside the harassed city, and disciplined the army. A new, orderly chapter in the occupation of Song'hai began, to end with the death of al-Mansur in 1603.

The Victorious' three sons quarreled over the succession, each occupying a strongpoint. The youngest, Zidan, took Marrakesh, and eventually prevailed over his older rivals. But Sulayman had been recalled at the death of the old Sharif, and the Sudan was rocked by only partially repressed risings of Song'hai, Twareg and Fulani.

When Mulaï Zidan had finally established his position at home, he sent Ammar Pasha back to the desert to restore order. Ammar returned with a report that offered little hope of an ordered occupation and – after twentyeight years of death and desolation – the Moors were finally ordered withdrawn by the young Sharif.

The army on the Niger was now, however, a law to itself. From 1612 onward, it elected its own Pashas and qaïds (Monteil says there were two hundred Pashas between 1612 and 1750). It promoted and demoted its officers. It had filled its ranks with Arma – the mulatto offspring which the soldiers had produced with the local Song'hai. Despite the new Sharif's decision to renounce Song'hai, Timbuktu remained a Moorish town, nominally governed by an Askia appointed by the army – which had now decided never to go home at all. Weaker garrisons ruled in Gao, Jenne and Bamba.

To all intents and purposes, the Moors on the Niger were now independent, although the Friday prayer was still said in the name of the Sharif – and when al-Mansur died, the Niger Moors were quick to recognize Zidan. In 1660, however, the Timbuktu Pasha or 'Askia', Muhammad esh-Shetuki, repudiated the Sharif and had the prayer said in his name instead. Decades passed, and soon there were more Arma in the Song'hai cities than 'pure' Moors. Their hold on Timbuktu weakened, and finally they were over-run by the pagan Bambara.

By now, the Sa'adian dynasty in Marrakesh had given way to the Hassanids or Beni Filal, who faced a struggle with the supporters of the former ruling house. One of these raised a Negro army in Timbuktu to support his claim, then came to terms with a new Sharif and became this ruler's army commander, using the intended rebel troops as a sort of loyal guard. These *élite* black soldiers were so genuinely disinterested in politics, they soon became the best troops each succeeding Sharif had, and appeals were made to black Moroccans – the descendants of prisoners of the Sudan campaign, or of other slaves – to join the army. Negro children were reared as professional soldiers almost from their birth, and raids were made into the Sudan to capture or to buy more potential troops. By the 18th Century, according to Monteil, there were one hundred and fifty thousand Negroes in Morocco.

Meanwhile, the lost 'white' army on the Niger disappeared, over the years, into the Bambara and Song'hai poulations – although in the streets of Jenne and Timbuktu one still sees, in the merchant class, physical reminders that the pioneers of the great invasion of West Sudan were largely European troops.

*

Despite the catastrophe into which the campaign foundered, the invasion had brought considerable treasure to the Sultan's court. Laurence Madoc, another English merchant in Morocco, records seeing a thirty-mule train bringing gold back from the desert to a modern value of over two million dollars. Timbuktu's annual tribute was nearly as much; Gao's was more than Timbuktu's. Even as the occupation was collapsing, a trader reports the transport into Marrakesh of over three million dollars-worth of unrefined gold.

The Sharifian kingdom could thus afford luxuries; Captain John Smith of Virginia, in his *Travels,* records the presence in Marrakesh of English artisans, plumbers, stonemasons and watchmakers, who were well-paid for the time – seven dollars a day, free food and free clothes of wool, silk and linen, plus exemption from customs taxes. The watchmakers are thought by one authoritative historian to have been probably employed, in part, on maintaining the Sharif's navigational instruments, then much used in the desert.

The war had, as the merchants feared, spoiled rather than improved their business – and (as they had correctly predicted) the source of Sudanic gold had never been discovered. But at no time had the royal lust for conquest disappeared. Morocco had only one ally – England, its arms supplier. England's prestige, in Sharifian eyes, had risen with Elizabeth's defeat of the Sultan's old enemy, Philip of Spain. In 1600, the Moorish ruler had sent an envoy to wait on Queen Elizabeth at Nonsuch Park, there to propose a joint war on the Spanish King – after which Morocco and England would share the Spanish Empire in both the Old World and the New. Elizabeth, who needed Moroccan saltpeter, and could therefore not say No directly, prevaricated until al-Mansur's death, three years afterward.

Still the relatively advanced world had not found the location of the primitive redoubt whence came their huge and essential supplies of gold. It seems almost incredible that for two thousand years this colossal secret had not been pierced. Al-Adrisi had correctly named one of the sources – 'Wangara'; but where was Wangara? The name (the equivalent Hausa word to 'Mandingo', meaning someone or some place subject to a reigning monarch) came to apply to each and all the sources of the ore. As used by the Negroes themselves, it is not sure to which alluvial deposits reference was made – Ashanti, Lobi, Bambuk-Bure? By Adrisi's account, it may

67

well have been the latter, where dumb barter was still practised until the 18th Century.

References in Cà da Mosto and Jobson to women with 'saucers' buried in their lips suggest Lobi, where these adornments can still be seen. Again, such tribal characteristics need not necessarily identify the region where such things are seen today: Africa has always been a land of great migrations. The richest 'Wangara' was almost certainly Ashanti.

*

The 17th Century was to see a surge of European activity on the Guinea coast. Small but wealthy kingdoms developed. But in what might still be described as pre-European Africa – the part unseen by Europeans except for the occasional Christian slave or apostate eunuch officer in Morocco's armies – there was an age of decadence through most of the upland area known as the West Sudan. By the 18th and 19th Centuries, Hausa alone had any real claim to interest.

The Hausawa – whose Hamitic-origin language embodies Arabic and the Temajegh of the desert Berbers, and is written in an ideogrammatic form of Arabic script – are Negrified Berbers who occupy what is today Northern Nigeria and the desolate territory, Niger, just to the North. Legend says the tribe began when a Berber hero, Abu Yazid, arrived in what is now Daüra from Bornu in the 9th or 10th Century, slew the sacred serpent and married the Queen. The similarity with the legend of the Ethiopian Dynasty is too strong to be unnoticed: the story also recalls that of the Song'hai hero, Za Aliamen. Theoretically, from Abu Yazid's union came seven sons, whose descendants, in the 14th Century, founded Daüra, Kano, Zazaü, Gobir, Katsina, Biram and Rano – the Hausa Bokwoi or Seven States.

What is certainly true is that Hausa was founded by the Zaghawa or Twareg Berber invasion of the area, the invaders bringing with them such novelties as horses and the art of sinking wells in rock. Today the direct descendants of the Zaghawa are called Habe, and have included the first federal Prime Minister of Nigeria, Sir Abubakar Tafawa Balewa. Their capital appears to have been Gobir, for it is here that their nobility, the Imajeghan, settled. Bovill notes that it is perhaps significant that the Sarakuna, the ruling family of Gobir, have under one eye the same tribal mark found under the eyes of certain Pharaohs of Ancient Egypt. Muslims from Wangara, Mali and other points North converted Hausa to Islam, probably in the 14th Century.

The Hausawa are today best known as traders, and their language has become a lingua franca of the Western Sudan. They are also still famous as tanners, weavers, dyers, smiths and craftsmen generally. They have not distinguished themselves in war, although in the 15th Century, Queen Amina of Zazaü won notoriety for her conquests both on the battlefield and the sleeping rug. She toured her queendom regularly, taking a new lover at each resting-place and having him strangled in the morning.

The Hausawa states were always relatively small. They fought among themselves and against Gao (Song'hai), Bornu and the Malis. Government, by Kings, ministers, judges and other officials, was good by Sudanic standards. An abundant literature was produced, including Mohammed al-Maghili's 16th Century work 'On the Obligations of Princes'.

The other great people of the area are the Fulani, who arrived from the Futa Jaloh in the 13th Century. The Fulani divide into Cattle Fulani (Bororoje) and Fulanin Gidda. The former are nomadic, pagan pastoralists and bear the features of the Berbers and Jews from whom the tribe emerged. Even today, they rarely if every intermarry with their Negro neighbor-tribes. The Fulanin Gidda or City Fulani are Muslims who have intermarried very freely. The pale-skinned Cattle Fulani, who have been variously described as one of the Lost Tribes of Israel or as being the original gypsies, play no role in politics, stay primitive and ask only to be left alone. The black city Fulani are today the most powerful political tribe in Nigeria.

The Fulani hero of Hausa, Usuman dan Fodyo Dem, came from Gobir, where he was born in 1754. In the Fulani's original Futa heartland, he would have been called Usman Fode Dem: Dem is a Tukolor clan name. A devout Muslim and earnest preacher, author of nearly a hundred books, and hundreds of epistles, he soon attracted the venom of the King of Gobir, Nafata, whom he had criticized for encouraging the city's marked reversion into paganism. Nafata decreed that only born Muslims could practise Islam; he forbade the wearing of veils or turbans.

An uneasy peace between the Crown and the zealot lasted only until the monarch's death. He was succeeded by his son Yunfa, a former pupil of Usuman's, who decided the pious leader was too dangerous to live. A plot to murder Usuman then failed, and won the learned *mallam* even greater popularity.

Yunfa acted vigorously. He marched on Degel, Usuman's village, forcing him to flee. The date of his *hijra* or flight – February 21, 1804 – is still held quasi-sacred by the Fulanin Gidda. At Gudu, he collected an army of disciples, believers in a liberal Islamic trend which proned religious teaching for slaves and women, and approved Usuman's act in translating the Quran from the holy tongue, Arabic, into Fulani. Four months later, this force had defeated Yunfa and oathed itself to a *jihad* on infidels.

The crusaders now proclaimed Usuman 'Sarkin Musulmi' – 'Commander of the Faithful', a title still borne by the Sultan of Sokoto. The rulers of Katsina, Daüra, Kano, Adar and Zazaü, alarmed by Yunfa's fate, set upon Usuman's followers in their own realms; in reaction, almost all the Fulani rose against the dominant Hausawa – although with several Fulani fighting for the ruling pagans, and many Hausawa slaves and churls siding with the reforming, Islamic zealot.

Usuman dan Fodyo gave to each of his most trusted followers a flag, which he blessed, bidding them rid the world of infidels. Later these generals were to be given the Emirates of Katsina, Kano, Zaria, Bornu, Hadeïja, Adamawa, Gombe, Katagum, Ilorin, Nupe, Baüchi, Daüra, Messaü and Kazaüre – where, for the most part, their descendants rule today.

In Kano, the Hausawa army of ten thousand spearmen, some of them in chain armor (still seen in Northern Nigeria on days of celebration), were swiftly defeated by the Fulani archers. Soon the Hausawa states were under effective Fulani control. Bornu alone resisted; with the aid of Hausawa refugee troops and leaders – and, above all, the powerful assistance of al-Kanemi, the ruler of Kanem – Fulani hegemony was halted in the Bornu country west of Chad. Al-Kanemi, whose real name was Muhammed al-Amin, was a devout

70

Muslim, like Usuman, but was concerned at the spreading of Fulani power.

One of Usuman's disciples, Ahmadu Lobo or Seku, a man of great piety and humility, founded an Empire of his own to the west of Hausa. Starting from the village that became Hamdallahi (roughly, Halleluia in Arabo-Fulani), near Mopti, he defeated the Bambara at Masina and the Arma at Jenne, establishing control of a region from the Black Volta to Timbuktu. Usuman blessed his standards, and he took the honorname Sise (also written Sisay and Cisse) indicating a scholar versed in Arabic. He also called himself Amir ul Muminina – Commander of the Faithful. He ruled a strict, puritanical, theocratic régime composed of four Tukolor clans (Jallo, Ba, Sibide, Sangare) and a substantial slave class, until his death in 1845. The little Empire fell to al Haj 'Umar in 1862.

By 1810, the Fulani advance had reached its furthest point, although not the limit of its ambitions; further serious progress was checked by the forested South and the military power of such pagan tribes as the Yoruba and the hill peoples. In the East, the Fulani reached Yola market. To the West, they occupied Birnin Kebbi but failed to defeat all the Kebbawa. The Fulani established a loose form of government based on Quranic law and the payment of tribute to the joint capital Emirates. Usuman himself retired from the struggle once history had defined the limits of his conquests; he devoted himself to religious study, first at Sifawa, then at Sokoto, where he died in 1817 and where he is buried.

After Usuman, the religious zeal of the Empire died, and raids on recalcitrant Hausawa villages were more concerned with the acquisition of slaves than with the propagation of the Prophet's Faith.

*

Another empire which lasted until colonial times was that of the Mossi. Originally, there were five states between the Black Volta and the great bend of the Niger River: Wagadugu, Yatenga, Fada Ngurma, Mamprusi and Dagomba. By oral tradition, these states had a common origin. In the 13th or 14th Centuries, people from the Lake Chad area described as 'red men' – that is, light-colored Africans, presumably of Berber descent – conquered the

71

Gur- and Mande-speaking aborigines of the region. They installed a system similar in organization and ritual to that of the Hausawa Bokwoi. They tamed horses and used cavalry in war. The ruling caste favored the Mande traders, but treated the Gur majority as serfs and slaves; however, the Gur language prevailed over all the others, as did Gur religious beliefs. Islam came later, but failed to make a deep penetration until recent times.

The first state appears to have been Mamprusi. In the 14th and 15th Centuries, the empire spread north-ward, seizing Timbuktu in 1338. A six-year expedition which began in 1477 actually reached Walata, where it was finally driven off by Sonni Ali. The power of the Askias in the North eventually contained the movement of the Mossi states, which were then consolidated into Wagadugu, Fada Ngurma and Yatenga. Later, the possibility of an advance South led to the creation of the Dagomba state. The Mossi states are in modern Voltaic Republic, except Dagomba, most of which lies in modern Ghana.

Pressures from Song'hai in the north and Ashanti in the South failed to break up the Mossi-Dagomba states. When Europeans arrived at the end of the 19th Century they found them intact, and ruled by direct descendants of their founders. The frontiers had barely changed. The principal Mossi ruler, the Mogho Naba, is still a great figure in Voltaic national politics.

*

Kanem, which aided the Hausawa against the Fulani, was another state of long duration, roughly corresponding to the modern Nigerian region of Bornu, and land across Lake Chad. The origins of Kanem go back to the 8th Century, and its peak period lasted until the 13th. It reached its widest frontiers under *Maï* Dunama Dibbalemi (1210–1224). The Saïfawa dynasty ruled from the 9th to the 19th Centuries. The people, much influenced by Mediterranean culture, cast pottery and bronze (by the lost wax process). Women enjoyed a power role in government, and the Kanemi were great trading folk.

There has been a long tradition of iconoclasm in religion; even today, the Bornuese reject the spiritual authority of the

Sultan of Sokoto, the Sarkin Musulmi. Leo Africanus found the Kanemi masses still pagan in 1526. When Denham and Clapperton penetrated Kanem four centuries later, they found that the *Maï* (King) still spoke from behind a curtain, surrounded by the trappings of a power which had much diminished. In 1870, the German explorer Gustav von Nachtigal found authority had been taken over by the palace serfs and slaves – whence it was to be wrested by the mighty Rabeh, whose story belongs in a later chapter.

One of the mysterious ruined cities of Darfur in the central Sahara, Djebel Uri, may have been a Kanemi district capital in the 13th Century. Several drystone buildings remain, with walls still standing to about twelve feet.

An historian says: 'Kanem was truly in the Middle Ages the civilizer of the central Sudan, just as Mali . . . was the civilizer of the Western Sudan. These were the centers which saw the elaboration of Sudanic civilization as we know it today: so different from the civilization of the Arabs and from that of the purely Negro tribes of the South.'

In this regard, two contemporary historians have this to say: 'The typical "Sudanic" state was not feudal. It was based on the hereditary position and power of great families within the state. It was in principle something nearer to a bureaucracy – a bureaucracy without paper, ink, desks or telephones – in which power was wielded by officials, who held their office during the King's pleasure, and who could be transferred from post to post, promoted, demoted and even destituted, by a nod of the divine head or a syllable from the divine mouth.

'Around the royal person circled a galaxy of titled office-bearers, as numerous as the economic organization of each particular state was able to support. The pre-eminent offices were nearly always those of the Queen Mother – (actually) the Queen Sister – and of a limited number of titled "great wives" of the ruler. At the head of the administration were a few high officials, often four in number. From these depended a descending hierarchy of provincial and district chiefs, often recruited from the pages, sons or nephews of the great, who had been educated at the royal court.

'The main concern of such administrations was the raising of tribute for the support of the King and of the semi-urbanized inhabitants of his capital – on the one hand, articles of consumption such as wives and labor, beer and foodstuffs; on the other, the materials of long-distance trade, such as ivory, skins, gold, copper, salt and kola-nuts. External trade was always in some sense a royal monopoly. Artists, craftsmen and other specialists were located at the royal capital, and were an important attribute of the royal power; there was indeed a tendency for the rulers of such states to be themselves identified at least with the mysterious craft of the smith.'

An authority notes that 'the longer an Empire lasted, the more corrupt and inefficient its administration was apt to become, and the more its rulers tended to concentrate on ensuring their own wealth and pleasure, so that provincial Governors and subject peoples had both more incentive and more opportunity to rebel or to co-operate with the new invader.'

The Sudanic states rarely pushed far into the forested South, where their cavalry was at the mercy of the tsetse and the technique of combat gave advantage to defenders. Nevertheless, many West African traditions, such as the Akan legends of the Ivory Coast and (modern) Ghana, claim that the people of these areas came 'from the North' or 'from the East'; some degree of migration, and therefore of invasion, must be assumed.

*

The forested South developed in a different way. If the great parched wastes of modern Mali and Niger bear obvious traces of the influence of the peoples of the desert, and of the Mediterranean, the catalytic force on the West African coast was Atlantic Europe. Here the influence was long, constant and – by Sudanic standards – extremely peaceful. It begins in earnest in the 15th Century. Slaves from what is today Saint-Louis-du-Sénégal reached Lisbon in 1444.

By 1475, the Portuguese had reached the Bight of Biafra – the shores of modern Nigeria. In the same century, Portuguese traders went inland and reached the Benin kingdom. When Europeans 'returned' to Benin in 1897, they found much evidence of Portuguese influence still, including the habit of crucifying the King's enemies. By the late 19th

Century, Benin had become synonymous with horror and barbarity – a 'city of blood' – but when the first Portuguese arrived it was at its *apogée*. In the heart of the rain-forest, it had been a remarkable achievement.

Benin illustrates, as the Sudanic Empires do, that the dynamics of rise and fall were much the same in Africa as in Europe and in Asia – with the hard core of savagery lurking, as in Renaissance Europe, in the near background, ready to reappear at the first hint of anarchy or disagreement. Some contemporary writers have sought emotionally to relate the fallow period of history which preceded colonization in West Africa to the slave trade, and thereby to blame it on external forces; but the evidence suggests that the Sudanic and Guinean cultures flourished, became exhausted under the weight of their own intrigues, corruption and incompetence, and justly died – much the same story as Egypt, Athens, Rome and Lisbon. The inference that the slave trade was principally the initiative of foreign powers should also be rejected, in the light of historic evidence: the slave trade was, first and foremost, Africa's greatest industry.

Some Guinean cultures show similarities with the Sudanic. The art of the Nok civilization, both abstract and naturalist, suggests influences from the North. Remarkable figurines over two thousand years old have survived. Other elements of Guinean life with a Kushite or Egyptian flavor include the whole conception of divine kingship, and the use of ram's heads in religious decoration. A distinguished modern scholar, Dr Saburi Biobaku, finds in his own Yoruba tribe 'Egyptian, Etruscan and Jewish influences'.

Populations closer to the coast tended to be thinner, because of the forest. The choice of Liberia as a place of settlement by the American Colonization Society, and of the Freetown area by the British Abolitionists, was largely dictated by the absence of population in these rain-forest regions. The tsetse eliminated mules and horses and made head-loading the only form of transport – thus retarding real development toward the coast. But the West African coast, later to be known to historians as the Coast, with a capital C, had great rivers. The Niger is navigable for most of its two thousand six hundred miles. Steamships can use it for considerable distances, and the Benue, the Niger's great tributary, is navigable below Yola. In the wet season, the Senegal is navigable for five hundred and sixty miles, to Kayes. The Gambia can be used for three hundred miles. Another advantage was a relative profusion of natural harbors – today's Lagos, Freetown, Dwala, Bathurst, Saint-Louis, Port Harcourt and Dakar.

The arrival of Europe on the Coast was to turn the face of Sudanic trade away from the desert, especially when the colonial development period brought roads, river traffic and lines of rail. This was timely in every way, for the passage of the years had not made Sahara crossings any easier. In 1805, a train of one thousand eight hundred camels and two thousand men perished totally on the way back to Taghaza, from Timbuktu.

Only the great value attached to gold – and salt – made these incredible journeys purposeful. For long after the heroic period, a caravan known as the Azalaï or Taghalam would set out each fall from Aïr for Bilma, the capital of Kawar, to fetch salt for the Hausa country. As late as 1908, when the Azalaï was in decline, Bovill records trains of twenty thousand camels.

The Azalaï camels were gathered from the Kel Geres and Itesan tribes over a long preparatory period, and grazed for the journey at Tabello. The round trip took only three weeks, but the track is still marked today by hundreds of camel skeletons. The trains were frequently beset by raiding Twareg. The journey was made in October, and the traditional trail boss was the Sarkin Turawa of Agades, vizier of the Amenokal (Sultan).

Corn and cloth from Hausa were taken to barter for the salt, and great quantities of fodder, there being no camel food but dates in Kawar. The Kawar outpost of Fachi was reached in five days, and there the Azalaï was joined by another caravan coming from Damagaram. Bilma was reached three days later.

The return journey followed the same route back to Agades whence, after a short rest, the Sarkin Turawa took the caravan on to Sokoto, Kano and other Hausa markets. The camels then returned to Aïr with grain and dyed cloth. The latter was so admired that cloth would be sent from Ghadames in the far-away Fezzan of the Libyan desert to

76

Kano, to be dyed and sent back for sale in Tripoli. Mediterranean markets also prized Hausa leatherwork.

Today, Kano cloth is still seen worn as far away as Mauritania. It often goes there today, of course, by sea, and it is by sea that the Hausa country now imports its Manchester cottons, French rayons, sugar, tea. Older trade goods like Tripolitanian silk, Venetian glass beads, mirrors and needles from Styria, once staples of the camel routes, are no longer found; but desert caravans still bring kola nuts and other more localized delicacies as far as Kano, which lies on the twelfth parallel – the dividing line between the desert savannah and the central African tropical belt.

Although the Fezzan-Kawar trail carried great quantities of salt South from Bilma, it was essentially a slave-route. Bovill says: 'Every European who traveled this blood-stained highway recorded his horror at the thousands of human skeletons with which it was strewn. They were mostly those of young women and girls, and were particularly numerous around the wells, showing how often the last desperate effort to reach water led only to death from exhaustion.

'There had long been a big demand for Negro slaves on the North African littoral, partly for local use, but more particularly for export to Egypt and Turkey. . . . Hausa slaves were more highly valued than any others, the men for their skill and intelligence, the women for their good looks, cheerfulness and neatness.' So great was the demand for slaves, and the Arabs' profits on the traffic, that frequently camel trains took nothing else; Denham records that Mediterranean merchants trading into Bornu would accept payment for their goods in nothing but slaves, which Bovill calls the 'chief currency' of Bornu.

Bovill goes on: 'In their own interest the slave merchants saw that their slaves were in good condition before they set out to cross the desert. The men, who were mostly youths, were coupled with leg-irons and chained by the neck, but the women and girls were usually allowed to go free. Only the strongest survived the desert march, and these were little better than living skeletons by the time they reached Fezzan. There they were rested and fattened for the Tripoli and Benghazi markets, where prime slaves could be sold at a profit of five hundred per cent.

77

'An important but particularly hideous branch of the trade was the traffic in eunuchs, for whom, as guardians of the harem, there was a big local and foreign demand. It was customary in the Sudan to geld the most robust of the boys and youths captured in slave raids, and some tribes, notably the Mossi, punished crime with castration – in order, no doubt, to foster a lucrative trade. Only about ten per cent of the victims survived the brutal mutilations which were performed in the crudest possible manner.'

Bovill quotes a Kano source, in 1919, for a description of the gelding of one hundred Ningi: ten survived. Barth gives the usual survival percentage as being 'less than ten per cent'. The Mossi were said to have greater relative skill than other tribes at the operation, and to keep their surgical methods secret. Says Bovill: 'They and the Bornuese enjoyed international reputations in the trade in which the principal foreign buyers were Turkey, Egypt and the Barbary states.' Because eunuchs were a home-consumption product as well as an export, prices were competitively high. (The practice of gelding, usually associated with Africa and the Middle East, also existed in Europe, notably in Spain, France and Italy, where the male sopranos of the Sistine Chapel were world-famous – and where the practice continued until late in the 19th Century.)

Slavery as a whole was both a home and foreign market activity; many strong tribes spent most of their time raiding weaker ones. Bovill describes how, mounted on mares – which are less inclined to neigh and squeal than stallions – the attackers would surround a village silently, in the night, and capture everyone at dawn. 'Only the young men and women were taken. The older men, who had little value, and the aged and infirm of both sexes, who were unsaleable, were usually slaughtered.' In Bornu, Barth saw '170 men in the prime of life being left to bleed to death' after such a raid.

The European Abolitionists helped, indirectly, to destroy the Sahara camel traffic in general, not only by killing trade in the most profitable of Africa's homespun industries, but also because the cultivation of the oases – on which the camel trains depended for existence – was the work of chattel slaves. With the neglect of the oases came the death of the camel caravan as it had been known for countless centuries.

All this, of course, had certain disadvantages. An historian writes: 'Desperate need compelled the people of the desert to prey on each other. Anarchy, such as even the nomads in their long and troubled history had never known, became general. The desert boiled over, as it had done when the Romans tried to deny the nomads their traditional grazing grounds, but on a vaster scale. The raiding of the sedentary agriculturists of the peripheral areas reached proportions which none could stem. Within the desert, the oases continued to shrink, the wells fell in, and the water-holes dried up.

'Through human neglect the desert became more sterile than ever before, and the ties which for countless centuries had bound Barbary to the Western Sudan were for ever broken.'

But, long before the abolition of slavery, global interests in the African trade had much diminished; this perhaps accounts best for the few centuries of political and economic twilight which preceded the brief colonial era – which suddenly ushered what was by then a largely stagnant continent into the relatively prosperous century in which we live. The desert journey, with its dependence on oases, on the *takshif* getting through to Walata and bringing a supply train with water four days out to meet the caravan – and similar fallible elements – could only be justified by enormous profits. Deaths from disease on the Coast were so high that the sea route was an ordeal too. By the end of the 16th Century, Africa had almost ceased to be worth such risks. Drake's *Pelican*, in 1580, on an investment of five thousand pounds, showed a return of one and a half million pounds – which was why he renamed the vessel the *Golden Hind*. A New World, or new worlds, had been discovered, and European commerce began to look toward Asia and especially the Americas. Neither slaving, palm oil, the Rand or colonial development ever quite restored sub-Sahara Africa's comparative importance in the world of trade; but by its very size, and potential wealth, Black Africa could never be neglected, either.

2 SHIP AND SHORE

The Age of Trade and Exploration

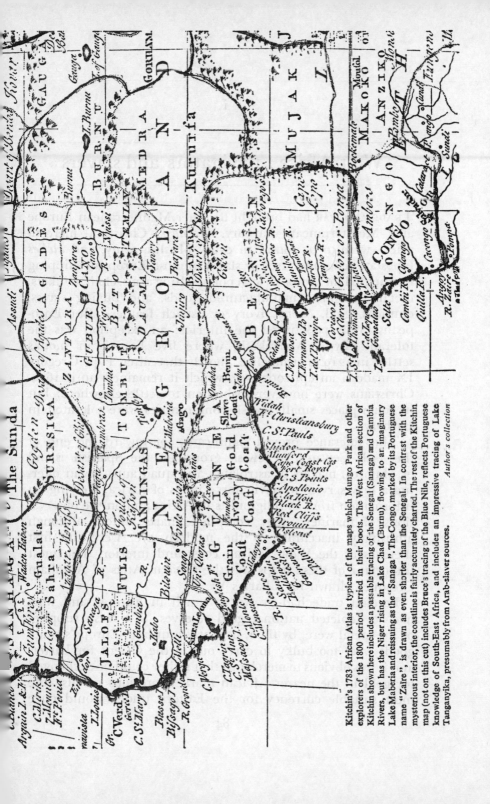

Kitchin's 1783 African Atlas is typical of the maps which Mungo Park and other explorers of the 1800 period carried in their boots. The West African section of Kitchin shown here includes a passable tracing of the Senegal (Sanaga) and Gambia Rivers, but has the Niger rising in Lake Chad (Burnu), flowing to an imaginary Lake Maberia and reissuing as the "Sanaga". The Congo, marked by its Portuguese name "Zaire", is drawn as even shorter than the Senegal. In contrast with the mysterious interior, the coastline is fairly accurately charted. The rest of the Kitchin map (not on this cut) includes Bruce's tracing of the Blue Nile, reflects Portuguese knowledge of South-East Africa, and includes an impressive tracing of Lake Tanganyika, presumably from Arab-slaver sources.   *Author's collection*

West Africa : navigators and slavers

TRADE AND WAR had brought together Mediterranean Europe and Mediterranean Barbary. *Frendji* – Christian mercenaries – were to be found in every Muslim army, and *elches* (apostate renegades, free or slave) in most. European shipping frequented the Arab-African ports, selling arms, cloth, trinkets, metal and other manufactured goods, and buying slaves, eunuchs, gold, ebony, ivory or ostrich feathers. But Europeans rarely penetrated the interior: an exception was the tolerant city of Marrakesh, where five Franciscan monks settled in 1219 to evangelize. Shortly thereafter, Pope Gregory IX made it an episcopal see, which it remained until 1639. Christians were however forbidden to settle elsewhere; but in some places small Jewish communities were tolerated in Barbary.

This tolerance proved significant, for toward the end of the 14th Century, a Jewish group on the Spanish island of Majorca, makers of astrolabes and quadrants, began offering a new service to navigators – maps of Africa. Relying on information from co-religionists in Africa and on the observations of mariners, they compiled charts which, although amusingly inaccurate to the modern eye, were the first sketches of the West African coast and interior. The most important of these maps was the Catalan Atlas of Abraham Cresques, drawn for Charles V.

Foreign trade had grown so much in Europe, and wars had so depleted national gold reserves, that fresh supplies of the metal were, by then, urgently required. Europe's trade goods were too bulky to carry out to the Orient for barter, and it was obvious to merchants that if they could be exchanged for gold in the nearer African market, precious metals – the most suitable currency for the Eastern trade – would once more be available. Although the Majorcan maps were so hopelessly inaccurate as to be frequently more of a danger than a help to pioneer travelers, they gave men the encouragement to dare the overland Sahara route to the Moors' source of Black African gold.

Hesitations about the hazards of such a journey were partly resolved by the landing in Marseille, in 1413, of a Toulousain, Anselme d'Isalguier, who had left home eleven years before and not been heard of since. Historians have assumed that he took part in the Norman expedition of Jean de Béthencourt, which departed in 1402 to conquer the Canaries. Isalguier had spent some years in Gao (the *Tarikh el-Fettach* refers to a Christian slave in Gao at that period), had won favor at the court and married a Song'hai princess, Kasaïs.

Isalguier landed with his wife, her rich dowry of gold and jewels, their daughter, three Song'hai maidservants and three eunuchs. The eventual arrival of this exotic party in Toulouse caused something of a stir, and one of the eunuchs set up practice as a doctor there; the Dauphin Charles became one of the eunuch's patients.

One man encouraged by Isalguier's experience to set out for the African interior was a wealthy, couragcous, Genoese merchant, Antonio Malfante, who penetrated deep into the Sahara, learned useful information about the route – but discovered no gold. Others are thought to have followed, and to have secured some limited success in trade. Benedetto Dei, representing the Florentine banking house Portinari, is recorded as being in Timbuktu somewhat later – in 1470 – selling Lombard cloth. He returned to Florence safely, but his records have not survived.

If one man can be said to have opened up Africa to the outside world more than any other it was Prince Henry the Navigator. Portugal's national hero won his spurs at the capture of Ceúta (today a Spanish enclave in Morocco) in 1415, when he was twentyone. He became royal Governor of the city. This early African experience fired him with a lifetime ambition to explore the unknown continent, monopolize its gold resources and convert the heathen.

At this time, the sea journey held almost as many terrors for superstitious medieval man as the Sahara. Beyond Cape

Bojador, legend said, were impenetrable mists from which no ship could escape; the mist was inhabited by devils who swept craft into a seething lake of liquid fire. Henry insisted all this was nonsense. An inspired subject, master mariner Gil Eannes, set out to prove his sovereign right, and returned to Lisbon in 1434 with a sprig of rosemary picked in what is today Senegal. The dead flower was a court sensation; it proved that Eannes had gone beyond the desert coast to the green country to the south – and that the devils and brimstone were not there. Several ships set out in Eannes' wake, mostly caravels (wide-sterned craft of great stability), registered as ships of fifty tons (that is, over one hundred tons by modern reckoning).

The passion to open a new frontier made the blood run fast in hundreds of young Portuguese of the age. Many volunteers to sail to Africa had to be turned away, some to be recruited by pirate vessels. Converting Africans to Christianity was one of Henry's stated aims; although it was not as important as trade, it was the purpose he emphasized – for obvious political reasons – and he used it as a lever to secure from the Pope a decree that whatever countries might be discovered *between Bojador and India* would be Portugal's.

The first 'discoveries' were of course repeats of those of Carthaginian times. The mouth of the Senegal at modern Saint-Louis was assumed – with Herodotus as the authority – to be a 'western branch of the Nile', and so charted. On a tree the seamen carved Henry's arms, and his motto, *Talent de bien fayre*. Here for the first time they saw a country where the people were in majority black. Borrowing from the Berber words Akal 'n-Iguinawen (Negroland) and Aguinaou (Negro), they called the area Ghinea. The modern spelling, of course, is Guinea.

Later, the Venetian mariner Alvise Cà da Mosto was chartered by Henry to prospect the Gambia River, which it was rightly believed led into the 'Wangara' gold country. Cà da Mosto went up the river, but failed to reach the mines. Portugal then obtained permission from Sonni Ali to send a mission overland from Cape Arguin (in modern Mauritania) to Timbuktu; only one man survived the awful two-way march, and the journey proved fruitless for trade.

By the end of the 15th Century, Portugal had established a number of trading stations along the coast between the Gambia and the Bight of Benin, but had failed to make any advance into the interior, where forest, swamp and hostile tribes barred the way. In 1481, eleven years before Columbus landed in Cuba, the Portuguese built a fort, São Jorge da Mina, on the Gold Coast. Still standing and in use as a police center today, just outside a village called Elmina (modern Ghana), it is an extraordinary monument to Portugal's determination to establish itself in Africa – and to the value, at that early date, of the coastal gold trade. At that time, King João II of Portugal was permitted by the Pope to style himself Lord of Guinea, a title which only died with the advent of the republic in this century. The use of the word Guinea for the area became general at the end of the 15th Century. The English coin of that name was first minted in 1662; it was so called because it was cast from highly pure West African gold, and was worth five per cent more than sovereigns made from other sources.

By the end of the fifteenth century, Portuguese knowledge of the coast was considerable, but the interior remained a mystery. How long this would have continued if Africa had remained the tempting new frontier can only be a question for speculation. As it was, the discovery of America at once began to push interest in Africa into the background.

*

Eventually, however, it was to be the discovery of the Americas that re-launched a major trading drive in Africa, by providing a burgeoning market for the African slave industry. The Portuguese, the first great African 'colonial' power, were already sending ten thousand slaves a year to Brazil one hundred years after Columbus' voyage, and this rhythm was maintained from about 1580 to 1680. In all, about a million Africans, mostly Angolans, crossed the South Atlantic to Bahia in the 17th Century. A story, perhaps apocryphal, but possibly true, has the Bishop of Luanda satisfying the Vatican mandate to the Portuguese monarchy by sitting in a chair on Luanda harborside, hand upraised, baptizing the crowds of slaves as they rowed past, out to the ships, under the shadow of the whip. The great British port of Liverpool was largely built from the profits of slaving, which reached a peak in the 18th Century. During the single decade 1783–1793, Liverpool ships were to handle three hundred thousand slaves on the Middle Passage. This may have involved a profit of as much as three million dollars yearly.

Portugal was the earliest of Africa's major European trading partners, and to begin with slaves were a relatively unimportant part of barter. Portugal had trade with the inland port of Benin, now in modern Nigeria, in the late 15th Century, when America had only recently been discovered and all the African trade was still directed to the needs of metropolital Portugal. The Benin kingdom welcomed the appointment of a resident royal agent from Lisbon, Duarte Pires, and also accepted missionaries. From Benin and neighboring ports, such as Warri, young men of chiefly family went off to the court in Lisbon, to be returned as intellectuals and Catholics. When Richard Wyndham, a captain out of Bristol, anchored at Benin in 1554 and bought eighty tons of pepper, he found many of the people spoke some Portuguese.

Also in the 15th Century, Portuguese and some Spanish navigators explored the West African coast as far South as the Congo estuary and beyond. With the new prosperity opened up by shipborne trade, the hitherto backward coastal kingdoms of Atlantic Africa began to eclipse in importance and wealth the vast savannah states which had for centuries conducted trade with the Mediterranean world along the desert routes.

The initial attraction of African trade, apart from the great, permanent need for gold, and before the development of the Americas boosted the trade in men, was connected with the traditional spice traffic with Asia, an overland commerce which passed expensively through many middle-men, each specializing in some commodity – silk, sugar, precious stones, ivory, or spices proper. Portugal, France, Spain and Britain all sought to break the spice trade monopoly of Venice, Genoa and Trieste, the great maritime city-states which bought with timber, iron, Christian slaves, and occasionally gold and silver. Earlier, the Crusades had been fought to make the spice routes to the Orient more open. The western kingdoms sought cheaper, closer sources for 'spice'.

The Guinea coast was also an attraction for the Barbary pirates. The Genoese themselves had set the Guinean trading pattern. In 1270 they had sent an expedition to the Canaries. In 1291, some Genoese ships had set out to circumnavigate Africa. The convoy never returned, but in recent years some evidence has been turned up that they may have reached East Africa. As the power of Genoa declined, Genoese navigators – including, of course, Columbus, who sailed for Spain – offered their services to wealthy foreign courts. Portugal's Prince Henry the Navigator was one of their most dynamic employers.

Two centuries before, Spain had reduced the Arab occupation of Iberia to the single Emirate of Granada, leaving independent the Christian kingdoms of Castile, Aragon and Portugal. All these kingdoms sought three things: to monopolize West African trade and escape dependence on the Levantine-dominated trade routes with the Orient; to find a passage into the Indian Ocean and buy, direct, those products which it still would be worthwhile to bring all the way from the East; and to make Christian converts who would be allies against the permanent threat of Islamic imperialism. Prince Henry, at least, was to some degree successful in all these aims.

In 1448, the Portuguese erected a fort on Arguin, where the fishing, then as now, was good. It was from this date that Portuguese exploration of the coast became systematic. By 1460, when Henry died, the Senegal and Rokel rivers had both been charted for navigation, and the first Negroes had been brought to Lisbon for conversion and education.

In 1469, the Crown granted Fernão Gomes a five-year monopoly of the Guinean trade on the condition that his ships should go a hundred leagues (four hundred miles) further into the South Atlantic every year. A one-year extension to the agreement gave Gomes control until 1475. By then he had established a base on Fernando Póo and discovered El Mina, with its opportunity for side-tracking the Muslim gold traders. At this point, the Portuguese Crown reassumed control of the coastal commerce.

In 1482 the Congo was reached, and six years later Bartolomeu Dias rounded the Cape and entered the Indian Ocean – a feat comparable to the first orbital flight of an astronaut in modern times. In 1497, Vasco da Gama also

89

rounded the Cape, and went on to visit India. By then, the West African trade, except in gold, had fallen short of what its entrepreneurs expected. West Africa, as a source of supply, could not compare to India, and neither could compete with the Americas.

The complaints found in West African traders' records of this early period are all much the same. The West Africans were reported 'unreliable' in furnishing the ivory in the quantities promised and at the periods agreed. West African pepper proved less successful on the market in Europe than Indian pepper. Sample loadings of slaves were brought to Western Europe, but the shippers reported back to the African exporters that demand was poor. The European countries that bought slaves, and Turkey, already had a source of supply in Barbary. Gold alone justified the long voyages to West Africa, at this early stage; and it was to warehouse gold, protect traders and mariners, and prevent smuggling that the fort of El Mina was built in 1481. A royal governor and garrison were then installed.

Competition developed, despite papal bulls in 1451, 1455 and 1456 restricting Guinean exploration and trade to Portugal. In 1494, the Treaty of Tordesillas gave the New World to Castille, Africa and Asia to Portugal; but lesser naval powers, such as England, France and Denmark, continued to interlope. Among skippers chartered to sail to West Africa by merchants during the century that followed (the 16th) were three famous names: Jean Ango of Dieppe and William and John Hawkins of England. These men were in fact little more than seaborne gangsters; but the greater part of British and French energies were devoted, not to West Africa, but to plundering Spanish ships in the Caribbean – the 'Spanish Main'.

European atttention in West Africa was concentrated mainly on 'Upper Guinea', from modern Sierra Leone to Mauritania. There was less interest in the Grain Coast (modern Liberia) and the Ivory Coast, where the surf approaches were dangerous and there were no ports, no useful natural anchorages. Further east, the Gold Coast and what was to become known as the Slave Coast (Dahomey) attracted somewhat more attention. For over a century the Portuguese remained the dominant power; as well as the

El Mina fort, they erected a few smaller fortified trading posts, and a watering station in the Cabo Verde Islands.

*

The Portuguese who came to Africa africanized themselves, rather than attempting to convert the natives to their own customs and religion. Despite the monopoly on trade conferred by the papal decrees, many Portuguese acted as agents for non-Portuguese interests. In these and other ways, the Portuguese 'Coasters', divided by many mail or travel months from the mother country, inevitably showed their independence from Lisbon control; as a consequence of this and certain other factors, Lisbon's ambitious plans for converting and developing Africa largely failed.

But there was some money to be made in the area, and the Gold Coast soon became the most successful trading center on the littoral. By the 16th Century, the forts at El Mina, Shama and Axim were supplying one-tenth of the world's total gold supply. The dust was bought with cloth, pots, beads, trinkets or cowries, and with slaves from other parts of the Coast. But the Portuguese were prevented from trading directly with the Gold Coast interior. Their penetration of Benin, in the 'Nigerian' interior, in 1483, was assisted by two elements: it was reachable by ship, and the Bini had a surplus of slaves – prisoners acquired in their conquest of the Niger Delta, then in progress. The principal ultimate buyers were the Fanti of the Gold Coast. In 1486, the Portuguese established their own Delta port at Gwato, near Benin.

In 1493, the Portuguese built a settlement on Fernando Póo (now a Spanish province) and began one on São Tomé. Sugar plantations were sown on these islands, and on the neighboring Atlantic islets of Principe (still Portuguese) and Annobón (now Spanish). This venture might have developed, and possibly even led to plantations on the mainland, if Brazil had not then appeared on the historical scene as a much larger and more promising area for Portuguese agricultural settlement. In the latter half of the following century, the Dutch, having finally thrown off Spanish rule, began to take an interest in West Africa also.

It was at this time that the Spanish conquest of much of

South and Central America and the Caribbean raised labor problems for the mines and for farming in the New World. The indigenous population they had found was small, and peculiarly unsuited for intensive work; slave labor appeared the natural solution to an imperial power which, by working the West African coast, had come into touch with populations which looked on slaves as a normal trade commodity. West African slaves suited the tropical climate of the Americas, and Guinean chiefs had been seeking for years to boost this profitable commerce. With the winds, the voyage from the Coast to the Caribbean only took a month. Slavery thus provided an easy answer to what could have been an insuperable economic problem. The African leadership and their European partners-in-trade were satisfied, and the terrible traffic in living human flesh began.

The Spanish government gave *asientos* to Portuguese merchants for a fixed number of slaves. During most of the 16th Century, Portugal had a theoretical monopoly of the traffic, although piracy naturally began. The famous English mariner John Hawkins slaved in 1562 and 1568. This century saw the beginnings of the trade in earnest.

In the 17th Century, the Dutch became serious competitors in the slave trade and colonial commerce, opposing the Portuguese, the Spanish and the British. They occupied part of Brazil and joined with English and French buccaneers in the Caribbean to cause Spain to lose the balance of maritime power in the Main. At one point, the Dutch occupied nearly all the Portuguese trading posts in West Africa; by 1642, they held all the Portuguese forts from Arguin to Luanda, and were in a position to block and control all slave traffic to Brazil. The great Dutch figure of this buccaneering age was Maurice of Nassau.

By 1648, the Portuguese had recovered part of their losses and by 1654 they had managed to drive the Dutch from Brazil. But the Dutch remained the dominant West African trading power for a decade longer; they retained a quasi-monopoly of the slave trade with Spanish America, as well as with the new French, English and of course Dutch possessions in the West Indies, where labor was required in the sugar, vanilla and tobacco fields. Later in the century, however, the English and French began to rely almost entirely on their own merchant shipping for the slave trade to their own Caribbean possessions.

The ships of the Dutch States-General took their flag into the Indian Ocean. Churchill has written that 'great Dutch fleets, heavily laden, doubled the Cape of Good Hope several times a year'. England, which had become Britain by the Restoration of the Scottish Stuarts, was as concerned as Portugal at this sudden rise in naval power. Tangiers, part of the dowry of Catherine of Braganza, had become a fief of the English realm, and this invited new concern with the balance of power in West Africa. Britain, with one hundred and fifty ships, crippled the Dutch fleet off Lowestoft in 1665; but the following year the Dutch, under the great Admiral de Ruyter, held off two major attacks and finally drove the British vessels into the Thames. A British victory in the Channel two months later (August 1666) was followed by British reverses at the hands of both Holland and France. In 1667, the Dutch sailed into Chatham harbor, burning ships of the line. But when peace came in 1668, with both sides exhausted, Holland had lost by default some of her control of the Guinean trade.

The era was also one of exploration, for much remained unknown about the African Atlantic. In 1618, a ship under Captain George Thompson sailed four hundred miles up the Gambia River, where Thompson was killed in a riverside quarrel. Two years later, Richard Jobson repeated the voyage, getting higher up the river. He found game in abundance, and reported that the natives had an easy and 'most idle kinde of life'. There was 'musicke . . . dancing . . . and hethenish noyse' most nights. Possibly Jobson arrived in the late rains, when the harvest is gathered and men relax from their toil, and when religious festivities like circumcision, initiation, marriages, and so on, are the order of the day. Islam had penetrated the area, and Jobson expressed admiration for the Almoravids or marabouts – which he picturesquely spells 'Mary-buckes'.

An important pioneer of the period who has left an interesting record is William Bosman, whose African descendants are now a distinguished Ghanaian family. Bosman was fourteen years in Guinea for the Dutch West India Company, finishing his career as Chief Factor at Elmina. His *New and*

Accurate Description of the Coast of Guinea was published in London in 1705, and includes accounts of the castles of Elmina, Cape Coast and Anomabu as they were in that active period. Bosman's book shows the great wealth of trade then done with the Gold Coast, where the Fanti tribe had a quasi-monopoly of commerce with Europeans. On the Slave Coast – modern Dahomey – Bosman reports that the people showed great respect for authority, for the elderly, for parents. Women showed deference approaching awe before their husbands. The folk, says Bosman, were harder-working than on the Gold Coast.

Bosman gives his account of slaving. 'Markets of Men are here kept in the same manner as those of Beasts with us,' he says acidly. He reports that slaves selected for purchase by a buyer were branded on the breast to prevent the wily traders replacing good slaves by the old or maimed. Women, he says, were a quarter to a fifth cheaper than men. Feeding slaves in the barracoons on bread and water cost two cents a day per head in Bosman's time. When the slaves went aboard ship, the sellers removed all their clothes. An average cargo was six to seven hundred slaves. Bosman, perhaps biased, says the Dutch ships were the cleanest. At sea, slaves were fed thrice a day. Men and women were kept apart. Slave revolts were common.

The development of North America increased the slave trade. By then the main countries trading in 'ebony' – the traders' expression – were Holland, England, Portugal, France, Denmark, Brandenburg and Sweden. Governments supported their slavers in the fight to compete with the Dutch, and the concept of charter companies grew. The first were not very successful; in short succession, three English and four French charter companies were wound up. Then in 1660 the English Crown chartered the Company of Royal Adventurers into Africa. This made good profits for some years before running into difficulties; it was replaced in 1672 by the Royal Africa Company. The French West India Company was founded in 1664 to try to monopolize slave traffic between the Coast and the French Antilles.

All these companies worked the 'three-way passage': trade goods went from Europe to the Coast, where they were used to buy very little except slaves at the height of the traffic;

slaves went from the Coast to the New World, and the produce of the New World went to Europe. The slaving areas of the Coast were dotted with moored hulks, or barracoons or forts on dry land; all these changed hands frequently as a result of intra-European fighting on the Coast, and of piracy. But to the imperial policymakers of Spain, England, Holland, Portugal, France and the lesser powers, West Africa appeared to offer no interest as an area for colonization; the whole West African trade, and particularly the trade in men, was seen as an adjunct of their American colonial systems. Only Portugal made tentative beginnings of imposing an administration. During the 18th Century, England finally overtook the Dutch leadership in the slave trade; English companies held the Spanish *asientos* from 1713 to 1750.

The French made the Senegal River their base in 1630, and built a fort at Saint-Louis in 1659. In 1677, they captured Arguin and Gorée from the Dutch. The roads between the little fortress island of Gorée and the fishing village of Dakar which it protected became the principal French anchorage. But the French were the least successful of the major European powers and, except for a brief period at the end of the 18th Century, never got more than eight thousand slaves a year; at no time were the French traders able to meet the labor demands of the French West Indies, particularly Haiti.

The most profitable area was the Gold Coast, where the Dutch had wrested eleven forts, including El Mina, from the Portuguese. The British captured Cape Coast – in much later years to become the Governor's castle – from the Dutch, and built nine other fortified trading posts. The Danes concentrated on Christiansborg, Ada and Keta. Although the slave trade was now the principal justification for these voluminous, armed warehouses, the gold trade from the Gold Coast was still worth over six million dollars a year, at modern values, in 1700. At this point, Holland controlled about half the Gold Coast trade, England about a third. By 1785, when Gold Coasters had boosted their slave production to ten thousand a year, Britain held about half the buyers' market – the rise of Britain in West Africa being in part a reflection of the rising importance of Britain in European trade.

95

The great slaving fortresses, barracoons and hulks built or anchored in Upper Guinea and as far South as Ewe-land could not be duplicated east and south of Keta. The Dahomeyan and Nigerian chiefs wanted slaves stored in temporary mud buildings, inland, near their palaces, and forbade permanent bases to the European countries, companies and individuals with whom they did their business. The promising Portuguese beginnings in Benin had turned to mutual suspicion.

In 1750, the Royal Africa Company was replaced by the Company of Merchants Trading to West Africa. This grouped all private merchants in the area who wished to join. The Company did not trade itself; it left trade to private enterprise, but the organization kept up facilities, including forts, and for this it got a 'grant-in-aid' from the Parliament in London. Largely by leaving coastal enterprise to private traders – rather than to government-sponsored schemes which, in the final analysis, could always afford to fail – Britain gradually achieved a superior position over all other European nations on the Coast.

During the Seven Years War, Britain captured all the French West African posts, although Gorée was restored to French control by the Treaty of Paris in 1763. The following year, British control of the rest of this area of Upper Guinea was emphasized by the founding of the Crown Colony of Senegambia. Until then, only Portugal had had colonies in Africa, all in the southern part of the continent. But it would be deceptive to regard colonialism in West Africa as starting at this early date; it was still a trading situation, and the colonial status was merely a defensive one against foreign trading interests. Nevertheless, Senegambia had a Royal Governor, an appointed Council and a Judiciary. The project failed.

During the period 1778–1783, during most of which time Britain was involved in the American Revolution, France managed to take back Saint-Louis and most of the other formerly French stations on the Coast, as well as some 'traditionally' British ones, including the Gambia River mouth. By the Peace of Versailles, 1783, British rights on the Gambia River were restored, and control of the area was given to the Company of Merchants. The advantage taken by France of Britain's trans-Atlantic pre-occupations proved to be a purely temporary, localized set-back for British fortunes. By 1785, Britain held more of West African trade than all other countries put together, including an estimated thirty-eight thousand of the annual output of seventyfive thousand slaves. At this prosperous time, France was handling up to twenty thousand slaves.

The concept of a colonialist solution to the development of West African trade was always there in some peoples' minds; but as Britain's prosperity tended to increase after the loss of the thirteen American colonies, predominant British political philosophy was against becoming involved in further responsibilities overseas. Trade alone, not administration, was the British aim.

But the situation, even for trade, was far from static. In 1807, Britain 'abolished' slavery by law – partly for humanitarian reasons, but mostly because of the dictates of British economics. This is perhaps the moment to take a closer look at this revolting, revealing institution which (as at other moments of world history) played such an important role in 'solving' problems of manpower and development.

*

Slavery was a common feature of African society, as of most societies in their pre-literate stages. Slave castes existed, so that the slaves inter-married and bore children theoretically condemned to life-long bondage. Slavery was also widespread as a punishment for crime and debt, and children were often bonded as a guarantee for a father's debts. Prisoners of war had no rights, and were traditionally enslaved for life; their children became slaves also.

Much of this slavery was roughly benevolent; no pyramids were being built, and there was no point in working a slave to death. Manumission was common. There appears to have been little gratuitous cruelty, although punishment for offenses, such as theft, could be terrible. Most of the slaves sent to North America found an equivalent system. Except in a few cases, such as parts of Virginia, most American plantation farmers were modest yeomen employing only a handful of labor; the expatriated African found himself one of a small group working for a roughly paternalistic master. The master and his sons often inter-bred with the slave

97

women, as in Africa. However, whereas in Africa the children of these unions were usually freemen, in America they almost always only belonged to the upper caste of slaves – house Negroes (that is, domestic servants who avoided field work).

Since the whole history of slavery arouses much emotion and provokes our just indignation today, it is important to be objective in our study of it. Much that has been written leaves the impression that thousands of Africans who enslaved and sold their compatriots did so in such a trance-like stupidity that they did not know what they were doing; in truth, of course, the most obvious fact about the trade was that it was an African initiative into which African slave merchants – many of them of the same class as small Coastal storekeepers or housing sharks of modern times – went with enthusiasm. Broadly speaking, there were always more slaves for sale than there were buyers, except in certain areas of Upper Guinea, where the French slavers had difficulty meeting the Antilles quotas. Europeans, except in a minor way in the early years, never captured slaves themselves; they bought from the Africans the fruit of the local manhunts. But by encouraging the trade, and by supplying firearms to such eager slavers as the Efik, the Yoruba, the Fon or the Ashanti, the European merchants and mariners helped to make it a bigger, more evil thing than it had been before.

Slaves came down from up-country in manacled lines – slave-trains. The inevitable comparisons to the driving of cattle seem justified. On the Coast, middleman tribes interposed themselves between the big capturing tribes and the European buyers. There were small slave-brokers who dealt in mere half-dozens, or at best in scores of slaves. In this respect, the pidgin diary of Antera Duke, an 18th Century chief of Old Calabar, is interesting for its picture of the slave trade seen as a small merchant's means of earning a few 'honest' extra dollars.

It was an anarchic commerce, both by its fluctuating prices and greatly varied trading customs. On what came to be known, later, at the height of the 19th Century palm-oil boom, as the Oil Rivers (the Cross River and Niger Delta), the chiefs exacted an 'export' duty on the slaves. At Wida – then spelled Whydah (modern French spelling: Ouidah) – slavers had to buy licenses. There, the King of Dahomey's

slaves were sold first, at an exaggerated price. There was
'dash' (obligatory tipping), corruption and much confusion.
To try to check the more obvious abuses of the fringe finances
of the trade, European factors were appointed to reside on
the Gold and Slave Coasts from the 17th Century –
although they did not get these limited residence rights on
the Oil Rivers until a century later.

Slaves were not usually traded for cash. They were purchased
for iron or copper bars, cloth, gold dust, cowries, brass basins,
knives, guns and liquor. Values varied with the scarcity or
abundance of slaves, and also with the scarcity and abundance
of European commodities or 'bar' currency on the Coast at
a given time; the presence of over-paying interlopers frequently
boosted the market price temporarily. The accounts of traders
that have survived contain continual references to the prices
obtaining at this or that port at the time they called, expres-
sions of satisfaction if the price of slaves had dropped since
their last visit, or complaints if the value of textiles, guns or
basins, in terms of men, had fallen since the previous year.

Men were usually taken between the ages of ten and thirtyfive. Women were taken from ten to about twentyfive.
Purchasers examined their quarry principally for fitness; the
journey was to be arduous; most of the slave work was manual;
the women were not a good investment if they could not
produce a fair number of healthy children; even the branding
formality would be hard on the weak. In the Delta, in the
early 18th Century, slaves varied in value from eighty dollars,
for a borderline choice, up to one hundred and seventy
dollars for a powerful young male or a well-built virgin.

Although no overall statistics have survived, piecing
together disparate records gives us a fair idea of the immensity of the commerce. About a million slaves were exported
by West Africa in the sixteenth century, and a further *twenty
millions* in the 17th, 18th and 19th Centuries. Deaths in
transit could vary from very few to five-sixths (in the case of a
shipboard epidemic); the average death toll on the voyage was
said by some sources to be about twenty per cent. Others
would have already died on the march to the coast, or in the
filthy hulks, barracoons and forts, so that the total West
African population involved, as victims, in the slave trade
was well in excess of twenty millions over the four centuries

99

affected by the trade. Where wars were conducted to capture slaves, many more persons were of course killed or maimed. If we assume a round figure of thirty million victims; if we round off the period of the slave trade from the mid-16th to the mid-19th Centuries – three hundred years; if we assume infant mortality, then, to have been about seventy-five per cent (and assume that this brought the West African life expectancy average down to about thirty years) then we get a figure of thirty million victims for ten lifetimes – about three million victims in a given generation. The population of coastal West Africa (the coastal states except the Northern region of Nigeria) is today about sixty millions, and cannot have been much more than twenty millions in those days. This means that, on average, one West African in seven could expect to be a victim of the slave trade while it lasted – perhaps one man in five, one woman in ten. The proportion would have been less in the 16th Century and toward the end of the trade, more when the traffic was at its boom period in the late eighteenth and early nineteenth centuries.

At Wida, the most famous slave port of all, English factors were purchasing fourteen to fifteen thousand slaves a year by the 1680s, according to the slave trade historian André du Casse. Here the surfbound roadstead, with its strong east-flowing current, was dangerous, particularly at the onset of the wet season, when Bosman noted that 'dismal accidents are very frequent . . . great quantities of goods are lost, and many men drowned; for the sea-burning is so violent, and rolls so, that a canoe full of people is overturned, and the canoe shattered into splinters in a minute.' In compensation, the Wida brokers were 'so diligent in the slave trade that they are able to deliver one thousand slaves every month, if there are no ships at Jakin.' Wida probably reached its zenith about 1716: in this year the French, for whom it was an exceptional year, bought six thousand slaves, the English and Portuguese nearly seven thousand together and the now considerably displaced Hollanders fifteen hundred. By this time, the Dahomeyans were getting much higher prices for their 'commodity'.

The trade goods used to buy men were then reckoned in monetary 'ounces', with each trade article – rum, iron bars, gunpowder – having a fixed ounce value; by this token, slaves averaged fortyfive dollars at Wida in the middle of the 17th Century. The price rose in 1669 as the value of gunpowder rose in Europe, and with the competition from pirates; it reached one hundred and twenty dollars for an average adult male. The development of the trade led to employees of 'legitimate' trading companies doing business on their own account with African brokers – some of whom were similarly cheating their own principals. The French fort at Wida had twentythree directors between the years 1704 and 1779, as violent deaths arranged by chiefs, expulsions, or firings from Paris followed one upon the other. In contrast, however, between 1700 and 1807, when the English fort at Wida was abandoned, this establishment had only fourteen directors; one of these, Lionel Abson, spent twentythree years at the station. The incredible life and customs of these Coasters is well recorded in the writings of Captain John Adams of Virginia.

The number of people who battened on the trade in their unfortunate compatriots was considerable, and chieftaincy grew fat on the traffic. When a three-masted slaver dropped anchor off Wida, the master was required to pay the value of twelve slaves (about fifteen hundred dollars at the end of the 17th Century) to the Yovogah (the King of Dahomey's representative). A two-master paid the value of nine slaves). The Yovogah then gave permission for the ship's trade goods to be beached. Ashore, the trader was burdened with a horde of mostly useless and unnecessary messengers, porters and servants provided by the Yovogah; he had to pay a certain number of other fixed duties to tribal officials and to the distant Abomey king. Guards stood over his barter goods; messengers sought out brokers he already knew; even the guides who conducted the slaves to the surfside were paid off by the purchaser. There was a confusion of volunteer small boys, bearers and washerwomen whom it was politically difficult to turn away. The Yovogah in turn employed a retinue of spies to see that no obligations were missed or skimped.

A century later, things had not greatly changed. In 1791, the English slaver Johnston recorded in his *Journal* the fees he paid in connection with slaving at Wida. The figures are here converted into the modern dollar equivalent of the gold sovereign:

To begin with, the Yovogah was 'dashed' two slaves, some rum, cloth and a Dane gun 'as Customary on opening trade'. A guide and two messengers cost equal amounts of rum and cloth. Miscellaneous servants and boys took payments totalling one hundred and ninetysix dollars. Johnston sent the King two slaves, cloth, twentyfive Dane guns, gunpowder, cowries and rum to the value of thirtyeight 'ounces' – between one hundred and sixtyfive and three hundred dollars. Johnston bought slaves from six different Fon brokers, who could not be paid in guns. These went only to the King and to the Yovogah; only the King got powder. A French trader wrote that 'If a Black is found to have more than one hatful of powder in his hut he is looked upon as a rebel and sold as a slave for the King's account.'

The abusive incidental costs of slaving in some ports – Wida is, perhaps, the outstanding case – make it clear that although the European profits of the traffic were immense, they were probably not as immense as some recent writers have suggested in figures based on the net cost of a slave on the Coast and his sale price in a Mississippi Delta auction. These faulty figures tend to ignore all overheads except those of chartering and sailing a ship and crew – some writers even seem to ignore these as well. The European slavers' profits were, almost inevitably, proportionally less (except in the very early years of the trade) than those of the African slave-exporters, whose investment was negligible.

Other ports were less complicated than Wida in their means of extorting payments, but everywhere trade had a quaintness of custom that seems, to the modern mind, revolting for persons trading in human flesh. Here is an account by Lieutenant Edward Bold of the Royal Navy of trading in Grand Popo, a port not far from Wida, as related in Bold's *Merchants' and Mariners' African Guide*. The reader should recall that the 'prices' quoted usually meant so many slaves:

'The mode of proceeding is thus on arriving, it is necessary to go on shore, (for the natives will not bring their trade to the ship) with samples of each of your articles of merchandize, and pronounce before an assembly of the Caboceers their various prices, which you must maintain as high as possible, (though obliged sometimes to abate.) When the prices are agreed on, by both parties, a piece of cloth and a few gallons of rum are paid to each Caboceer, for custom; upon which you open trade.'

Bold also describes the sale of an elephant's tusk, apparently also subject to special 'taxes':

'The owner of a tooth of ivory sells it through the medium of a broker, who according to its size makes a demand, which never fails to be exorbitant, however you must patiently abate until he reduces it to a price you can afford to give; observe, that independent of the assortment that is given, the broker on commencing will desire you to hold back a certain number of ackeys in proportion to the size of the tooth, which afterward are to be paid to him.' Ackeys were the metal-bar currency.

Between the Dahomeyan coast and the Niger Delta, there was relatively little slaving, although Captain Adams of Virginia noted the sale of members of the traditional slave caste (that is, not specially captured prisoners of war) at Porto Novo, Badagri and Ijebu at the beginning of the 19th Century. What importance Lagos acquired in the slave trade, as in the case of Porto Novo, was due to the arrival shortly afterward of Brazilian slavers who settled permanently on the Coast, just as the slave-producing Yoruba wars were at their height. As a result of their presence, numerous African families in Togo, Dahomey and in the part of Nigeria around Lagos have Portuguese names. Some of the settlers were mulattos. All had direct business – sometimes family – connections with buyers in Bahia and other great Brazilian ports.

A particularly colorful Brazilian was Francesco Felix da Souza, whose extensive Togolese and Dahomeyan clans still deeply revere his memory. This handsome, bearded, fearless, brutal swashbuckler, who lies buried under the main bedroom of the family house in Wida, arrived in the late 18th Century and was for a while commander of the historic Portuguese fort at Wida. He went into slaving on his own account, as broker at Badagri (modern Nigeria) and Anexo (modern Togo), where he became the creditor of King Adandozah of Abomey. An historian writes: 'While trying to reclaim his debts he was imprisoned at Abomey; and there he entered into an alliance (cemented by a blood-pact) with Prince Gangpe – later King Ghezo. Released with Gangpe's help, he supplied his "brother" with rum and tobacco to increase the number of the prince's partisans and enable him to seize power at Abomey in 1818. Ghezo reciprocated by installing da Souza at Whydah as a Fon customs official with the title of Shasha and with the privilege of conducting the King's own business with visiting vessels.' There were obvious opportunities for graft and 'his riches and hospitality became the legend of the coast'. He is credited with having stimulated the palm oil industry – which, when Dahomey became a modern independent state over a century and a half later, was all that stood between the country and bankruptcy. Several writers have related in detail the incredible escape from Abomey; da Souza made the whole journey to the coast concealed in a head-loaded rum barrel.

Altogether the slavers were a mixed bag of tough, even sometimes engaging, ruffians. The biggest slave-dealer in Porto Novo when Captain Adams visited the lagoon harbor was Tammata, a Hausa slave who had been to France. At Anexo, a major operator was George Lawson, a Gold Coast Fanti who had sailed from Accra as steward on a slave vessel and returned to West Africa from England in 1812. The Lawson clan is today extensive, and part of the lineage holds a chieftaincy in modern Anexo, the township which Lawson helped considerably to put on the map. Lawson dealt in slaves and palm oil, 'saluted all flags and supplied false information to naval officers,' one historian remarks. Anexo, then as now, was divided into two 'cities' by a lagoon fertile in fish, and the ruler on the landward side was a Brazilian who had taken the mixed Portuguese-Ewe name Pedro Kojo (Kojo means a boy born on Monday). Pedro raided for slaves and 'bought Manchester cottons from the Gold Coast firm of F. and A. Swanzy,' according to the same source. (Swanzy's is now a part of the Unilever group.)

Tammata the Hausa was succeeded as top slaver of Porto Novo by a mulatto, Domingo Martinez, who also sold palm oil and had contracts with the Gold Coast company Forster and Smith. Trading in oil as well as men became a real necessity (as well as a profitable enterprise) early in the 19th Century, because of the need to have an honest 'cover' for slaving when Britain abolished it by law. The explorer Richard Lander, in his account of Clapperton's journey, refers to attempts by the slavers to elude detection:

'As soon as a vessel arrives at her place of destination, the crew discharge her light cargoe, with the manacles intended for the slaves, and land the captain at the same time. The vessel then cruises along the coast to take in country cloth, ivory, a little gold dust etc., and if a British man-of-war be near, the crew having nothing on board to excite suspicion, in most cases contrive to get their vessel searched while trading with the natives. . . . They return to the place where the cargoe had been loaded, and communicate with the captain on shore . . . who then takes the opportunity of acquainting his crew with the exact time in which he will be in readiness to embark. The vessel then cruises a second time up and down the coast till the appointed day approaches, when she proceeds to take in her living cargoe.'

Speed became essential; narratives record the presence of Spanish, Portuguese and American clippers. Illegality raised prices; slaves purchased for two hundred and twentyfive or three hundred dollars at Wida and Lagos in the 1830s and 1840s sold for seven hundred and fifty to twelve hundred dollars each at Bahia auctions in this period, the higher figure being for 1844, one record tells us. This writer notes that import duty had to be paid in Brazil, but gives no estimate of other 'overheads' or indications of profit. To calculate this, the cost of the long voyage would have to be known, and the pro rata value per slave of the considerable pork-barreling of African middlemen and traditional officials. An average twenty per cent of slaves bought died at sea, and were therefore a commercial loss. There was of course the profit on the original legitimate trade in European manufactured articles, since slave values are estimated at the 'retail' value, on the Coast, of these articles; but if this legitimate aspect of trade is ignored, it seems unlikely that the profit on slaving went above one hundred per cent of the investment – a fairly low profit for an illegitimate traffic, with the risks of seizure of ship, loss of all cargo, fines and imprisonment. It must often have been less than one hundred per cent. In especially difficult years, the profits presumably went higher, since one historian records Brazilian prices for average slaves reaching the equivalent of eighteen hundred dollars per head in 1846 – falling to twelve hundred dollars in the following year.

The history of slavery exists principally in terms of statistics, with some anecdotic material on methods of capturing, trading and transporting the human material. The subject awaits a dispassionate enquiry into its historic uses, misuses and effects. It can be reasonably assumed that the theory that this abominable traffic crippled West Africa's development is not entirely justified. At the time, Africa's elementary farming methods could barely support the limited population of the area, and some thinning out of population – by sickness or by the war instinct of non-affluent peoples – undoubtedly would have taken place. The 'slack' – the over-reduction in population figures caused by the slave trade – was soon taken up in the 19th Century; today, the fact that Africa is relatively under-populated is one of its brightest economic assets. In terms of emigration, and other loss of population associated with the trade, the figure of thirty million people over a period of more than three centuries was modest compared to Europe's loss of fifty million emigrants in the 1880–1930 period alone.

In the days of the trade, even more than now, Africa depended on Europe for the import of medical and other sciences, including improved farming methods and business opportunities making the countries richer commercially, and able to raise themselves. The profits of slavery went into goods, equipment and other tools of development, including education for African slavers' children. Proportionally to living costs and man's requirements, which of course have changed considerably since slaving days, it may well be that no African export so enriched Africans; certainly, no other export business of like importance has ever remained so totally an African monopoly; even the gold trade finally fell to the technical superiority of European firms.

On the debit side, slaving much increased the tendency to warfare, creating a sort of feudal chaos. If the vast panorama of human unhappiness occasioned by the trade is not a fit subject for history, the insecurity created by slaving 'war-lets' may perhaps have some influence on the shortcomings of modern African life, and may therefore deserve study. Slave-trading seems likely to have encouraged the belief, still widespread in the area, that to get rich quick is cleverer than working hard. In the advanced societies, easy money is regarded with disapproval and suspicion, even when it happens to have been honestly and reasonably acquired: there is no equivalent of this reflex on the Coast, and the slaving tradition may bear some blame.

Conversely again, slavery caused the rise in West Africa of Negro kingdoms comparable in size to all except the largest of the Berber or Berber-founded kingdoms of the desert fringe. Ashanti, Yoruba, Dahomey and Benin were realms that grew prosperous and significant on slavery. The mess of potage for which West Africans sold their brothers to the pioneers of the New World has grown into fields of relative abundance.

ii

Guinean kingdoms

THE WEST AFRICAN COASTAL OR 'GUINEA' KINGDOMS had varying fortunes. The story of Yoruba begins sometime between the years 600 and 1000 when, according to a partly documented legend, immigrants coming 'from the North-East', of partly Hamitic stock, established Ile Ife. In later years the Oni of Ife acquired spiritual supremacy over the tribe, and in modern times this was the reason the Oni Sir Adesoji Aderemi became the first Governor of Western Nigeria after independence. In the mid-18th Century, the political power of the Alafin of Oyo appears to have been as great as the divine power of the Oni. What is now called 'Old Oyo' was then the 'capital' of the people, and the Alafin ruled Egbaland – the southern part of modern Western Nigeria – plus part of modern Dahomey and a section of modern Togo, as far as Anexo. This influence gave Oyo trading rights at Badagri, Porto Novo and Benin.

Ibadan, now the principal Yoruba city, was then a sprawling camp of mercenaries which drew men who sought the warrior life. There was a war every dry season. Individual armies would be given a set task to perform, and it was common for unsuccessful commanders to commit suicide or banish themselves.

In the early 19th Century, the far-flung provincial chiefs began to defy the authority of the Alafin; states withheld their tribute. In this divided condition, the kingdom became vulnerable to enemies. Ilorin fell to the Fulani. An historian comments: 'The southern chiefs became emmeshed in a devastating series of wars which lasted for nearly a century. The Alafin of Oyo and the Oni of Ife were left high and dry among the wreckage of a once powerful empire, and the ports of Lagos and Badagri were so stocked with the human spoils of war that they became for a while the chief slaving ports in all West Africa.'

Prospering under the slave trade, the provincial chiefs were even more reluctant to share their profits with the Alafin, and this helped further the cycle of disintegration of Yorubaland. Only the advent of British rule halted the permanent threat from the North and rescued the remains of the empire from total collapse.

Benin originated when a group of minor chiefs from Ife, who had established their domain to the East, quarreled among themselves and asked Ife to appoint a King over them. In the 15th Century, Benin broke away from Ife, whence the Bini, as they had become known, had brought the knowledge of casting brass and bronze – an art which was to reach its greatest African expression in Benin.

With the arrival of the Portuguese in 1485, Benin became a trading center. With money, goods and firearms, the city state expanded; in the 17th Century, it occupied Bonny and even Lagos. Warfare, including slaving campaigns, weakened the realm. The kingdom crumbled, and by the late 19th Century had become little more than the notorious 'city of blood' of the adventure books.

The Fons established the kingdom of Dahomey, with its capital at Abomey, in 1625, when Dako, a son of the King of Allada, moved north to Uhwawe with his followers, usurping the powers of the local chief, Awesu. Dako began encroaching on the neighboring territory of a chief, Danh, who quipped of Dako's incursions that the young chief would 'soon be building in my belly'. Dako conquered Danh, and

108

called his palace Danh-homen, '(in) Danh's belly'. Having thus named his still modest Empire, he enjoined his son who would succeed him to enlarge the nation, and to bid his successors, in their turn, to do likewise. The oath to expand was taken and kept by nine successive Kings.

All the stools of the Dahomeyan Kings are still to be found in the royal palace, now a museum. In the 18th Century, under King Agaja, the kingdom conquered the coast in order to be able to sell slaves direct to the Europeans, occupying Wida and forcing Porto Novo to pay tribute. The European merchants had inevitably sided, in the war, with the coastal chiefs, with whom they had treaties. An alliance of coastal peoples, Coasters and Yoruba warred on Abomey. Compromise was reached: in 1747, Tegbesu, who had succeeded Agaja on the stool, made an agreement with the Europeans to sell direct to them through his pro-consul, the Yovogah, at Whydah. Abomey agreed to pay tribute to Oyo and the Alafin withdrew his forces.

Tegbesu set about the slave-hunt energetically, sending armies to the primitive North and others to the West, where they allied with the Akyem and the Kwahu against the kingdom of Ashanti. The Ashanti won, and entered the Fon country for reprisals, driving Tegbesu back as far as Atakpame in modern Togo.

In the 19th Century, as Yorubaland degenerated into chaos, Abomey repudiated its tributary duty to Oyo and made sallies into Yoruba country; apart from a temporary occupation of Badagri, these were however unsuccessful, and Dahomey never recovered its earlier importance, although it made a spirited two-year resistance to colonial occupation under the leadership of King Behanzin.

*

Ashanti seems to originate in the 11th or 12th Centuries, when its Akan founders appeared from the North. They adopted the language of Tswi which they found in the country, and absorbed some of the local customs. A pushing, fighting people, the Ashanti advanced down the Volta valley and through the Akwapim Gap to reach the coast, where they turned West. In the 16th Century, they were joined by the Ga people from Calabar, who appear to have marched (or canoed) eight hundred miles up the beach after a violent tribal conflict. The Ashanti who had reached the coast founded the Fanti states and, North of modern Accra, the powerful kingdom of Denkyera. All these Akan states were engaged in sporadic warfare among each other, and finally some of the smaller tribal principalities of what is now Ashanti came together under the Chief of Kumasi to resist the Denkyera and, to the West, the Doma, another fellow-Akan group.

Around 1700, Chief Osei Tutu, who is said by legend to have been born from a cloud, successfully led the alliance against the Doma. Guided by his high priest Anokye, Osei Tutu announced that he would bind the alliance in a mystic bond that would enable them to defeat the mighty Denkyera also. At Anokye's call, according to Ashanti legend, a golden stool came down from heaven and became the bond-symbol of the Ashanti brotherhood. To this day, no king has sat on this stool, but only beside it. It is from this heroic period that the Kumasihene (the Kumasi Chief) became known as the Asantehene (the Ashanti Chief).

The Denkyera were defeated. Naturally, the Asantehene followed this up by the conquest of many minor tribes and established a firm stronghold on the sea, trafficking in slaves and acquiring a considerable armory from Europe.

In the course of one of the local wars, Osei Tutu was killed in action. His successor, Opoku Ware, extended the empire both to the South and North. Later in the 18th Century, another Asantehene, Osei Kojo, pushed his dominion even further, reaching the Dagomba country in the far North of modern Ghana, where he exacted an annual tribute of cows and slaves.

Of all the coastal states of any significance, Ashanti was the only one still at its peak when the colonial era began. Kumasi was only finally conquered by a Nigerian force led by British officers. Ashanti was given special recognition in the administration of the Gold Coast, and survived as a kingdom until Ghana's independence, when the South finally had its revenge, forcing the realm into a presumably temporary decline by intimidation and legislation.

Mapmakers and pathfinders

THE GREAT HANDICAP to all Europe's early work in Africa was the absence of proper maps. The African peoples produced none themselves. The charts based on Leo Africanus' journeys and the various Majorcan atlases were still pathetically in use, with few changes, in the 18th Century. Even the plots of the extensive African shoreline were untrue for long stretches of littoral. D'Anville's 18th Century map of Africa was hardly more accurate than Ortelius' African Atlas had been two centuries earlier. The Niger was still shown as flowing from its (highly variable) source to the West. Ortelius had it rising near the Equator in an expanse of water called Lake Niger, whence it was supposed to flow about sixty miles North to Lake Chad, usually then called Lake Bornu or Borno; it then passed through another fictitious lake, Guber, before splitting into two – the Senegal and the Gambia. D'Anville had it rising in Lake Chad and flowing West, roughly along what is now the Niger-Nigerian frontier, to Timbuktu. Then it entered an imaginary Lake Maberia and re-issued as the Senegal.

Timbuktu was believed to be a great city. Some thought it was on the Nile, some on the Senegal. No one had the remotest idea where the Congo rose, and when Livingstone found the Lualaba – the Upper Congo – he thought it was the Nile. To the North, the Senegal was for centuries believed to be a much more important river than it is in reality.

Muslim control of Barbary was mainly to blame for European ignorance of the African interior. The Moors driven from Spain established a series of little realms along the African Mediterranean shore, whence pirate princelings harassed the Straits of Gibraltar and the Detroit of Malta, capturing and enslaving Christians. They frequently attacked the coast of Spain itself. Eventually the Moorish pirates, mostly under the leadership of Berbers but with Negroes and

Arabs in their hosts, plundered the shores of Ireland, Iceland, Scotland, England, France and Denmark; in a few places they settled, and they left a clan of partly African descendants in Scotland now called Moore, Morris, Morison or Morrison; in France the memory of these lusty pirate ancestors lives in such African-descent names as Morisot or Moricaud. To Scotland, the Berbers brought the bagpipes and, probably, the plain-silver, square-stoned jewelry of the medieval Highlanders.

Corsairs from Salee, now a twin city (with Rabat) on the Atlantic coast, occupied Lundy Island in England's Bristol Channel. They harassed the great Irish port of Cork with their shipping. The major powers could of course have broken the pirate hold on the Barbary Shore but for centuries the African interior was apparently not lure enough to warrant a serious challenge to the Berber-Arab barrier.

The interior was equally impenetrable from the Atlantic. Slavery was so profitable that the great slave-trading tribes feared that if the white man established himself up-country, he would buy direct from the simpler, often easily cheated tribes on whose internecine warfare the slave trade depended for a constant supply of raw material. The chain of middlemen and coastal sharks made sure the land just beyond the shore was one of unbreachable hostility for the white stranger. Another check to traveling up-country was of course sickness, which was bad enough on the Coast itself. As late as 1841, the well-equipped and adequately doctored British Government-sponsored expedition on the Niger lost fortyeight out of one hundred and fortyfive men in two months. The MacGregor Laird expedition of 1832 had lost thirtynine out of fortyeight men from sickness.

The founding of the African Association (the Society Instituted for Exploring the Interior of Africa), on June 9, 1788, at a meeting of the Saturday's Club at St Alban's Tavern, was perhaps the first concrete step to putting Africa, literally, on the map. The Association's first task was to find the Niger and plot its course to the ocean. After two expeditions from the Mediterranean had failed, an attempt from the West Coast was decided. A Major Houghton set off up the Gambia but lost his life up-river. There must by then have been considerable pessimism in the ranks of prospective explorers; so when, in 1795, a twenty-year-old Scottish ship's physician, Mungo Park, offered his services he was accepted at once. He was told to go up the Gambia, find the Niger and follow it to its mouth. He set off from England in May, 1795. He left the coast in October, and after nine months of tortuous trekking through Serer and Fula country he finally encountered the Niger at Segu – on July 20, 1796. His description of his excitement is part of a great classic of adventure, *Travels in the Interior Districts of Africa*. He saw 'with infinite pleasure, the great object of my mission; the long sought for, majestic Niger, glittering to the morning sun, as broad as the Thames at Westminster, and flowing *to the eastward*'.

Park, who was traveling with a freedman and a friend's slave – whose freedom he purchased on his return – a pony, two asses, never more than two days of food in hand, and trinkets and tobacco for barter, continued his journey through months of appalling suffering. He nearly died and was nursed back to health by a kindly Negro slaver, on his way to 'trade flesh' on the Gambia with Europeans. He returned to Europe after three and a half years' absence, to find that he had been given up for dead. Through his privations and sickness, he had fortunately maintained and preserved a voluminous diary.

His book makes most 20th Century adventures seem modest. One is left with the impression of a man of nerveless ego and self-control. When in Kaarta, he recounts, King Desi Kurabari warned him not to continue into Bambara country: war was in progress and, coming from the enemy, he would probably be killed. Park not only persisted but persuaded the King to furnish guides, including three of the royal princes.

Like all the early travelers, Park had great difficulty convincing his bearers to continue forward. They very reasonably feared enslavement once beyond their tribal or tribal-ally boundaries. Park's physical peculiarity of being white caused fear or astonishment almost everywhere. At Benowan, 'people who drew water at the well threw down their buckets; those in the tents mounted their horses; and men, women and children came galloping toward me'. He was pinched, examined and threatened. The women unbuttoned his clothes to look at the whiteness of his skin. His toes were counted.

The local potentate tested his respect for Islam by offering him roast wild pig – to have eaten it would presumably have led to his murder. He was virtually a prisoner, subjected to continual tortures. His tormentors were mostly Moors, whom Park found 'the rudest savages on earth'.

He was, of course, robbed of everything; but his compass was returned because it was feared to be magical. At a sinister trial before the Chief, the elders deliberated as to whether he should be killed, deprived of his right hand or blinded. Even when he fell sick again, his tortures were applied with regularity. He was finally freed on the fortunate instigation of the local Queen.

It was from here that, pursuing his journey through country infested by lions, he finally came upon the Niger. Here too, at Segu, Park was poorly received by the local chieftain; he decided to return to the coast. He notes that the chief, on hearing of the object of his journey, 'inquired if there were no rivers in my own country, and whether one river was not like another'. Swamps, wild animals and more sickness dogged his return march. He reached the coast in rags, following his new-found friend's 'coffle', as slave-trains were known.

His book appeared in 1799 with an introductory *mémoire* by Major James Rennell, the leading geographer of the period, who wrote: 'On the whole, it can scarcely be doubted that the Joliba or Niger terminates in lakes, in the eastern quarter of Africa; and those lakes seem to be situated in Wangara and Ghana.' Rennell's misinterpretation is the fruit of other misunderstandings. It was not then known that any country from which gold came might be called Wangara, nor that the kingdom or kingdoms of Ghana had long since ceased to exist. But disconnecting the Niger from the Senegal and the Gambia, on the strength of its eastward flow for all its early course, was a step toward accuracy.

Rennell regarded Wangara and Ghana as the 'sink of North Africa', where the waters of the Niger became so widely dispersed in lakeland that they evaporated. The theory was not entirely new, and was widely accepted. Leo Africanus, by placing 'Wangara' (a Hausa word) in Hausa and identifying it as a specific place, had confused geographers for centuries; it was known that the Niger flowed from or through 'Wangara'. Rennell, notes an historian, 'assumed that Adrisi's

Wangara and Leo's were the same, and he accepted the current belief that the Hausa city of Kano was identical with the Ancient Ghana'. Rennell wrote: 'Of course Ghana, which in the 15th Century was paramount in the center of Africa, is now become a province of Kassina.'

While Park had been suffering up from the Coast, a young German, Frederick Hornemann, had set out from Cairo. In April, 1800, despatches were received from him showing he had reached Murzuk in the Fezzan. It was later learned that he had reached the Niger in Nupe country, where he died. His records did not survive.

Shamed by the efforts of the Association, the British Government at last accepted to finance an expedition which would navigate the Niger to the evaporating lakes – or the sea. Mungo Park willingly abandoned his Peebles practice to lead the party. He decided to march to Segu and there build a boat which would sail down the river through Katsina, Hausaland and Nupe 'to the kingdom of Wangara'. If the river ended there, he would either return up the Niger and across to the Gambia, or cross the Sahara, or mount the Nile, or trace a new route to the Gulf of Benin. Park himself actually expected to do none of these things: he was convinced the Niger and the Congo were one and the same river – a mistaken but much more intelligent guess than Rennell's – and he expected to reach the Atlantic in his Segu craft. The Government instructed Park to investigate trade conditions and do what we should today call market research.

Park was accompanied by two fellow-Scots, five naval artificers who were to build the boat and, from Gorée onward, by two seamen, an army officer and thirty-five soldiers from the Gorée garrison. Except for one Mandingo guide, no natives could be induced to join the expedition.

Park left England in high fettle in January, 1805, heartened at the extra help and companions and the advantage of having traveled across the same country before. But the expedition was an unmitigated disaster. The soldiers were a total liability, collapsing and dying from fever and dysentery. Despondency settled on the team, and only Park's driving kept them moving forward. He sent messengers ahead to Segu to tell Mansong of his arrival, and explaining that if the Niger proved navigable European goods would reach Segu more cheaply than through the Moorish middlemen; hence the party's wish to build a boat and descend the river. While an answer – which proved favorable – was awaited, two more men died; and while preparations to set out downstream were going ahead, Park lost yet another two, including his deputy leader, Dr Anderson.

All the artificers were dead by the time the party reached Bamako. Three-quarters of the soldiers had been buried along the route. At Sansanding, where the building of the boat was finally done, Park – in November, 1805 – drafted his last despatch.

'I am sorry to say,' he reported, 'that of the fortyfour Europeans who left the Gambia in perfect health, five only are at present alive. . . . But though all the Europeans who are with me should die, and though I were myself half dead, I would still persevere; and if I could not succeed in the object of my journey, I would at least die on the Niger.' Fate took him at his word.

The despatch and a last letter to Park's wife were carried down to the Coast by the faithful Mandingo guide who was later sent back to determine what had become of Park. On this subsequent investigation, he found that in spite of hostile tribes, Park and three surviving companions had sailed down the Niger for a thousand miles, reaching the Busa rapids. In an historian's words: 'Finding the banks thronged with apparently hostile natives and not daring to land, and probably unaware that their frail craft could not possibly survive the terrible rush of waters ahead, they had continued downstream and perished. Some have thought that the wild gesticulations of the armed natives on the banks were no more than a warning to the white men of the perils toward which they were heading. Against this must be set the great reluctance of the natives in later years to discuss the incident at all.'

Of this mighty effort, only the Mandingo survived. Despite the great overwater distance covered, no records remained of this part of the trip; it was still not known where the Niger ended. To compound this tragic waste of heroic effort, it was thought back in Europe that Busa was eighty miles from Timbuktu; actually it is eight hundred miles downstream. As a consequence it was not known that Park's ill-fated journey had at least demonstrated the probability that the river flowed into the sea, not interior lakes; but the belief grew that Park had been right, and that the Niger and Congo were one.

In 1816, Britain officially sent two expeditions to test the Niger–Congo link by sailing up the Congo and trying to sail down the Niger. All members of both teams came to an early end. Two years later, Captain F. G. Lyon led a mission out of Tripoli, which got no further than the Fezzan but mysteriously concluded that the Niger flowed into the Nile 'to the southward of Dongola'.

Sheer doggedness was to overcome the long line of brave failures and heroic limited successes. In 1821, the British Government sent a further expedition from Tripoli, led by Major Dixon Denham, seconded by naval lieutenant Hugh Clapperton and Dr Walter Oudney. Halted by hostile attitudes at Murzuk for several months, they finally managed to push on South, reaching Lake Chad. They were received by the Shehu, al-Kanemi, who wrote to George IV saying he would accept four or five small traders, but no more – and no 'heavy traveler' (rich or big trader). A man called Tyrwhitt, who had joined the expedition in May, 1824, was left as Consul in Kuka, the Shehu's capital.

Denham, who thought the Niger and Chad were part of the same watercourse, was excited at the discovery of the great lake, then much bigger than it is today. But since no real river issued from, or flowed into, the lake, the belief was sustained – another old theory – that the river flowed underground. Oudney and Clapperton set off West to explore Hausa and look for the Niger there, while Denham concentrated on Bornu. Oudney died at Murmur near Katagum, aged thirtytwo, but Clapperton reached Kano, where he was told that the Niger, known as the Kworra on its lower course, flowed into the sea at a place called Raka, in Yoruba country, where European shipping called. This was said to be only a month's march away. But the information was limited, for the people feared Clapperton was spying out the ground for an invasion, which may explain why what he was told was partly correct – that the river flowed to a port frequented by European ships – and partly wrong: the Niger Delta is not in Yoruba country, and there is no such place as Raka.

Clapperton went on westward to Sokoto, the capital of Muhammad Bello, the Sarkin Musulmi, who had heard of the British and told Clapperton he would like to trade with Britain. He asked for a British Consul and physician in Sokoto, and promised to help Clapperton reach Yaüri and Nupe and study the Niger: but the Arab residents, the natural enemies of Europeans seeking to trade with inland Africa from the Atlantic, persuaded Bello – Usuman dan Fodyo's son – to go back on his promise. The continual insistence of Clapperton that the price of a treaty of friendship with Britain would be the abolition of the slave trade also influenced Bello against the visitor. Slavery was then the chief industry of the Fulani.

Having collected the first acceptable account of the Western Sudanic tribes along the caravan trail to Chad, Clapperton, unable to advance, returned to Bornu and found Denham. They set off North, across the desert, back to England.

Clapperton impresses more than Denham, from their accounts. Denham, although the expedition leader, was in many ways a caricature English gentleman; his courage and endurance were often artificially sustained by the resources of his snobbery. His book is littered with boorish comments, and the troubles into which he falls when – for instance – he refused to give a Bornu chieftain a military salute are characteristic of the cases in which his attitude made the difficulties of such a trip through usually hostile, often savage peoples still more difficult. But of his courage there can be no doubt; he accompanied Bornuese troops into combat, saw a panther speared to death before his eyes and was arrowed in the face in battle. With his Bornuese 'allies', he was routed and captured, stripped of all clothes and tormented with spears. He escaped from his torturers in a naked dash through the bush, brushing death once again in an encounter with a snake. With arrows falling about him like a light summer shower, he was swept up and rescued by a Bornuese horseman. Back in Kuka, he weathered the wet season watching wrestling and dancing and hunting buffalo while he waited for Clapperton. He explored Lake Chad thoroughly.

After Denham and Clapperton, the problem of the Niger was a little nearer solution – but not much. There was still a big, long, uncharted river which most of the world called by the Latin word for black, but which naturally had many different names as it flowed through different African nations. There was still no clear picture of the river's course – of whether it ended in central or eastern Africa or whether one of the numerous estuaries on Africa's Atlantic shore was in fact the Niger.

In 1825, Clapperton was sent back to the Niger search, this time from the Atlantic side. He was to uncover the river's lower course and, hopefully, to get Bello's signature on an anti-slavery treaty. This time, he had four Europeans with him; ever resourceful, the young aristocrat had persuaded his twentyone-year-old valet Richard Lander to be one of the group marching into the unknown – a fact for which the scientific, political and business world was soon to be eminently grateful.

The ports mentioned by Bello – Raka and Funda – being unknown to Coasters and mariners, the party started its journey inland from Badagri. By then, one of the group was already written off as dead: he had landed at Wida on a visit, and was never heard of again. Two more died soon after setting off inland, leaving only Clapperton and Lander. The two men traversed Oyo and reached the Niger at Busa, where they got confirmation of the nature of Park's death.

Their trek through the rain forest had weakened both men, especially Clapperton. Kano and Sokoto were cooler and healthier, but Clapperton was still ailing. In Sokoto, he was received with great suspicion, preceded by a rumor that the British planned to displace Fulani rule. The disappointment at Bello's attitude hastened Clapperton's death, which took place sometime in April, 1827. He was twentysix.

Lander, also sick and with almost no money or equipment, was permitted to leave the city and made his way to Kano. He marched from there to the confluence of the Niger and the Benue, whence he hoped to sail down the Niger to the Gulf of Benin – where, like Clapperton, he correctly believed the river ended. But at a place called Dunrora, a hostile tribe barred his way, and he had to turn back. He finally reached Badagri overland, momentarily cheated of the greatest geographical discovery of the time. Lander's perseverance was, however, to be rewarded.

From Badagri he took ship for England, where he let it be

known that he was eager to return to Africa and complete the work. Without class, education or connections in the Establishment, he was disgracefully exploited by the Government of the day; the youth was packed off to the Coast, accompanied by his brother John, with a promise worthy of Scrooge himself – their mother would get twentyfive pounds every three months while they were away, and a fee of one hundred pounds would be paid to Richard if he managed to return. John was to get nothing at all.

The two boys, scarcely out of their teens, successfully completed their march to Busa – where the Emir still wears, as part of his regalia, a British medal presented to his forebear by Richard Lander; from there, they coasted down to the confluence in two light, leaky canoes. The two brothers became the first foreign eyes to see the religious rites of the riverain tribes of the lower Niger. As they grew closer to the sea, the natives became more and more unfriendly, and the area was in any case wracked by slaving warfare.

The Landers were finally captured by Ibo warriors, after their frail embarkations had been surrounded by fifty warcanoes, each bearing about forty people and six-pounder guns; the assailants waved Union Jacks and were dressed in European shirts, but nothing else. The Landers put up some resistance, but were soon overpowered and robbed of their few possessions.

As prisoners, they encountered people who spoke pidgin; they realized they must be close to the Atlantic. Some notables wore sarongs of Manchester cloth, and top hats, while one man wore what had obviously been an English mariner's jacket – plus a lace handkerchief across his loins. These signs of the closeness of shipping gave the Landers hope. Finally, they were ransomed for twenty sovereigns (about three hundred dollars) by a notable, Prince Boy, from the Delta village of Brass, whom they had assured would be repaid. But at Brass, a British captain refused to settle with the helpful prince. The Landers suggested Boy come with them to Bonny, a Delta island, but for reasons of tribal hostility the prince hesitated to go. This whole chapter of their experience, following their incredible escape from death and their epochal achievement, has a weird flavor in Richard Lander's terse account: half the crew of the British brig were dead from fever, and Lake, the captain, was sick and more than a little mad.

Finally, Lake unexpectedly relented and gave Boy a written assurance that he would be paid off, somehow, before the brig sailed. This, it was assumed, would enable the Landers and their eight Nigerian bearers to take refuge on the vessel. By then, the explorers had decided the palm oil ruffians and white slavers were as hostile as the Nigerian warriors – and Boy was distrustful, as well he might be, of the value of Lake's word. After much hesitation, Boy brought the party to the brig; Lake treacherously drove the prince off with gunfire.

The choleric skipper sailed the Landers to Fernando Póo; here they rested while awaiting ship for England, where the Government magnanimously gave Richard the promised pittance. The greatest mystery of African geography had now been solved; half a century was to go by before Henry Stanley – on a more remunerative basis – was to solve the second greatest in behalf, not of his government, but of the *New York Herald*.

*

Other discoveries were afoot. In 1818, the Frenchman Georges Mollien had traced the Senegal, Gambia and Rio Grande rivers to their sources, and a compatriot of the Scotsman Mungo Park – Major Gordon Laing – had become the first European, since the renegades of the Moroccan forces, to reach Timbuktu – whose site was another major cartographical mystery. Laing went from Tripoli, through Ghadames and In Salah. He reached the 'forbidden city' in August, 1806, seriously wounded in a brush with Twareg At the start of his return journey he was murdered by his Berabish bearers; his records perished with him.

The following year, René Caillé, a Frenchman of simple origins, set out from the Rio Nuñez to emulate Laing's feat. Disguised as an Arab, he trekked to Jenne, whence he canoed down the Niger to Timbuktu. The whole trip took a year. Like later visitors, he was appaled at what a dull, dirty little village the romantic, legendary city really was. He returned across the desert, through Arawan and Taghaza to Tafilelt, with a caravan of fourteen hundred camels taking slaves, gold, ivory, gum, ostrich feathers and Kano cloth. The desert journey was particularly hard and nearly fatal; but he finally reached Fez, where he hid in the French Consul's house until passage to France was found.

Richard Lander made a third trip to West Africa, in 1832, this time for what seemed a slightly less difficult task than his previous two journeys: with two capable companions, MacGregor Laird and R. A. K. Oldfield, and a large expedition of over one hundred persons, he was to go up – instead of down – the Niger. Fighting and disease made the river voyage a nightmare. Laird was gravely ill. The party's Kru bearers were poisoned. Leaving Laird to recover, Oldfield and Lander pushed on, exploring and charting the Benue. There was more hostility to follow, and at Hyama Lander finally died of spear wounds.

*

At the middle of the century, West Africa was to encounter perhaps the most energetic, certainly the most thorough of a remarkable generation of great explorers. This was the German Heinrich Barth. An official British mission led by James Richardson, and consisting of Barth and his compatriot Dr Hans Overweg, left Tripoli late in 1849 to negotiate commercial treaties with chiefs in the Western Sudan.

Midway in the desert, the three companions separated, with the intention of meeting up again in the savannah. Barth went through the Aïr and studied Agades before continuing South to Hausa, where he rejoined Overweg to visit Katsina and Kano. By then, he was short of money, but the Emir grudgingly agreed to bail Overweg and himself as far as Bornu. On the way, Barth learned of Richardson's death: this made him leader of the expedition.

The Sultan of Bornu was not unwilling to trade with Britain: he needed the profits of commerce to buy guns to capture slaves to sell to other trading powers; but he was suspicious of the now notorious British policy of trying actively to abolish slaving, West Africa's best-loved trade. Largely defeated in his commercial mission in Bornu, Barth went South to find the Benue, through Kuka, Adamawa, historic Kanem, Mandara and Bagarmi. He reached the

Benue at Yola, but the Fulani there were so hostile he made a hasty retreat.

Barth charted much of the Benue, then, returning North, explored Lake Chad; he saw the slave trade in practice at first hand, and was appalled. Barth's intention was to continue eastward to the Nile, but a shortage of funds decided him instead to return to Tripoli and England. Then, unexpectedly, despatches arrived across the Sahara Desert from Lord Palmerston, the British Foreign Minister, and with them a new stock of dollars. Palmerston wanted Barth and Overweg to visit Timbuktu, an idea which at once appealed to the German adventurers. Then came the almost inevitable next chapter in all these great odysseys: Overweg died.

Barth set out alone except for guides, through Zinder, Katsina, Kano and Sokoto to Gwandu, where he discovered an extant copy of the *Tarikh es-Sudan*. He crossed the Niger at Saï and found himself in lands engulfed by warfare between, on the one hand, the Twareg and Arabs, and on the other what Bovill crisply calls 'the fanatical Fulani'. Posing as an Arab, he made a difficult and often dangerous trek toward the North, reaching Timbuktu seriously ill. Here his true identity was discovered and execution seemed to be inevitable.

Fortunately for Barth, something of Timbuktu's scholarly traditions remained: his profound knowledge of Islam, together with his impressive defense of his own faith, astonished intellectuals. Sheik al-Bekkai, head of the Kunta Arabs, took Barth under his protection. Fortunately, the Kunta, the Berabish and the Twareg were at that time in control of the city – although their power was hotly contested by Barth's tormentors, the Fulani. Al-Bekkai alone saved Barth's life, despite considerable pressures, including an offer from the Fulani to cease plaguing the Kunta if Barth would be handed over to them.

During his eight months in Timbuktu, in spite of his vulnerable and unusual situation, Barth collected more information on the city than any traveler has done, before or since. At last he was able to escape, and relieve the stubborn al-Bekkai of the responsibility of his life. Six years later, when the Tukolor under al-Haj 'Umar were at the gates of Timbuktu, al-Bekkai sent messengers across the desert with an appeal to Queen Victoria for help. The appeal went un-answered; but in later days, the French Sudan administration erected a tomb to Barth's courageous benefactor.

Barth returned to Hausa, where he briefly rested. Thence, he proceeded to Bornu and across the Sahara, reaching England in September, 1855, after five years of travel on foot, by canoe or by camel. He had covered more of the northern half of Africa than any traveler, foreign or native. In London, Barth, like Lander, was not exactly drowned in a surfeit of generosity. He got a handshake from Palmerston and Lord Clarendon, a medal from the Royal Geographical Society and reimbursement of some of his unpaid expenses. Of the one thousand pounds which was all the five-year official Government expedition had cost, Barth had to find two hundred pounds out of his own pocket.

Public interest in Africa, stimulated at the time of Clapperton and Lander, had died; Barth's return to England was not mentioned in the newspapers of the day. The two thousand two hundred and fifty copies printed of the first three volumes of his *Travels and Discoveries in North and Central Africa* sold so badly that his publishers only did a run of one thousand copies on the fourth and fifth volumes. These books contained an encyclopedia of detail – historical, ethnological and geographical, as well as mercantile and political – of an area of country larger than the United States, divided into scores of languages and nations, where the fastest means of travel was a walking camel, and where the author's life was constantly endangered by warfare, malice or disease. His maps pinpointed with painstaking accuracy not only the unknown middle course of the Niger and the Upper Benue, but cities, villages, mountains and minor rivers, many of which had never been heard about before. To modern Africanists, Barth surpasses all his brave contemporaries of African exploration; his work contains more information than the books of Burton, Stanley, Park and Lander put together. This, of course, is not to decry the efforts of men whose work, although contributing less to the sum of knowledge, nevertheless involved the same super-human courage and incredible endurance: Barth's superiority lay in brains.

*

In 1863, Richard Burton, principally known for his work in East Africa, was sent by the then Foreign Minister of Britain, Lord Russell, on an embassy to King Glele of Dahomey, whom he found holding court at Kana. Burton's mission – to encourage 'legitimate' trade and discourage slavery – was only a limited success, but his account of his trip is illuminating.

Burton describes the king and his concubines, who held a gold spittoon when he spat, prostrated themselves when he sneezed and howled blessings when he ate. The English traveler made sketches. He accompanied the monarch to his capital, Abomey, where he witnessed and drew part of the gruesome 'customs'. Burton was not allowed to witness the final slaughter, in which about forty men and a like number of women were immolated.

An exception among the West African explorers was the only woman, Mary Kingsley. She belongs to a later period, beginning her travels in 1893. An eccentric, hob-skirted figure, who tried to be all things to all men – soldiers, mariners, palm oil ruffians, chiefs, bearers – and woman to none, her most exciting and amusing experiences were probably those along the Ogowe, the main river of the Gabun. She fell into elephant traps and rivers, and was confronted by gorillas or mutinous followers; but she lost neither her honor nor her sense of humor, and she survived – three considerable achievements in that area and that period.

iv

Abolition, Sierra Leone and Liberia

TRADE AND POLITICS in much of 19th Century Africa had to be completely re-vamped as a result of the Abolition of slavery, imposed by Europe gradually in the years following several British initiatives. The actual campaign against slavery in Europe – which was only partially responsible for its Abolition – was a simple humanitarian move; in many ways, it was surprising, for it seems likely that slavery did not shock average persons then as it would today. One West African authority writes:

'Men and women who were accustomed to seeing their own fellows executed for petty theft and imprisoned for debt, to the forcible impressment of men to serve in the navy, and to the transportation of criminals as a normal means of peopling the colonies, were not likely to be troubled by the inhumanity and injustice involved in the slave trade and plantation slavery. In practice most Europeans saw and knew next to nothing of either the slave trade or slavery. There was no demand for African slaves to work in Europe. Although the ships and men engaged in the slave trade began and ended their voyage in European ports like Liverpool, Nantes and Amsterdam, slaves were on board only on the stage between West Africa and America. The only African slaves that were normally seen in Europe were the few brought as personal servants by American planters returning home on leave or retirement.'

It should be added that some slaves were in fact auctioned at London, Liverpool, Bristol and other ports, and that British high society, from royalty down, kept black retainers: once lightly educated, many of them do not seem to have had much difficulty asserting their equality with the lightly-educated British population, and they were absorbed into upper, middle and lower class English families by marriage.

All the major European powers, and some of the minor ones, were involved in slaving, although the Spanish, who possessed slaves in Spanish America, were not much involved in trading; (the ever-supple Church finally ruled against slave-trading but tolerated slave ownership). The case against slavery was first forcefully put toward the end of the 18th Century by Granville Sharp, Thomas Clarkson and William Wilberforce. In 1772, in a judgement over a runaway slave from America, Lord Chief Justice Mansfield declared slavery unlawful in England. In 1807, the campaign of Wilberforce and his 'Clapham Group' bore fruit: an Act was passed making slave-trading illegal for British subjects. Denmark had passed a similar law in 1804. The United States followed in 1808, Sweden in 1813, Holland in 1814.

A Vice-Admiralty Court was established at Freetown in 1818 and during the next twenty years two hundred and eightytwo ships' crews were prosecuted and condemned. Following 1838, when the 'equipment clause' was passed (making prosecution possible even if there were no slaves actually on board, providing manacles, numerous feeding utensils or other arrangements for the stowage of humans were discovered) the number of prosecutions doubled: there were two hundred and eightyfour convictions in ten years – a quarter of them being obtained in the year following passage of the equipment clause. Abolition was thus a difficult and slow decision to apply; in 1845 alone, thirty ships were captured. But the Royal Navy, basing its anti-slavery squadron on Port Clarence (now Santa Isabel), the capital of Fernando Póo, applied the 1807 law strictly; from 1824, the Freetown court was empowered to give the death penalty to recalcitrant slavers.

France outlawed the trade in 1818, Brazil in 1825. Portugal and Spain, by laws passed in 1815 and 1817 respectively, had limited slaving to 'waters South of the Equator'. Other countries could not or would not apply restrictions, and in practice only Britain took continuous naval measures to repress the trade. Abolition came at a time when the British West Indies no longer required fresh imports of slaves, but when other markets, notably the United States, needed as many or more than ever. Despite the patrols from Fernando Póo, slave-trade figures actually increased from eightyfive thousand in 1810 to one hundred and twentyfive thousand in 1830 to one hundred and thirtyfive thousand ten years later.

In 1817, Spain and Portugal authorised the Royal Navy to stop their flags and search ships for slaves. They were given reciprocal rights against British slaving pirate clippers. France made a similar agreement with Britain fourteen years later. But in practice, although the agreements were reciprocal, only the R.N. searched foreign ships; it is staggering to think what the extent of the trade would have been by 1840 without the Fernando Póo squadron. Given the death and severe injury figures in slave wars and the losses in forts, barracoons and on the passage, a West African born in the slave-trade area in 1820 had one chance in four of becoming either a slave or a victim of the slave campaign in some way or other, during his or her next thirty years.

France accepted the 'equipment clause' in 1833, Spain in 1835, Portugal in 1842. The United States signed the Reciprocal Search Treaty only in 1862. But in 1840, the R.N. estimated it was stopping about a quarter of the slave ships. The captured vessels had to be brought up the Coast, often against seasonal winds, to Freetown. Caring for the arrested crews became a problem and an average of five per cent died under arrest; on some captured ships, the death rate was ten per cent. Between 1825 and 1865, a total of 1,287 slaving ships were captured and one hundred and thirty thousand slaves were released alive. Wilberforce, still active in the anti-slavery movement in the first part of this period, recommended that slavery be stopped on the Coast itself by 'Christianity, commerce and colonization'.

Anti-slavery patrols stopped not only outbound vessels, but also ships bound for slave ports, and examined their papers. As a consequence, although it was just as easy for European traders on the Coast to procure slaves after Abolition as it had been before, it was often difficult for them to procure the goods or money with which to pay for them, as these were very often seized. José Francisco dos Santos, the Wida trader from Brazil who exported to Bahia and Rio, and whose extensive African lineage now lives in Togo and Dahomey, is found writing desperately to his principals in 1842 saying he will accept 'any currency'.

Slavers began to avoid well-known spots like the Wida beach, and marched or canoed their human cargo to secret rendezvous further along the coast. 'Transactions', says one historian, 'were completed as quickly as possible, and payment made in dollars and doubloons rather than in goods. The demand for coin increased. The papers of a slave ship captured in 1844 revealed that she had carried a consignment consisting of eighteen hundred and thirty dollars in gold for da Souza. . . . Cowries, too, began to be imported into the Slave Coast market about 1847 by the Hamburg trader Lorenz Diedrichsen.'

Captain Diedrichsen, a free-lance trader, coasted in a Flensburg brig from about 1843 onward, and brought cowries from what later became German East Africa. A head of cowries (about two thousand shells) was worth two dollars in 1847; but as cowries became commoner, a head was worth only sixtysix cents by 1849, when Santos reported to Bahia that in the Wida area the natives were becoming reluctant to accept such a bulky and unstable currency.

An historian says: 'The dispersal of the slave markets was helped by the topography of the region. Apart from the Lagos lagoon, the heavy surf made an outright attack on the barracoons difficult, if not impossible; and the thick bush obscuring the lateral creeks enabled the trader in human flesh to ship his cargo where and when least expected. Such conditions explain the foundation by the Fon of a secondary slave port at Kotonu in the late 1830s. They explain, too, the incentive given to the smaller brokers from Anexo to Lagos to make a precarious but profitable living as agents for (or rivals of) da Souza and Domingo, and the efforts of Domingo himself between 1845 and 1850 to shift his barracoons further West from Porto Novo to Ajuda' (now part of Wida).

The most obvious product to replace slavery as a moneyearner for West Africans, and their European trading partners, was palm oil; but so relatively reduced was 'legitimate' trade right up to the British capture of Lagos in 1900 that until that time European trading companies not buying slaves numbered only six in the area from Porto Novo to Benin. An historian records: 'The agent of Victor Regis at Wida and Thomas Hutton's men at Anexo, Wida and Badagri were joined in 1849 and 1850 by Legresley, acting for the Gold Coast firm of Banner Brothers, and by J. Sandeman with two or three employees, acting for the firm of Stewart and Douglas. Where they could not supplant the Brazilians (as they eventually did at Badagri and Lagos) they were obliged to trade with them.'

The high import duty on palm oil was lowered in Britain in 1817. Imports rose, reaching sixteen thousand tons in 1840 and thirty thousand in 1851. As duty fell, prices gained. At Liverpool, oil sold for twenty pounds per ton in 1816. The price reached fortytwo pounds in the late 'Forties and a high of fortyeight pounds a ton was achieved in 1854. By then, the gross oil trade was worth over thirty million dollars in modern money. But outside Britain, purchases were light, and Africans were for many years reluctant to rely on this new – or on other, more traditional – agricultural crops; delegations of African leaders succeeded each other in London, pleading for the restoration of the slave trade.

The missions, understanding the African reluctance to give up such a profitable commerce, without lucrative alternatives, backed schemes for colonization and development. The British Missionary Society sent representatives to the Coast from 1792 onward, followed in 1798 by the London Missionary Society, in 1799 by the Church Missionary Society and in 1803 by the British and Foreign Bible Society. The Missions joined forces with the Abolitionists to help launch Sierra Leone, and gave backing to the African Association, inaugurated in 1788 to explore the African interior. Explorers found the hinterland in many places decimated by heavy slaving; all humanitarian voices joined in urging colonization, and their doctrine was embodied in the book *The African Slave Trade and its Remedy,* published in 1839; this was the work of Sir Thomas Buxton, who had succeeded Wilberforce to the parliamentary leadership of the Abolitionists.

*

Lord Mansfield's 1772 judgement had freed fifteen thousand slaves in Britain. The end of the American Revolution in 1783 created, among other things, the problem of Negro veterans who had served with the defeated, loyalist British forces. Encouragements for them to colonize Nova Scotia had not been successful, because of the pitiless climate and other factors, and a similar Negro colonization scheme in the Bahamas had not greatly prospered either. It was the London Abolitionist Granville Sharp who was first attracted to the idea of re-grafting the Afro-Americans on to the original African tree by purchasing land for them in relatively under-populated Sierra Leone. Although most of the African Britons remained in England, and were absorbed into the population, and although the greater part of the Bahamian settlers also decided not to go 'back' to Africa, some of the black British and the majority of the black Nova Scotians eventually volunteered for Sierra Leone; a 'Nova

Scotian Society' still exists, as a registered club, in modern Freetown.

Henry Smeathman, a humanitarian butterfly-collector who had visited West Africa, had recommended the stretch of West African coast known by the Spanish words for 'Lion Range' as suitable for the settlement. The immediate object of the humanitarians was to help destitute Negroes in London. Some had fled West Indian plantation owners following Lord Justice Mansfield's ruling in 1772 that slavery was not 'the law of England' – so that a bondsman became free when he reached the British Isles. Others were servants or former servants of planters who had retired to Britain. But most, according to Granville Sharp, were American Revolution veterans, particularly sailors, who had avoided the Nova Scotia project and reached England. In 1786, Jonas Hanway became the chairman of a 'Committee for the Black Poor'. They distributed a tract offering land in Sierra Leone to those who desired it. The British Government offered modest financial support, including the ship to take the emigrants.

The pan-Africanist leader and former Red Army colonel, George Padmore, said of Sierra Leone, in a book published shortly before his death: 'This African community . . . was inspired by confidence in the Negro potential to assimilate Western civilization. The founders were not concerned with trade and commerce and the exploiting of Africans.'

The first colonization group consisted of four hundred and fiftyone Negro ex-slave volunteers, sixtyseven impressed (in the circumstances, one is tempted to say enslaved) British prostitutes taken from jails, notably Portsmouth prison, and a few white men, including surgeons, a chaplain, a town major and a gardener. According to a Sierra Leonean historian, over fifty persons died between Portsmouth and Plymouth, giving some idea of conditions on the vessel the Government had provided. At least twentyfour persons were set ashore at Plymouth as unsuitable for the settlement; twentythree more ran away. Finally, four hundred and eleven sailed.

Their ship, under a Captain Thomson, was hit by considerable sickness, and by the time she moored in the estuary of the Rokel in May, 1787, only three hundred and seventyseven of the passengers were still alive. The colonists were given twenty square miles purchased by Sharp and his friends from a local chief, King Tom, and food stores for six months. The harbor was named St George's Bay and the settlement Granville Town. The site proved unhealthy, and no one seems to have realized that as the wet season was about to start the following month, planting would not be possible for several months. Nor was there time to build substantial houses.

Captain Thomson, who stayed with the colonists for four months, returned to report on the problems and to announce that another eightysix persons had died, including most of the high-jacked whores. Other settlers had hired their modest abilities for writing and arithmetic to local slavers. The following year, a ship, the *Myro*, was sent out by Sharp with fresh provisions, including livestock, and thirtynine new colonists, mostly white. By then, there were some brave signs of a permanent village; but in November, 1789, the colonists were dispersed by attacking tribesmen, and the settlement burned down.

In 1791, the London parliament passed an act setting up the Sierra Leone Company, absorbing the St George's Bay Company created the previous year; the company's trading profits were to cover the costs of the Government of the colony. Henry Thornton, a banker, became the chairman of the firm. An agent, Dr Falconbridge, advisors and technicians were sent out.

Falconbridge and his wife found the settlers dispirited and quarrelsome. By then, only sixtyfour of the original emigrants remained, and these were re-established on a better site – the present Sierra Leonean capital of Freetown. During the year, one hundred and nineteen white settlers were expatriated to get things moving; but they received no apparent preferential treatment, and the basic aim of a regenerated African state remained that of the promoters. The whites succumbed greatly to the humid climate. Then came the most substantial single immigration: twelve hundred volunteer colonists arrived from Nova Scotia. The relatively high figure suggests that they had been told nothing of the galloping death rate.

They came after a former loyalist sergeant, Thomas Peters,

had made his way to London, and impressed both the directors of the Company and the Secretary of State, Grenville, with the need to do something for his destitute fellow war veterans in and around Halifax, in the maritime provinces of Canada. Naval Lieutenant John Clarkson, brother of the Abolitionist, Thomas Clarkson, had then gone to Nova Scotia with an assistant, Hartshorne, to interview prospective settlers; he had been much impressed with the 'good, moral character' of the black Nova Scotians. Clarkson found that 'the majority of the men are better than any people in the laboring line of life in England.' The emigrants were urged to vindicate their race and not to take jobs as servants when they got back to Africa. Clarkson's flotilla of fifteen ships, bearing eleven hundred and ninety volunteers, sailed on January 15, 1792. Sixtyfive people died on the passage; the remainder arrived between February 28 and March 9. These were pre-Abolition days, and shortly before arriving, the convoy passed a slaver, the *Mary of Bristol*, on its way to Anomabu.

The Nova Scotians and the remaining early settlers were gathered into the new site of Freetown, as the city was called; land was distributed. There was great disappointment when the twenty acres per family originally promised were whittled by necessity down to four, and when rents were exacted to help pay for Government. Local administration in the settlement was organized under 'tithingmen' (one for every ten families), and three 'hundredors', who represented a hundred families each.

Many West African Coasters viewed the new colony with suspicion, particularly the French traders. In 1794, French ships stormed the settlement and burned it down. This tragedy forced England to take more interest in its distant offspring; a new and energetic Governor, Zachary Macaulay, was then appointed. He introduced a measure of self-government among the 'Creoles', as the colonists were already known.

Another mishap had a similar advantage in 1800, when local indigenes revolted against Creole control. To help the hard-pressed Government, Britain agreed the same year to grant an annual budget subsidy. Also in 1800, the Colony was increased in numbers by the arrival of Maroons – former rebel slaves who had lived an outlaw life in the mountainous Cockpit country of Jamaica, and who had later been transferred to Nova Scotia.

In 1808, Britain finally agreed to give the little settlement the status of a Crown Colony. The extreme reluctance to found colonies in Africa had been overcome by liberals, who had argued successfully that the Rokel would make a good naval base. By this time, liberated slaves had begun to be added to the existing Creole population.

In 1827, Fourah Bay College was founded – not on its present cliff-top site, but down in the city. A theological college to begin with, it was to be the first university South of the Sahara, and the first university in Africa in the modern sense. Freetown by then was already a tiny outpost of Western civilization in Africa, a society of Christians (Wesleyans, Baptists or members of a sect known as the Countess of Huntingdon's Connexion), eating a partly European diet (they imported from England salt beef and pork, biscuits, flour, oatmeal, barley, cheese and butter), dressing in European jerkins and flowing crinolines – and keeping their social distance from the admiring, wondering native. The settlers were viewed in London as black Britons, whose task was to civilize and evangelize the barbary surrounding them, and eventually to leaven the civilization of Africa.

Most early Governors were impressed by them, especially when comparing them to the white settlers. Perronet Thompson, a Methodist, had written to his betrothed in England in 1808: 'The state of European manners is bad beyond description. The black subjects are infinitely more orderly and decent. So much for this religious colony! And while the white inhabitants are roaring with strong drink at one end the Nova Scotians are roaring out hymns at the other.'

*

Like Freetown and the French-founded city of Libreville – later to become the village-capital of Gabun – Monrovia, named after President James Monroe, was founded by freed slaves. The concept of Liberia really dates from 1816, when the American Colonization Society, a body for freedmen under white philanthropic patronage, was established by Judge Bushrod Washington of Virginia – General George

Washington's brother. Judge Washington was succeeded by a Maryland lawyer, John Latrobe.

Quaker and other Abolitionist concern for destitute freedmen, and the opportunity to evangelize Africa through Afro-Americans, were two predominant spurs to the enterprise. Another was the desire of some state governments to rid their states of freed slaves. The previous year, 1815, a Quaker Negro shipowner and master, Paul Cuffe (or Cuffee), had taken thirtyeight Negroes to Sierra Leone at a cost of three or four thousand dollars to himself.

In 1819, the Society secured a Government Charter to establish a free state for Negroes in West Africa. Two white men, founder-member Samuel J. Mills and Ebenezer Burgess, were sent to Africa to purchase land: on the advice of Governor MacCarthy, whom they saw in Freetown, land was bought on Sherbro Island. The following year, eightyeight immigrants were brought there under Dr Samuel A. Crozer, the Society's agent, and two other white men appointed by President Monroe. The Sherbro chiefs reneged on their treaty: while palavering at Sherbro, the three whites and twentytwo of the settlers died: the rest, under Daniel Coker and Elijah Johnson, moved to Freetown.

In 1821, after a reconnaissance early in the year by Ephraim Bacon, a fresh group of twentyone Negroes, under Dr Eli Ayres and Captain Stockton, set off for the Coast. The party made a brief stop at Freetown before their first settlement on an island (now Bushrod Island) near the center of what is now the capital. They suffered numerous native attacks until relieved on August 8, 1822, by the arrival of fiftythree new settlers under a Colony 'director', Jehudi Ashmun of Newhaven, Connecticut.

Many more native attacks, using arms supplied by Cuban and Spanish slavers, tormented the newcomers. On December 1, about one thousand warriors attacked, and the siege was only repulsed when a Georgia widow, Matilda Newport, fired a hitherto temperamental cannon by shaking the embers of her pipe on to the magazine. December 1 has been a Liberian public holiday – Matilda Newport Day – ever since.

A British warship, the *Prince Regent,* called, and a midshipman named Gordon and eleven men volunteered to stay at Bushrod and help the defenses. All but three died, probably of yellow fever. Finally the American warship *Cyane* brought new colonists and badly needed ammunition. Colonization was extended along nearby Cape Mesurado; several other coastal settlements were founded, following the purchase of land by different philanthropical societies, including the Maryland Colonization Society, which was capitalized at two hundred thousand dollars. The MCS sent out several hundred new colonists under Jamaica-born John C. Russwurm, the first Negro to graduate from an American university. Russwurm arrived on the Coast in 1836.

New York, Pennsylvania, Georgia, Mississipi and Louisiana were other states that sponsored schemes aimed largely at 'getting rid' of Negro freedmen, who were a source of envy to slaves. More emigrants arrived, and the US Government contributed food supplies. The main colony was named Liberia, and the capital that grew up from Cape Mesurado was named after President Monroe at about that time.

Until 1841, the Colony of Liberia (but not of Maryland) had white Governors. Then J. J. Roberts, a thirtytwo-year-old settler who had arrived in 1829, became the first Afro-American head of the nascent community. Together with the more obvious problems of establishing the colonists – even worse than in Sierra Leone because of the almost total disinterest of the 'mother country' – Roberts had to face challenges to his authority from an alliance of the indigenes and European traders.

In 1845, the point was diplomatically raised as to whether Liberia was under American protection. This was after a dispute with a Sierra Leonean on harbor dues had led to the seizure of his ship and a British warship's counter-seizure of a Liberian freighter. Washington's answer was equivocal. Left to some extent to their own devices, and faced with Britain's insistence that it would not recognize a 'commercial enterprise' as a sovereign state, the settlers decided in 1846 to declare themselves sovereign; but it was over a year later – on July 26, 1847 – before a Declaration of Independence was actually issued, after a meeting in Monrovia of representatives of the four settlements then in operation: Montsenado (Mesurado), Grand Bassa, Sinoe, and Maryland. The latter 'State' did not join the Union until ten years later, however.

A flag modelled on the American standard, but with only eleven stripes and one star, was adopted. The constitution at the time governed less than three thousand people, but provided for a bi-cameral legislature: representatives were elected for four years, senators for six, presidents for two. (Presidential terms were increased to four years in 1907, eight in 1938; now, additional terms of four years are also permissible).

The year following the 1847 declaration of independence, Britain recognized the new nation. Gradually, other countries followed. American recognition came only in 1862.

In 1848, President Roberts had made a successful trip to Europe, receiving encouragement from Palmerston, Queen Victoria – who closely resembled Mrs Roberts, also an octoroon and Prince-President Louis Bonaparte. He also visited King Leopold I of the Belgians, Holland, Denmark, Lübeck, Hamburg and Prussia. The Scandinavian and Iberian countries and some states in Latin America also extended recognition.

From the outset, and until very recent times, government was the monopoly of the Afro-American colonists. Deprived of skills and capital, the country progressed only slowly until recent years, when it has become one of the most prosperous West African states. Threats to its existence as an independent country were numerous, but never came to anything – although in frontier problems with France, Liberia lost a huge stretch of land in the Mount Nimba region to French Guinea. (This has turned out in the past decade to be rich in iron deposits, and as a consequence the Liberian claim to the area persists). Liberia also had frontier disputes with Britain, persisting until the Boundary Commission's work in 1903.

Liberia's most distinguished son was Dr Edward Wilmot Blyden, who had been born on the Danish West Indian island of St Thomas – now part of the American Virgin group – in 1832, the son of Ewe slaves shipped from Keta. In 1847, he sailed to New York to complete his limited high school education, but found that none of the better schools would accept him on racial grounds. The Colonization Society of New York offered him a free passage to Liberia, where he arrived in 1850. He became editor of the *Liberian*

Herald the following year, at the age of nineteen, then a teacher at – and later President of – Liberia College. Although this school's standards were abysmally low, Blyden used its library to self-educate himself. He became a cabinet minister (Interior) and was twice ambassador to London. An astonishing linguist, he spoke or read English, French, Spanish, Italian, German, Greek, Hebrew, Latin and Arabic, and was rated an international authority on Islam. From 1872 to 1873, he was employed by the British Government to negotiate a peace between warring Muslim rulers in the hinterland of Sierra Leone Colony.

*

By 1840, Sierra Leone had progressed to the point where Sierra Leoneans were helping to pre-colonize other parts of the Coast. Although all or nearly all the Creoles had taken English names, some of them knew themselves to be of 'Gulf of Benin' stock, and the first of these began 'returning' to Badagri and Abeokuta in 1838 and 1839. By 1844, about three thousand Sierra Leoneans, mostly Yoruba by descent but including some Hausa and Nupe, had settled in Abeokuta.

The main reason for the emigration was not the desire to discover the land of their fathers, but the overcrowding of the Freetown settlement. In 1833 – a generation after the abolition of the trade – slavery itself had been abolished throughout the British Empire, leading to mass manumissions in the West Indies, and fresh emigrations to Sierra Leone.

The Sierra Leoneans who went to Yorubaland through Badagri were welcomed cautiously by the populace. Those who landed in Lagos were robbed of everything they possessed. The four vessels that made the journey in 1838 and 1839 were all seized slave ships, bought and fitted out by the migrants themselves with the financial help of other members of the Freetown community and the Methodist mission. The migrants were mostly farmers and petty traders, some with a little education and nearly all with at least slightly more sophistication than the people among whom they settled. Missionaries soon followed their converts to Nigeria.

At once marked out as an *élite*, some of the Sierra Leoneans soon established themselves in Lagos on a similar footing to the Brazilian mulatto, Negro and white slave-dealers and traders. They had the advantage over the Brazilians of being able to expect some protection from the British Consul – a necessary privilege in the days of arbitrary rule associated with Oba Akitoye and his son Docemo. The Sierra Leoneans and Brazilians were almost exclusively traders and artisans; they kept domestic slaves; many became landowners and relatively wealthy people, especially the more successful export-import middlemen. They were both resented and respected for their superior knowledge by the Idejo chiefs.

The establishment of a regular steamship line to the Bight of Benin and the Bight of Biafra in 1852 enabled small factors to send their oil regularly to British commission houses, from whom they received goods which they sold on credit to the Brazilian and Sierra Leonean middlemen. Some of these, mostly Sierra Leoneans, engaged in export also. In the 1850s, Lagos exported four to five thousand tons of palm oil a year. The peak was reached in 1857, after which wars in the interior and some revival of slave-trading caused a fall-off.

The cowrie trade, mostly the monopoly of German traders, notably the firm O'Swald, was short-lived and was already in its death throes by 1859. A large sack of cowries was worth thirtyseven dollars of modern money in 1851 and could purchase thirtysix imperial gallons of palm oil in Lagos. By 1859, a cowrie sack was worth only fourteen dollars and fourteen gallons of oil. O'Swald imported over two hundred thousand sacks from Zanzibar during the decade beginning 1851. The French firm Régis imported just over half that quantity.

Although the trade itself was fairly small, profits on palm oil were considerable. In 1854, the Liverpool price was six hundred dollars a ton; it reached seven hundred and twenty dollars at the outbreak of the Crimean War. In comparison, in 1855 oil was costing three hundred dollars in Lagos; three-quarters of this price was estimated by the British Consul of the time to be middleman charges and other side costs. The price had declined to two hundred and seventy dollars by 1859, presumably increasing the European profits of the trade.

Pre-colonial British West Africa

BY THE FIRST HALF OF THE 19th CENTURY, the spheres
of interest were beginning to make themselves clearly visible.
Since France controlled the mouth of the Senegal, Britain
concentrated on the less accessible but more commercially
interesting Niger. The MacGregor Laird–Lander expedition,
1832–1834, was the most spectacular evidence of increased
British official interest in the river as a major source of trade.
The 1841–1842 expedition, also mentioned earlier for its
heavy death toll, was intended to establish a mission station
and model farm at Lokoja – the Benue–Niger confluence. It
was launched under pressure from scientific and humanitarian interests in London led by Sir Fowell Buxton. There
was spirited opposition from the palm oil ruffians, who were
inevitably opposed to any threat to the prevailing situation
of laissez-faire. This, tribal hostility and the onslaught of
fever contributed to the failure of the venture, which did
however produce a fairly accurate chart of the Niger valley.

The great figure in the Delta in these years was to be
John Beecroft, an Anglo-Spanish Eurafrican who first visited
the area as a merchant seaman. From 1827 to 1834, he was on
Fernando Póo working with the Anti-Slavery Squadron. He
stayed on to help slaves liberated there. Between 1836 and
1842, we find him exploring the Benin and Calabar Rivers
and the Niger as far as Busa. In 1842, Spain, which had
taken over Fernando Póo and Annobón, decided to lease
the island to Britain, and asked Beecroft to be Governor.
He accepted. In 1849, he became, also, British Consul to the
Bights (that is, the Bights of Benin and Biafra). A man of
great presence, honesty and sense of justice, he established
his word as law; both the rough, anarchic palm oil ruffians
and the ruthless, anarchic Delta chiefs bowed to the suzerainty of his decisions – behind which lurked of course, in
case of necessity, the metaphorical shadow of British gun-

boats. As will be seen later, his role in pre-imperial Nigeria was considerable.

In 1852, word reached the coast from Barth that he had located the Benue from the North; this, more than anything, inspired a third official British expedition up the Niger. Laird, a Liverpudlian shipowner, provided the vessels. The Royal Navy supplied navigators and cartographers. Beecroft was to have command of the undertaking. Unfortunately, he died; a naval surgeon, Dr William Balfour Baikie, assumed command. Shortly before the expedition set out in 1854, quinine was discovered, overcoming to a large degree the major barrier to Guinean exploration – malaria. The Baikie expedition set a new exploring record for West Africa: not a single member of the party died.

*

Growing interest in West Africa, and the discovery of the healing, prophylactic propensities of quinine bark sparked a missionary revival. The earliest Christian missions on the Atlantic coast of Africa, those of the Catholics, were mostly in decline or dead by the mid-19th Century; but British Protestants were becoming active, and American Protestants were starting to thrive in Liberia. After 1860, French Catholic missions began to appear again in some numbers. Portuguese Catholics, who had never completely ceased to be active, expanded their missions during the 19th Century.

Among the Anglicans, the SPG – Society for the Propagation of the Gospel in Foreign Parts – had been founded in 1701. Primarily concerned with education, it was particularly active in Cape Coast (modern Ghana) from 1752 to 1816. For the last fiftyone years of this period, the chaplain was an African – a Fanti of the area ordained in England, the Rev. Philip Quaque (Kwakwe). The activities of the British Missionary Society (BMS), the London Missionary Society and the British and Foreign Bible Society, at the start of the 19th Century, have been mentioned in connection with Abolition. The Church Missionary Society, CMS – born, like most of the other groups, in the 18th Century – began in 1806 to maintain a permanent mission in Sierra Leone.

The early 19th Century saw several other Anglican and non-comformist missions establish themselves in West

Africa. In 1827, Fourah Bay College was founded, in Freetown, to train African clergy; the first African Anglican bishop was to be appointed in 1852. Two CMS missionaries had accompanied the Niger expedition of 1841, including the Rev. Samuel Crowther, a Yoruba slave who had been freed when his ship was hailed. Put ashore with his fellow freedmen at Freetown, he had made his way to England, where he had been ordained.

Between 1839 and 1842 the Yoruba who returned from Sierra Leone to Abeokuta included several Anglican and Wesleyan missionaries. A CMS mission was established at Abeokuta in 1844, with Crowther on the staff. Shortly after, the Wesleyans also made their Abeokuta mission permanent. In 1848, the first Christian convert died in Abeokuta and there were tribal riots when he was buried according to Christian, not traditional custom. Persecution of Christians continued for a while. In 1851, a CMS mission was set up in Lagos, and two years later in Ibadan. In 1864, Crowther became the first Bishop of the Niger – the diocese still bears this name.

The Baptists, meanwhile, had established a mission in Port Clarence, on Fernando Póo, for freed men, in 1841. From here, this church expanded into Kamerun, where its missionaries produced the famous pidgin catechism. In 1858, Catholic Spain ejected the Baptists from Fernando Póo; they returned in the present century to minister to Nigerian migrant laborers, and school their children. The (Calvinistic) Church of Scotland established itself at Calabar in 1846.

German missions, on the coast and in the interior, were flourishing. The Basle Mission Society began in Keta in 1828 and proceeded West. In 1847, the Bremen Society also began evangelical work among the Ewe.

The Wesleyans were by then challenging the more austere Anglicans for the soul of the Fanti. The first great Wesleyan leader was the Rev. Thomas Freeman, son of an African freedman and an Englishwoman, educated in England. Freeman settled in Cape Coast in 1837. Two years later, he founded a mission at Kumasi, then moved to Abeokuta, where he worked until his death in 1890.

The mission schools provided cadres, and the sites of the schools determined the origins of clerks. The Gold Coast was first staffed with Sierra Leoneans; many descendants of these Creoles are among the leading families of Accra today – the Thompsons, the Hutton-Mills, the Casely-Hayfords, the deGraft-Johnsons, and many others. Sierra Leoneans particularly helped establish the growth of British trade on the Gold Coast after 1843. Sierra Leoneans and Fanti Cape Coasters helped establish British authority in Lagos, then throughout what became Nigeria. (In return, it was to be Nigerian soldiers that conquered Ashanti for the Queen.) Before the end of the 19th Century, these *élites* were to originate the area's first 'self-government' movements.

*

But in the decades following Britain's Abolition of slavery in 1807, colonization and its reactions were still some way off, except for the modest settlement of Sierra Leone. Britain's commitments in Guinea were only three: Sierra Leone, a Crown Colony of about three hundred square miles and four thousand freedmen families; the fort on the Gambia; and the Gold Coast forts. All the forts were the responsibility of the Company of Merchants.

There was strong opposition even to these limited commitments. Trade was not thought to justify the expense of maintaining and defending the little footholds on the Coast. Popular opinion was beginning to play a role in Government policy, and the public was for keeping only Sierra Leone – seen as a moral obligation and a naval base. But even Sierra Leone was expected to be self-supporting. Its subsidy was agreed to with difficulty, and was meager. Britain's colonies in the East, and the Caribbean, were justifiably seen as more interesting. But the humane societies argued for colonization, and committees and commissions met to discuss the concept.

A slight move toward official control came when the Ashanti occupied the Gold Coast littoral. Warfare affected trade. The British, Dutch and Danes, who all had Gold Coast forts, accepted Ashanti suzerainty over the coastal land, and the Danes received an Ashanti mission in some pomp at Christiansborg Castle. But the Ashanti proved to be warriors rather than traders, and commerce declined. After fruitless attempts to parley with the new suzerains, including two official missions to Kumasi, Britain abolished the Company of Merchants in 1821 and reluctantly assumed official control of all British forts on the Guinea Coast.

In 1814, Sir Charles MacCarthy, an energetic campaigner against slavery, had been appointed Governor of Sierra Leone: he extended the territory, by land purchase treaties, to accommodate the community, now numbering twenty thousand Creoles. In his ten years as Governor, the cost of the Colony to Britain rose from twentyfour thousand to ninetyfive thousand pounds.

MacCarthy annexed the Isles of Loos (off Konakri, the capital of modern Guinea) to prevent slavers using them as a haven; but what he called the 'pennypinchers' back in London forbade him to take over Bissagos (modern Portuguese Guinea) and Sherbro (modern Sierra Leone). When the Company of Merchants was abolished in 1821, MacCarthy, in Freetown, became Governor of all the settlements in Sierra Leone and Gambia and on the Gold Coast. Three years later, leading two hundred and fifty European troops, and Fanti levies, he was killed in action against the Ashanti. In 1826, Britons and Danes, together with Ga and Fanti troops, finally beat the Ashanti at Dodowa.

With MacCarthy's death, the liberals at home lost ground, and the anti-colonial business lobby won the favor of the Government. When Sir Neil Campbell came out as the new Governor in 1827, his instructions were not to extend British territory any further and not to form alliances with native chiefs, so as not to become involved in costly military operations. The Gold Coast forts were given back to merchant control, with a subsidy that varied from three to four thousand pounds a year. In studying the birth of British colonization in West Africa, observers have always been impressed with how widely British authority was to be established, largely thanks to the exertions of traders and despite the great official reluctance to colonize and the almost unbelievably parsimonious approach to budgets.

In 1830, the Gold Coast Merchants, through their London committee, sent out George Maclean to run their forts. A former officer who had fought the Ashanti at Dodowa, he was a determined man with an obvious colonial vocation. Maclean found the Ashanti still troublesome and the coastal tribes antagonistic toward Britain. They justly complained that Britain had first recognized Ashanti authority, then joined with them against the Ashanti, then left them to their own devices after Dodowa. Maclean found his authority did not extend beyond the forts at Cape Coast and Jamestown (the harbor district of modern Accra); his control of the British forts at Anomabu and Dixcove was more theoretical than real. The Dutch, occupying Elmina, were in league with the Ashanti. The Danes at Christiansborg (two miles from Jamestown) were intriguing to take over Akra, as it was then spelled, and territory inland as well.

In this climate of hostility, intrigue and ignorance, Maclean instituted some order, and courts of justice. His authority was extended, to some degree, to all the land between the Volta and the Pra and, according to one authority, 'about forty miles inland'. Exports through British forts increased from seventy thousand sovereigns – $1,050,000 in modern money – in 1831, to $4,875,000 in 1840. Imports rose from $1,965,000 to $6,345,000.

A brilliant man who did not suffer fools gladly, Maclean made many enemies. Back in London, some of them plotted their revenge. As a result, the Governor was severely criticized in an abrasive report. In 1842, a parliamentary select committee investigated, exonerated and praised him – but agreed that a large part of the authority he was exercising was illegal. The committee recommended he be instructed to negotiate formal treaties with the coastal tribes; the Government endorsed the proposal.

The following year, Britain appointed a Lieutenant-Governor of the Gold Coast, under the authority of the Governor in Freetown. Maclean, the Gold Coast Merchants man, was made his Judicial Assessor. From 1844 to 1856, and at a lesser rhythm for eighteen years after that, a series of 'Bonds' were negotiated with tribal chiefs. These concerned traders' rights and the administration of local justice. The African chiefs agreed to abolish all barbarous practices, especially human sacrifice; but the Bonds did not give Britain governing rights over any territories except the British forts themselves.

The situation at this time is easy to imagine. Maclean, the experienced, effective, authoritarian Coaster, was seen by the merchants as being the victim of petty London functionaries. The frequent changes of policy in Britain only added to the feeling that Government interference was amateurish and dangerous. It is probably fair to say that the merchants and Maclean, though less legally meticulous than the 'interloping' Lieutenant-Governor, were more acculturated to the people they were dealing with. Maclean died on the Coast in 1847, and the Coasters, fearful of more interference now that their strong right arm was gone, boiled over in resentment against the mother country.

It was a battle for power between Government and business, and Government put in more rank. In 1850, the Gold Coast got its own Governor – with a nominated Executive and Legislative Council, which went some way to satisfying the angry merchants. The boom in trade helped the liberal lobby, and Britain bought out the Danish forts, Christiansborg and Keta. In 1852, the chiefs linked by Bonds to Britain met in council, and agreed to raise a poll tax to develop education, medical services and roads – for British Government funds were still inadequate, even to cover the maintenance of the trading forts. The chiefs, however, were not successful at tax-collecting; after some fiscal shortfalls, the development scheme was abandoned. Enmity remained between Europeans and Ashanti, who could now export only a limited number of slaves through the Ivory Coast and Dahomey; the unsaleable surplus was sacrificed.

At this time, Beecroft was the most active suppressor of the traffic. He undertook a mission to Dahomey in 1850, calling at Lagos and reporting that the city had by then become the main slave port, surpassing Wida, because of the effects of the Yoruba wars.

Britain, impressed with the reported power of Abomey, decided the conquest of Dahomey would be too expensive. Beecroft reported Lagos was weak and urged armed intervention. Back in Fernando Póo, the Eurafrican pro-consul received an offer of alliance from Akitoye, the deposed Oba of Lagos. If aided against the usurper, Kosoko, and reinstated, he would abolish slavery. Apprised of the negotiations, Kosoko launched attacks on Abeokuta, which supported the dethroned King, and Badagri, where Akitoye lay. He fled to Santa Isabel in time to avoid capture. The following year, the Royal Navy occupied Lagos and restored Akitoye. British trade at the port developed; but, despite vigorous action, slavery continued.

The conquest of Lagos was surprisingly easy. London had at first been reluctant to intervene in the city throne dispute – beyond rescuing Akitoye from Badagri, and taking him to safety in Fernando Póo. But in October, 1851, Beecroft received his orders to blockade Wida and expel Kosoko from Lagos – both measures being aimed at the suppression of the slave trade. Beecroft entered Lagos lagoon in a small boat, found Kosoko intractable, returned with HMS *Bloodhound* and a landing party – which was repulsed – and finally attacked the city in force on December 26. Kosoko had barricaded the Marina with palm trunks and humid sand, and mounted his artillery all along the waterfront. The two larger British vessels used, *Bloodhound* and *Teazer,* went aground, and the defense had killed fifteen and wounded seventyfive before the naval guns drove Kosoko and his men to Iddo Island, leaving Beecroft – who oversaw the operation himself from an open boat – the victor. Akitoye and his forces paddled alongside Lagos Island on the twenty-eighth: the restored prince signed a treaty with the Consul.

In 1861, Britain annexed Lagos Island, a lagoon-locked swamp of about twelve square miles, to support lawful commerce, to try to check slaving and to defend the port, if necessary, against Dahomeyan incursions. Accepted by Docemo, the treaty of cession helped to reduce the anarchy prevailing in Lagos trade and gave the Crown 'all the rights, profits, territories and appurtenances . . . as well as the profit and revenue of the port.'

But the hinterland of Lagos was still in ferment. Kurumi, the able Are of Ijaye, died in 1862 while his city was under siege by the Ibadan Yoruba. Faced by famine, Ijaye sold many of its citizens to Ijaye's ally, Abeokuta, in return for food. The Egba of Abeokuta, aided by an American sharp-shooter called Pettiford, took Iperu from the Ijebu Remo Yoruba and successfully attacked Ibadan. The war divided the CMS protestant missionaries. Townsend backed the Egba in his mission paper, *Iwe-Irohin,* while Hinderer supported Ibadan in his *Anglo-African.* The conflict interfered with Lieutenant-Governor Glover's hopes of pushing trade

North into the friendly territory of King Masaba of Nupe. In 1863, Dahomey attacked Abeokuta, and at Townsend's request prayers were offered for the Egba throughout the Protestant world. The Dahomeyans were decisively defeated the following year.

*

In 1863, Ashanti invaded the lands of the Fanti and other 'Bond' chiefs. The Governor, Richard Pine, post-hasted despatches to London with plans for a counter-attack. London, true to form, refused the funds for the operation. The setback for British prestige was considerable; it was the fourth time in half a century that Britain had reneged on its promises to one side or other in the lingering Fanti-Ashanti War. The Ashantis plundered widely. Legitimate commerce was brought to a halt.

Lord Newcastle's miserly policy was also being felt in Lagos, where the new Governor, Henry Stanhope Freeman, set about cutting costs, and developing sources of revenue by more zealously collecting customs at Lagos, Badagri, Lekki and Palma. Customs posts were set up on the Ossa Lagoon, which brings shallow-draft vessels from Porto Novo to Lagos; but the Colonial Office insisted that even the need for revenue was not to justify 'any further expansion along the littoral'.

The anti-colonial lobby was once more in full war-cry. In 1865 a Select Committee recommended that Britain withdraw from all settlements except Sierra Leone. While arrangements were sought to protect British trading interests in the Gambia, the Gold Coast and Lagos, these would remain under the protection of Freetown. The Committee also recommended that Britain should accept no further territories in Africa. The proposals urged Africans in the areas of British influence to prepare for self-government. The report was adopted.

But the British were to learn slowly that there was no alternative – if trade was to be developed in an area with no effective, literate administration – to full colonial responsibility. In Lagos, the issue came to a head over traditional rivalry with Egbaland, with its capital at Abeokuta. In 1862, the Egba refused to accept a British Consul. The Alake

Okukenu died the same year, and what we should today call the 'war party' in Abeokuta grew in influence. In 1864, what was to prove to be the last of the Fon invasions was repulsed by the Egba, and the victorious Ologun, the Egba war chiefs, turned their attention to reducing Ibadan and its ally Ijebu Remo.

A considerable quantity of arms – over three hundred thousand dollars worth at modern values – was imported into Lagos during the thirty-month period ending at Christmas, 1864. Much of it went to Ibadan, through Ijebu middlemen in the Ikorodu market. In March, 1865, the Egba attacked Ikorodu. The Administrator, Glover, was forced to intervene in this intra-Yoruba conflict; he did so decisively. Once again the specter of expense appalled that most reluctant of empire-builders in Africa, the Parliament at Westminster. The Select Committee recommended that Lagos should be returned to native rule.

Administrator Glover remained, with less powers and, theoretically, less responsibilities. The principal result of the swing in policy in London was to leave the boundaries of Lagos undefined; in practice, the boundary was ethnic, and moved with people.

The Select Committee's recommendations for withdrawal were, of course, never fully implemented. In 1876, the self-governing Colony of Lagos was annexed to the Gold Coast. In the years that followed, British control was extended westward to Katanu (in 1879) and Appa (in 1884), although no decree to this effect was ever signed.

Glover's eight-year term ended in 1872. In the next thirteen years, there were to be fifteen acting Administrators, Lieutenant-Governors and Deputy Governors, acting under the authority of the Governor in the Gold Coast, who in turn was answerable to the Governor-in-Chief in Freetown. (In contrast, from the establishment of the Colony of Nigeria in 1900 to independence in 1960, there were only eight Governors and Governors-General).

The Lagos Administrator had an advisory council consisting of the Chief Magistrate, the Colonial Secretary and the officer commanding the West Indian troops and Hausa constabulary. Two traders who had been members *de facto* but not *de diritto* were dismissed by the imperious Glover. After

149

his time, a trading community representative, Arthur Porter of Banner Brothers, was appointed, and Administrator Fowler recommended admission of two Sierra Leoneans to the Legislative Council of the Gold Coast – to represent Lagos. But in 1874, the Lagos advisory council was abolished, together with Lagos representation in Accra.

The advisory body was not revived until 1886, when it consisted of five officials, one European trader, one native trader and a native clergyman. By this time, Lagos was a bustling business community, with the census showing 47.3 per cent of the population engaged in trade or artisanship. The Yoruba and Egun traders had by then largely outnumbered the Sierra Leoneans and Brazilians, whose adult population in 1871 is given by one authority as 'only a little over two thousand.'

*

In the Gold Coast, the British decision of 1865 to withdraw into the forts was to lead to the setting up of a Fanti Confederation to take over the administrative task vacated by the British.

To begin with, in 1867, Britain had exchanged all its forts West of Cape Coast for all Dutch forts East of Elmina – enabling both countries to concentrate their limited, poorly-subsidized administrations. Among Coasters, there was fear that the Select Committee's proposals would lead to complete withdrawal; the traders argued vociferously for continued British administration and subsidy of the forts.

The exchange of forts drew native reaction. The anti-Ashanti tribes resented being transferred to the sphere of the Dutch – Ashanti's allies. At Komenda, the people refused to allow the Dutch into their newly-acquired castle. The Komenda people attacked Elmina, where the population was allied to the Ashanti and friendly to the Dutch. In 1868, the Ashanti again raised the war cry against the British; but their reliance on Dutch assistance was ill-advised; the following year, Holland offered to sell Britain all its forts. Policy in London had changed and the offer was accepted.

The Asantehene, Kofi Karikari, backed by the people of Elmina, particularly resented the proposal that the British buy Elmina, the main outpost of Ashanti imperialism. Britain's allies, the Fanti, hoped Britain would fight the Ashanti. Instead, concerned with the expense of warfare, the British negotiated. The Fanti interpreted this, after the earlier decisions of the Select Committee – inviting them to prepare for self-government – as a sure sign Britain had no intention of retaining its limited control for very long.

It was then that the educated members of the Fanti tribes met with the Chiefs at Mankessim in October, 1871, and wrote the constitution of the Fanti Confederation. This was to be the organ of government and defense when the British left. Not too surprisingly, British opinion on the Coast did not follow the policy swings in London, and had resented the 'sell-out' of 1865. A hasty administrator arrested the authors of the Fanti Constitution for plotting against the British; the Colonial Office ordered their release – but by now bad blood had been established.

In January, 1873, the Ashanti rose. The war hosts crossed the Pra and the Fanti trembled. But dysentery and small-pox decimated the invaders within a month, and the threat momentarily withdrew. At this point, Britain reluctantly accepted the necessity for military action. At the end of the year, Major-General Sir Garnet Wolseley was appointed Administrator and Commander-in-Chief of the Gold Coast. He was given two thousand five hundred European soldiers and an indeterminate number of African auxiliaries, mostly Nigerians.

The main battles of the First Ashanti War were fought between January 31 and February 4, 1874. The defenders fought well, but on February 5 Wolseley entered Kumasi to find that the King and most of his people had fled the town. The expedition was not equipped for an occupation, nor for further fighting, so Wolseley burned the mud city and left.

Karikari's envoys caught up with the returning column at Fomena and signed a peace. The Asantehene agreed to pay fifty thousand ounces of gold and to give up his empire in Denkyera, Assini, Akyem, Adansi and Elmina. He promised to keep the Kumasi trail open for trade and to abolish human sacrifice.

In July 1874, Disraeli took office in Westminster with a Conservative administration and a more energetic policy. The protected areas in West Africa were to be annexed to the Crown and the administration of Lagos was to be detached from the Government of Sierra Leone. Disraeli opposed the Fanti Confederation on the grounds that it over-rode the Bonds of 1844–1845. Britain would ask for no rights to land, but insisted on legislative control. In Disraeli's decrees, we can see the modest precursor of what was eventually to become a decision to colonize.

*

The administration of Lagos had also suffered from the vacillations which preceded Disraeli; but where Westminster had failed, individuals had sometimes succeeded. At Badagri, an administrative officer who established a pattern of colonial administration at its best, under difficult circumstances, was Thomas Tickel, a Gold Coast Eurafrican who had come to the area to trade and taught himself Yoruba. For about twenty years, with various titles, he dispensed civil and criminal justice, contained abusive chiefs and hacked away at the authority of fetish priests. In his later period, as Political Agent, he helped maintain the British position against the French on the western creeks. Men like Tickel reduced smuggling and helped to keep down the frightening levels of theft and theft-with-violence which plagued the trading settlements.

Both Lagos and Badagri failed to pay for their administrations. After a rapid rise in the 'Sixties, palm oil and palm kernel exports through Lagos had levelled off at about seven thousand and twenty thousand tons annually, but prices fell. Palm oil dropped, at Liverpool, from thirtyseven sovereigns a ton in 1868 to thirtythree two years later. The price of kernels fell from fifteen pounds to thirteen. Not all this drop was passed on to the Nigerian farmer and the greatest losers were the traders. Profits per ton on oil dropped from twenty pounds in 1865 to about eight pounds in 1881; the profit on kernels was only two or three pounds. Since traders extended credit, many smaller ones went under.

An authority on the period writes: 'Of the eleven Sierra Leonean merchants consigning to European commission houses in 1886, only two or three had lasted through the two previous decades: the others were newcomers from Sierra Leone and the Gold Coast, or descendants of local families whose lands they mortgaged as credit to the European trading houses.' (The *Lagos Times* of July 27, 1881, notes that these 'often consigned to one house under a fictitious name and through other persons the produce due to another'.)

Of the early British companies, only Banner Brothers had survived. Two Lagos British companies had moved to the Delta; three had closed. German competition had entered the scene, including two companies still extant today, about a century later – G. L. Gaiser, and Witt and Büsch. By 1881, out of one hundred and twelve European officials, traders and others in the Colony and Protectorate, fortyfive were Germans in trade or German engineers running the five steam vessels on the Lagos-Porto Novo run. By 1885, German and French firms had secured over half the kernel exports from Lagos, and one-third of the oil trade.

*

The great nightmare of British administrators – in West Africa as elsewhere in the Empire – was finding the bare funds necessary to carry out the minimum. This had proved the undoing of the intransigent, energetic pro-consul Glover. When war had broken out again, in 1871, between the Ibadan Yoruba and the Egba Yoruba in Abeokuta, trade fizzled and Glover looked to still flourishing Porto Novo. The trading community backed him, helpfully providing him with petitions to annex the city. The German steamer *Eyo* was dispatched to Porto Novo with a threatening request to King Mikpoh to place his market under the control of Britain. To London, Glover argued that control of Porto Novo would enable him to blockade the aggressive Egba, and starve them into peace.

In Freetown, Governor-in-Chief Pope Hennessy refused to back Glover's policy, and ordered the *Eyo* withdrawn. Glover ignored the order. In March, 1872, the emotional, Irish Governor-in-Chief steamed into Lagos and decided Glover's removal. This remarkable administrator was merely switched to the Gold Coast – a bank-handed vindication by Hennessy – and applied himself to the Ashanti campaign. In 1875, he became Governor of Newfoundland.

Glover's successor in Lagos, Lees, soon found Glover's policy to have been right; he was faced with the familiar colonial administrative exercise of rewarding a rejected policy to as to justify a superior's mistaken rejection, while re-establishing what was rejected. Lees said nothing of war: he proposed extending the boundary of the Western District (Badagri) to include Porto Novo, and buying off the new King, a seemingly more pliable fellow called Tofa, with a share of the increased customs revenues.

Without waiting for complete approval, Lees hied himself to Tofa's palace in 1875, taking with him Commodore Hewett – who looked for evidence of slaving, which would give the Royal Navy the right to seize the city. The palaver with Tofa was not successful, but the Gold Coaster Tickel produced ample evidence that the King was engaged in human sacrifice. The Governor of the Gold Coast (now presumably advised by Glover) passed these facts on to London – where parliament was often more likely, now, to vote funds for humane causes like anti-slavery or reducing human sacrifice than for boosting trade. Governor Strahan, and the small official and trading British community in both Accra and Lagos, were convinced that the whole coast should be occupied, although they feared that if the Egun and Ewe communities of Porto Novo and the lagoon creeks opposed occupation, these tribes might be able to call on the help of the warlike Fon in Abomey. Fon trading access to the sea would be entirely under British control, and the tribe might engage the Europeans in a long and very costly war.

While Britain hesitated, the resourceful Tofa chartered a British steamer and used it as a gunboat. The *Renner* was used to bombard into submission several villages in the Lake Nokwe complex; a tributary chief was installed at Appa (theoretically under British control), and the Weme stream was closed to Lagos traders. Lees was sick. Tofa's action gave the new administrator of Lagos, Deputy-Governor Ussher, the excuse he needed for vigorous action. With the approval of the Accra Governor, he revived another Glover plan to cut off Porto Novo trade with Kotonu.

Ussher sailed to Porto Novo in September, 1879, levied a fine of fifty pounds and demanded that Tofa withdraw the embargo on Lagos trade. A blank charge was fired – and Tofa paid and signed his cross. Ussher seized the opportunity to extend the British protectorate to the Nokwe shore. At

Badagri a suitably staged deputation of Ewe chiefs and notables, led by a certain Kojo – whose brother was one of the chiefs Tofa had despoiled on the Weme – appeared to ask Britain to take Katanu under protection. Tickel assured Ussher that Katanu was strategic to controlling the Porto Novo–Kotonu trail.

The Anglo-Ewe celebrations were toasted in trade gin; the Union Jack was raised, and Ussher was enthused into projecting the capture of Porto Novo, where he estimated he could collect two hundred thousand sovereigns a year in customs – about three million dollars in modern money. With this, Ussher said in a despatch to Colonial Secretary Hicks Beach, Lagos could become 'the Liverpool of the Coast'. Hicks Beach disapproved Ussher, but allowed him to hold Katanu because of the promise of tolls.

Lagos trade with the interior was still disrupted by the Yoruba propensity for quasi-perpetual, internecine warfare. Governor Rowe, in Lagos, wrote in 1883:

'In the so-called war, but little actual fighting occurs; few are killed; capture is the object of the warrior on either side. Man-hunting is the real business of these fights . . . All these tribes trade more or less with the Ibadans, notwithstanding they are at war with them; the most saleable produce the Ibadans can bring to market is slaves; to the Egbas they sell the slaves caught from the Ijeshas; to the Ijeshas, those caught from the Egbas.

'The Egbas, the Ijebus, the Ijeshas are middlemen. When these tribes talk of making peace with Ibadan, they mean a peace on which Ibadan shall bring its produce to their frontier, but no further; no Ibadan trader must come beyond that market. On the seaboard they will exchange this produce with the Lagos traders for European goods, but no Lagos trader must come into their country beyond the market place on the seaboard. The Ijebus pay a high price for slaves. They use them for farm laborers.' Some modern researchers, including Professor Ade Ajayi, have contested this simple analysis of the Yoruba wars; but none would contest their deadly futility.

By then, it was clear that the economic survival of the Crown Colony of Lagos depended on bold British direct intervention in Yoruba affairs, a policy hard to sell in

London. In 1884, London finally agreed to pushing the Union Jack out to Appa in a forlorn bid to take the western creeks. 'By then,' comments an historian, 'a flood of petitions and memoranda from Lagos, the Gold Coast and the Chambers of Commerce of Manchester and Liverpool, complaining of the economic backwardness of the two colonies under joint rule had made formal separation' (of the Gold Coast and Lagos-Colony-and-Protectorate) 'a certainty. But by then, too, the French had returned to Porto Novo. The wheel had come full circle: it had taken twenty years to return to the position won by Glover in 1864; but the chances of occupying the markets of southern Dahomey had been permanently lost.'

In reality, much more had been lost. In the atmosphere of preparation for the Conference of Berlin, the chance to amalgamate the two coastal holdings had gone by default – and with it the historical promise that, in the colonial period that was to follow, Nigeria would have extended through its smaller neighbors (Dahomey and the two areas now described as Togo and Ghana) almost to Abidjan. The blame for what some writers call 'balkanization' must lie predominantly with Britain's Whig governments, to a lesser degree with the Tories – who lacked the courage of their notions – and to some of the Freetown pro-consuls, particularly Hennessy, whose good record in Sierra Leone was spoiled by his bungling in the other West African settlements.

vi

French and German Initiatives: the road to Berlin

A COLONIAL POWER with formerly only modest African ambitions had appeared more and more on the scene – not only in the Egun and Ewe creeks, but especially further North – in the middle decades of the 19th Century. This was France.

French interest had revived slowly after Waterloo. More than a century of conflict with Britain had cost France most of her empire in the Americas – notably Louisiana and Haiti – and in Asia. Africa remained an open field; but French overseas policy, like that of London, was wavering and uncertain for many years. In 1830, however, France did conquer her sparsely populated neighbor, Algeria.

Not until 1879 – the eve of Berlin – did France show more than a trading interest in West Africa. By then, Germany was already looking for places to stake the flag. It was the sudden challenge of these two nations that finally forced on Britain the realization that even its already much-diminished leading position in coastal commerce would not be maintained, unless it attempted colonial administration – with all that this implied.

France's first tentative return to the Coast, after 1815, had been the reoccupation of Gorée Island, of Saint-Louis and of Albreda fort on the Gambia. Attempts at cotton plantations on the Lower Senegal had failed.

Between 1838 and 1842, Bouët-Willaumez, a naval officer, signed trade treaties with chiefs at the Cape of Palms, Grand Bassam and Assini. The former is now in Liberia, the latter just inside Ghana. Grand Bassam is in the Ivory Coast, and was for many years its colonial capital.

The French fort at Wida was reoccupied in 1843; shortly after, Assini and Grand Bassam were fortified. Trading relations were set up at other points on the Guinea coast, notably Porto Novo, Kotonu and Anexo. The cession of Kotonu was negotiated in May, 1868, by a French naval officer, advised by the French factors, as traders' agents were known. At Abomey, a treaty was signed with Glele.

In the general Fon-Yoruba unrest that followed, all these Fon and Ewe posts were abandoned. Later Britain gave France its trading stations on the Senegal and France gave Britain Albreda, on the Gambia, so that each country now had complete control of 'its' river in Upper Guinea. About this time, French interest turned to some extent away from the Coast, which offered relatively stern British competition, and toward a vast area that at that date interested no power in Europe: the Western Sudan.

*

The great area West of Hausaland then contained four main states: Futa or Tekrur, the Bambara kingdoms of Segu and Kaarta, and Masina. The powerful Bambara were the remnants of Mali, regrouped after that empire's defeat by the Askias. Under the rule of Bitoh-Kululabi (1660–1710), Segu became a strong state to which even the Berber rulers of Timbuktu paid tribute. Kaarta was a breakaway from Segu. The two brother kingdoms warred in the 18th Century, and in the violent aftermath of these conflicts the confines of Kaarta were pushed West to the Upper Senegal.

Masina was the theocratic Mandingo kingdom set up on the Upper Niger by Ahmadu Lobo: its population was over-lorded by Fulani pastoralists who had their own chiefs, the Jallo – who had, before Ahmadu, paid tribute, first, to the Emperors of Mali, then to the Pashas of Timbuktu, then, from the late 17th Century onward, to the Bambara Kings of Segu. In the early 19th Century, many Fulani of Masina had become Muslims; under Ahmadu, who had fought beside Usuman dan Fodyo, Muslim reformers then overthrew the pagan Jallos, defeated the warriors from Segu who had come to the aid of the tributary Jallo chief, and established in Masina a strict Muslim state.

The Futa had had numerous rulers, being the historic dispersal point of the remarkable Fulani people. Its indigenous people, the Tukolors, who speak the Fulani language, had thrown off the imposition of Wolof rule and restored Fulani leadership. Partly descended from the Almoravids, they had been Muslims for centuries.

In the first half of the 19th Century, the Tijani Muslim Al Haj 'Umar extended the Futa kingdom to Tim-buktu. Widely traveled and fanatically pious, 'Umar, the son-in-law of Sultan Bello of Sokoto, then led a *jihad* against the pagan states of the Western Sudan. In 1854, he defeated Kaarta, and began his 'long march' on the pagan Sudan. It was at this troubled stage in Sudanic history that France appeared.

Masina refused to join 'Umar against Segu, so he attacked Khasso and Galam on the middle course of the Senegal. He met an advancing column of French troops and was repulsed. In spite of this reverse, 'Umar occupied Segu in 1861, and Masina the following year. In 1863, he sacked Timbuktu.

'Umar was a sincere fanatic, a meditator, a hearer of voices, an off-with-his-pagan-head type of missionary; but many of his levies were less spiritual in their approach to conquered lands. Both the Bambara of Segu and the Fulani of Masina rose against the exactions of the Fulani-Tukolor imperial forces. The hordes, estimated at thirty thousand, horse and foot, were driven back and 'Umar himself was killed in a cave (possibly, suicide) in 1864. In revenge, three hundred Muslim teachers of Masina were decapitated, tied head to head by their turbans.

His sons and nephews whom he had named as his pro-consuls in the areas he had colonized faced unanimous revolt at his death. But by 1872, the revolts were suppressed, the Futa empire was re-established, and the overall authority of the Governor of Segu – Ahmadu, 'Umar's son by the Sultan of Sokoto's daughter – was accepted. But his rule proved unpopular. In the following decade, in 1884, he was forced to withdraw his headquarters to Nioro, in Kaarta. In 1891, the French advance was to send him fleeing to Masina; in 1893, he retreated to a small village near Sokoto, where he died five years later.

(The links between Northern Nigeria and Senegal, al Haj 'Umar's home, persist to this day. 'Umar's grandson, Sedu Nuru Tall, has been a leading politico-religious figure of modern Senegal. Nigeria's first post-Independence High Commissioner in London, Abdul Maliki, was the son-in-law of Ibrahima Nyas, Grand Marabout of Kaolack – who controlled from Senegal part of the Murid electorate of Northern Nigeria.)

The Fulani-Tukolor Emperor, Ahmadu, left a son, Samory, who united the subject Mandingo people around him after the manner of a robber baron; he practised extensive slave-trading, selling his human booty into the Sahara – where the Arabs were still buyers and had never heard of Abolition. Born of a fleeting union between Ahmadu and a pagan concubine, Samory had been brought up as a pagan Jula and a trader. He converted to Islam in his twenties. From 1870, when he was about thirtyfive, to 1882, slaving was Samory's only occupation; but from then on he too, like his father, was bothered by French incursions. From 1889 until 1898, he was entirely preoccupied with defending his realm, vigorously, from the white invader. He was starved out, captured and deported to Gabun in 1898, and died there in 1900.

In Northern Guinea, where the greatest number of Mandingos or Malinkes live, Samory is looked upon as a national hero, and historians concede him a fine military and administrative record. The first President of Guinea, Ahmed Sékou Touré, proudly claims kinship with Samory, of whom he is the maternal great-grandson. Samory's character had its negative side, however: he walled up his own son to die, for counselling surrender, and the contemporary scholar Amadou Hampaté Bâ has recorded that he 'roasted people like peanuts'. Areas he conquered still use his name as a curse or insult. Islam was, for Samory, a weapon rather than a faith.

Up the coast, France had established separate administrations for Gorée and the Senegal. Gorée became a naval headquarters, protecting all French trading posts on the Guinea Coast. The Governor of the Senegal, General Louis Faidherbe, pushed his influence up the river. It was during this process that his troops met and checked 'Umar.

The name of France's main colony in Africa comes from the River Senegal, which derives its appellation from the Zenaga – the original Berber population of the right bank of the stream. The main tribe, the Wolof, are first mentioned by Cà da Mosto, who calls them the Ziloffi. The word *Wolof* appears to come from the nickname for the tribe used by the neighboring Mande – *wolo fin* (blackskin).

The Wolofs were originally grouped in the kingdom of Walo (Delta), the Braks (Kings) of the country being memorized in oral records since the end of the 12th Century. The founder of the kingdom was called Njai (usual gallicized spelling: N'Diaye). The capital, until the 18th Century, was at Jurbel. It was a fairly sophisticated, matrilineal, Sudanic state, divided into free and slave classes. The first contacts with Islam were in the 10th–13th Centuries, but in 1455 Cà da Mosto found Islamization largely nominal.

Resistance to Islamization, and wars with the Moors and with the tribes of the Futa Toro encouraged the 19th Century Braks to make treaties with the French – at least eleven, from 1819 to 1890. Some are signed by Queen Mothers – usually, sisters of the Brak. With colonization, curiously enough, came general Islamization of the Wolofs

160

(now eightyfive per cent Muslim) – about eight centuries later than their neighbors, the Tukolors.

An exception to pagan intransigence had been the independent Wolof principality of Kayor – Muslim since the 16th Century under its Damel (King), whose 'honor name' was always Fal. In 1861, under Lat Jor, Kayor resumed fetishism, despite the opposition of the Jakate clan of religious instructors. Driven out by the French and in hiding in the Salum area, Lat Jor converted back to Islam in 1864. He made his peace with the French in 1868, returning to Kayor with the Muslim instructor Momar Anta-Sali – father of Amadu Bamba, founder of the Murid sect.

Governor Faidherbe, who had come out in 1854, was to introduce method and system into France's hesitant interests in Black Africa. France had had a more or less permanent presence at Saint-Louis and Gorée Island since the 17th Century. At the end of the 18th Century, Saint-Louis had a population of seven thousand, including six hundred Europeans – the largest European community on the Coast North of the Congo River. The Europeans were mostly males, living with *signares* – accredited mistresses, whose children they acknowledged and educated. The descendants of the *signares* and their common-law husbands are today's mulatto and quadroon community known as the Saint-Louisians. By 1825, Saint-Louis and Gorée together had a population of sixteen thousand, of whom twelve thousand were domestic slaves, Administrator Guillet notes.

In 1833, a royal decree had given all men born free in French territories full citizenship. This applied in the little African stations, as in France. In 1848, as a result of the liberal revolution that brought Prince-President Napoleon III to power, France at last abolished slavery. The same year, Senegal received the right to elect a deputy to the French legislature, but this privilege was withdrawn in 1854.

This was the year Faidherbe was sent to Saint-Louis, which then had a population of 12,336, but by now with only one hundred and seventyseven Europeans. The Eurafricans, then as now, ran the city. Faidherbe raised his now famous Senegalese Rifles and pacified neighboring inland territories, including the Futa Toro hills. Dakar, across the straits from Gorée, was taken in 1857, and Pinet-Laprade founded what

161

is now one of West Africa's major ports. Reconnaissance missions penetrated the interior, reaching as far as the Futa Jaloh in modern Guinea. Organs of administration were set up on the coast, together with some schools.

Faidherbe must take most of the credit for this growth. He was cast in the mold of the early colonial administrators. His compatriot Richard-Molard says of this dynamic worker that he was 'an officer of the Empire, endowed with an abominable character and a sense of authority which bordered on vice. He was pro-consul of an authoritarian Empire.'

After Faidherbe's departure in 1865, French rule stagnated again for fifteen years. By then, Senegal had an estimated one hundred and fifty thousand inhabitants of whom fifteen thousand – in Saint-Louis and Gorée-Dakar – were black, brown and white French citizens.

The following year, after France had abandoned Porto Novo, Chasseloup-Laubat proposed that France cede to Britain its trading stations on the Ivory Coast and in Guinea – where Britain already held the Isles of Loos – in return for the Gambia. Governor Kennedy of Sierra Leone strongly backed the scheme, and Earl Grenville, at the Colonial Office, was sympathetic. But the Anglo-Dutch exchange of forts convention of 1867 removed the English as neighbors to the Melakuri stations of Grand Bassam and Assini, and robbed the scheme of some of its initial attractiveness.

By the time the Dutch sold out all their Gold Coast forts to the British, in 1871 – including those, like Dixcove and Shama, which were close to Assini and Grand Bassam – the Franco-Prussian War had closed negotiations over Guinea and the Gambia. If carried to fruition, these proposals would have produced a much larger, more viable Sierra Leone, in modern times, and saved the continuing problem of the British enclave of Gambia in Senegal.

France's defeat at Sedan in 1871 produced an interregnum in French affairs, but in the last two decades of the century France made up for lost time, gradually occupying areas of Africa almost as large as the United States. Negotiations for the Gambia–Guinea–Ivory Coast 'swap' were reopened in 1875, and again the following year – but by then French interest in the area had grown, and Paris bargained more ambitiously: for this and other reasons, the negotiations failed.

In 1871, Lat Jor had been restored by the French as Damel of Kayor. Four years later, he helped the French in their military campaign against Tijani resistance in the Futa Toro. But from 1877 to 1882, Lat Jor opposed the French railroad project, through Kayor, from Dakar to Saint-Louis. Finally, he took up arms, and went down to defeat in 1882.

*

Before Berlin, European influence was almost exclusively limited to the Coast itself, and a few miles inland. The biggest European settlement North of the Congo, at the time, was certainly Lagos – which in the 1884 map is already shown as having its racecourse and grandstand. Inland, British influence stretched as far as the Oluge Lagoon, and in the Western district – headquartered at Badagri – the administration also extended a few theoretical miles into the local swamp. The confining of European influence to the littoral was equally true in the Gold Coast, where the treaties on the trade route to Kumasi, for instance, were not ensured by any permanent European presence, at first. In the French area, sallies into the interior were likewise temporary. An exception to the general rule was the Volta region.

Missionaries of the Norddeutsche Missiongesellschaft had established evangelical stations among the Anglor and Peki Ewe and the Akwamu, as far inland as Peki and Ho, by the 'Sixties. Wars between the Peki Ewe on one side, and Ashanti and other Akan invaders on the other – and resistance to the extension of British rule from the coast – made the mission's life difficult in the 'Seventies; in addition, the death toll from disease was well over 80 per cent. By 1886, the Ewe Church of the Volta contained only about five hundred native Protestants.

German initiative was also making itself felt on the Coast. Five Bremen and Hamburg firms had established agents at Keta, Lomé, Anexo and Grand Popo. In 1867, Britain pushed its Gold Coast frontier eighteen miles East of Keta to Aflao (the present Ghanaian frontier post). The ports from Denu – West of Aflao – to Grand Popo (just inside modern Dahomey) were great smuggling stations for arms and liquor, and the

163

Germans played their role in this profitable traffic also. In the 'Eighties, the little village of Lomé became a palm oil trading center for the Agotime hinterland. Kernels were brought from as far afield as Salaga, on the Hausa caravan route between Kumasi and the Niger.

There was also an oil market at Bagida which received supplies across the Hako – better known today as Lake Togo. Porto Seguro, today the main village of the Hako, prospered too. Lagoon traffic also went to Anexo, sometimes then called Little Popo, and until recent decades there was a lagoon system running from Keta to about three hundred miles East of Lagos; today, most of it is silted up, west of Nigeria. The Germans also drew considerable trade from their possession of Grand Popo, which stood both on the lagoon and at the mouth of the Agome River; but Fon toll barriers on the bush trails and creeks to the East robbed Grand Popo of any trade in that direction, which went to the mostly French firms at Wida.

English coin and South American dollars were the medium for exchange at the lagoon ports, a tribute to the omnipresence of British traders and the role of the Brazilian settlers. Under the Germans, prices of commodities tended to stabilize, and there was a bold attempt to stabilize 'dash' and graft; but exchange rates between sterling and dollars varied. By 1883, Germany was buying three-quarters of the palm oil and half the kernels in the western lagoon area; France took the rest.

Wida had grown considerably, and had about ten thousand population in the 'seventies, under five chieftaincies. The European forts were recognized as extra-territorial – in return for dues paid to Abomey. Ships were customed, as in the previous century, according to the number of masts. King Glele was the principal trader in his country, and records show that he was a notoriously bad payer.

When the Brazilian Santos became agent at Wida, in 1872, for the British firm F. and A. Swanzy he was instructed to cut the King's credit. In 1876, an order for cloth by Prince Kondo – later King Behanzin – was refused, pending payment of the royal family's (by then) scandalous debts. Fon officials retaliated by seizing Santos and all his goods. Swanzy's European agent for the Slave Coast, Turnbull, arrived and intervened and was seized as well. Fortunately he had had time to send word to Commodore Hewett, commander of the RN Bights Division. Hewett sailed on to Wida Roads, raised his cannon sights and soon forced the release of both traders. He fined the King five hundred puncheons of palm oil, and in July, 1876, blockaded the coast from Porto Seguro to Porto Novo until the money should be paid.

The blockade lasted eight months. Then the French firm of Régis offered to pay half Glele's fine and to persuade the King's subjects to pay the rest over twelve months. The firm was worried by losses on stored palm products, unmoveable because of the blockade, and feared a further disruption of trade if the stubborn King should push the British into collecting the fine by force. Hewett accepted. The result was that Glele got off with paying nothing at all himself; his subjects never paid their half of his debts, either.

The incident had an historical sequel. The blockade persuaded the French how ephemeral was their trading hold on the area, in the absence of written treaties, and how determinant the power of Britain. Although the belief that Britain would march on Abomey to collect the five hundred barrels of oil was based on an angry remark by Hewett's subordinate, Captain Sullivan, to some French naval officers (Foreign Office records show Britain was disposed to accept 'reasonable excuses', and no fine at all) the fear of trade-disrupting war in the area pointed the need for the French to obtain territorial rights of real significance.

The French Foreign Office backed its traders; Rear-Admiral Allemand, in 1878, presented a draft treaty to the Yovogah of Wida giving France fourteen square miles of Kotonu and all customs rights. It seems likely Glele never saw or approved this doubtful document, especially since it contains no compensation for his loss of tolls. French presence in Kotonu was enhanced by the appointment of a Consul, Ardin d'Elteil, formerly Vice-Consul at Freetown.

By this time, conflict between French and British traders, and their Governments' representatives, had moved forward apace; d'Elteil soon became convinced the British would seize Porto Novo. Allemand thought this unlikely, and d'Elteil's proposals urging the renewal of the Porto Novo protectorate were shelved in Paris. The policy in practice at the time of the Kotonu Treaty had already changed. D'Elteil had received no military support and was out of funds; in Paris, by this time, it was considered enough that he hold on to Kotonu just long enough for the consummation of a new scheme – to exchange it for the Gambia. France's condition was that the western Slave Coast remain free of British customs posts; in addition to surrendering Kotonu to Britain, part of Guinea would be added on to Sierra Leone. The scheme fell through, and d'Elteil's policy was finally vindicated: a Porto Novo protectorate treaty with King Tofa was signed in April, 1882, and made public two months later.

Fears of British intentions were not stilled, and at Porto Novo Consul Bareste informed his Foreign Minister, Freycinet, that he thought Lieutenant-Governor Moloney might move down from Lagos; Governor Sir Samuel Rowe might link up with him, with troops from Accra. To forestall this, France – under a new Foreign Minister, Leclerc – made the protectorate official the following year, and the French trader, Colonna da Lecca of the company Régis, was installed at Kotonu as Resident: the French flag was raised over Porto Novo. Kotonu ceased to pay dues to Abomey. At Porto Novo, the Egun King was to be paid ten thousand francs a year in compensation for surrendering his toll rights there.

In July, 1884, the French colonel Dorat, with Senegalese riflemen, occupied Kotonu with instructions to contest British rights in Appa and to push the Porto Novo protectorate as far North and West as was practicable. With Dorat, the anarchic Franco-British trade 'war' hardened; similarly France took a sterner view of the successes of German traders on their western flank, and the Germans eyed uneasily the growth of the British on the Gold Coast. In Germany, the lobby in favor of colonizing had grown apace: in addition to the Chambers of Commerce of Bremen and Hamburg, there were two pressure groups, the Westdeutsche Verein and the Deutsche Kolonialverein.

In the area of particular interest to both French and German traders, the French had moved first. While both the Paris and Berlin governments dithered, the agent of Cyprien Fabre, the French shipowners, had in 1881 handed 'requests for French protection' to the chiefs at Anexo, Porto Seguro and Grand Popo; these gentlemen were encouraged to sign by promises that the threat of British customs dues would be removed, if the French navy was called in. The chiefs signed, but Paris hesitated to act – finally accepting the 'request' from Grand Popo in 1883, and not the others. France's position at Agwe, a settlement of Brazilian traders with a Catholic mission, remained equivocal, but for practical purposes it was recognized by the British and Germans as being French.

*

Meanwhile, by 1870, France had a real enclave in Senegal, where farmers were growing – with mixed success – cotton, olives, dates, coconuts and coffee. In the wake of the defeat by Prussia at Sedan, France – as previously in the Eighteen Thirties after Waterloo, and as in recent Gaullist times in reaction to France's fall in 1940 – underwent a wave of nationalism. As in post-Waterloo and more recent times, the nationalist reaction to humiliation took about a decade to gather force. In the 'Eighties, this nationalist spirit sought an outlet in Africa, where the Senegalese foothold already offered an opportunity for empire-building.

In 1871, France's black citizens in Senegal recovered their right to elect a deputy. A Council General was established in the Colony, and mayoral councils at Saint Louis and Gorée. In 1880, the port of Rufisque became a *commune,* birth within the boundaries of which thus conferred French citizenship.

In 1881, a military command for the upper Senegal River was established at Kayes (modern Mali), the highest navigable point. Bamako was occupied in 1883. Segu and Timbuktu fell to French forces in the 'Nineties. In 1887, Dakar had been administratively separated from Gorée. By then, the enclave-Colony of Senegal was comparable to Britain's enclave-Colony in Sierra Leone, although the intentions, at the time, of the two imperial powers – Britain's incipient 'dual mandate', leading to independence, and France's aim to integrate West Africa into France – were of course different.

A recent writer comments: 'This was as far as assimilation was to go in either Senegal or the rest of French West

Africa. Not until 1944 was there any extension of political rights in French Black Africa. Indeed in Senegal the citizens had to fight to retain what they had against an administration that came increasingly to regret the privileges it had granted the Senegalese in the first fine flush of colonial expansion. . . . Thus until the outbreak of the Second World War one had the paradoxical situation of the French regretting their assimilationist policy and the Senegalese citizens asking that it be applied more liberally.

'This is one of the main reasons why the activities of French Africans (in recent years), particularly in Senegal, were channeled not toward the attainment of independence but the assertion of their fundamental equality with the French. Their energies were for long directed to obtaining from the French those rights which in principle an assimilationist policy offered them.'

To the South, meanwhile, Binger was exploring and treaty-making in what are now Ivory Coast and Voltaic Republic. The Foureau-Lamy expedition went to the Chad area. Across vast inland areas, France laid hands on outposts of extensive, mostly desertic scrub which Faidherbe had called 'lunar' and which was described at the time by Lord Salisbury as 'what agriculturalists would call very light land'.

Most of the occupation task was the work of small groups of French officers, using mostly African troops. But hopes of creating great African legions, to compensate France for the military power of its permanent enemy and neighbor, Germany, had to abandoned: only the Senegalese – first used in action by France in the 'Fifties – and the Mossi of the upper Volta, proved to be 'natural' military material.

In the 'Nineties, a movement animated by the journalist Hippolyte Percher and promoted in the French legislature by Eugène Etienne, the Algeria-born leader of the Colonial Party, urged France to install a colonial Government 'from Algeria to Dahomey'. Some of the crops tried already in Senegal would be developed, as well as two other major export cultures, both introduced into Africa by the Portuguese: groundnuts and cocoa. French industrialists became interested in the concept and gave it lobby support. Soon, a genuine French colonial policy was to appear.

The Niger Delta: prelude to Nigeria

IN MODERN TIMES, Black Africa has produced only one power which potentially compares with the major European, Latin American and Asian countries: Nigeria. Not unnaturally, the pre-colonial story of the Niger Delta surpasses, in complexity, the vicissitudes of the rest of 19th Century West Africa.

The Delta was the region most stunned by Abolition – slavery having been, in the words of a Nigerian scholar, 'the economic mainstay of all the coastal principalities'. But it survived this blow to become the richest region of legitimate trade, and the channel for the principal colonization scheme in West Africa. Moreover, the economic revolution caused by Abolition led to deep political changes in the tribal governments. As a case study, the Delta presents a macrocosm of 19th Century Euro-African interaction in Atlantic Africa.

In this region of alluvial soil which – together with its hinterland was to prove peculiarly suitable for planting palm, rivers and channels made natural barriers between numerous, rich or relatively rich river-chieftaincies. Society was semi-military, and government in the first half of the 19th Century was consequently strong and despotic – so much so that European traders preferred to work from their sloops, rather than on land, limiting their shore installations to barracoons for slaves and for some of their barter goods. (In earlier centuries, African chiefs had insisted on this arrangement). Life was, in general, hard for these dynamic rogues, whether they dealt in flesh or, as later, in the product that gave them the name that has come down to us in history – palm oil ruffians. Mortality was high, mostly from disease but also from drinking and fighting. A Nigerian historian has written: 'It was trade, first and foremost, that brought Englishmen to Nigeria; it was trade which sustained them when the difficulties of climate and disease induced the missionary, the explorer and the pure adventurer to retire.'

Abolition hit West Africa like a natural catastrophe. The philosophic arguments were not only not understood; few African leaders of the period knew that a campaign for Abolition had been going on. The humane approach was too esoteric to win proselytes. Slavery had been an African initiative: its Abolition was a European one, and it was seen as a gesture of hostility; European forts were besieged by angry, violent native rioters clamoring for the restoration of slavery. Indeed, many kingdoms like Abomey, Lagos and Bonny were pure creations of slave economics. Captain Hugh Crow, in his memoirs, records the reaction to the Act of 1807 of the King of Bonny: 'We tink trade no stop, for all Juju man tell we so, for dem say you country can niber stop trade ordered by God A'mighty.'

The Reverends J. F. Schön and Samuel Crowther, on the Niger expedition of 1841, were informed by the Obi Ossai of Abo: 'We thought it God's wish that Black people should be slaves.' Lt. Levinge of the Fernando Póo naval squadron reported a belief that Britain must be at war with the nations still slaving. Levinge noted: 'We carried on the trade so shortly before ourselves, that I do not think they clearly understand why we should be so anxious to suppress it now.' King Pepple of Bonny, in his 1841 treaty with Britain, insisted on a clause stating that when Britain resumed slaving, Bonny would be at liberty to do likewise.

When slave-trading was already illegal, but still being practised, commerce with Atlantic Africa, especially the Delta, was made easier by an exceptional survey of the Coast undertaken by Captain W. F. W. Owen of the Royal Navy – whose charts form the basis of those still in use. This survey was conducted by the already much-traveled navigator from 1821 to 1825. At Bonny, his presence seemed suspect, and aroused the indignation of King Opubu, who complained that his 'brother' King George IV had not asked permission for his officer to cruise around the Ibo kingdom. Owen, who was surprised that the local traders showed such anxiety to placate Opubu, wrote that 'they administer to his whims and caprice, as if the advantages derived from their traffic were not mutual.' Although not impressed by Africa, Owen had a remarkably sympathetic ear for pidgin, and recorded for posterity the Delta chieftain's complaint:

'Brudder George send warship lookum what water bar ab gat, dat good, me letum dat. Brudder send boat chopum slave, dat good. E no send warship, for cappen no peak me, no lookee me face. No no no, me tell you, no! Suppose you come all you mont fool palaver, givee reason why do it, me tell you, you peak lie, you peaked n'lie. Suppose my fadder or my fadder fadder come up from ground and peak me why Englishman do dat, I no sabby tellum why.'

The matter was amicably settled, and Owen's work was to aid not only the use of the Coast by sailing ships, but also the penetration of the interior by the new steam vessels.

The Niger Delta area measures two hundred and seventy miles in breadth, at the sea, and can be said to extend for over a hundred miles inland. The two main mouths of the Niger are known as the Forcados Entry and the Nun (pronounced Noon); these are joined by such broad, deep streams as the Benin, the Brass, the Bonny, the Kwa-Ibo and the Cross, as well as many lesser creeks and an extensive lagoon system. In those days, a man could paddle a canoe from Keta in the East of the Gold Coast to the Rio del Rey, near Calabar, without entering the ocean. Consul Sir Harry Johnston was to note in 1888 that 'There are hardly any roads existing in the Delta; the most trivial distance that a native requires to go, he generally achieves in a canoe.'

Then as now, the coastal region of West Africa presented much less homogeneity than the Islamic area. The cities like Gao, Timbuktu and Jenne which grew out of the trans-Sahara trade with the Arabs and Berbers were all very similar. The cities like Lagos, Accra and Calabar created by European maritime commerce varied strongly. In particular, each maritime and riverain tribe of the Niger system was different in language, culture and socio-political organization. Living on islands in the Delta, they were all the more inclined to be insular. The Delta communities, to quote a Nigerian historian, grew in a 'haphazard way'. Atlantic vantage points were seized, and natural harbors like Calabar and Bonny quickly acquired importance.

These societies built on slave-trading were themselves traditionally organized on 'bond and free' lines. Moreover,

171

the surplus of slaves left over in the Atlantic villages by the suppression of the traffic had ensured that slaves outnumbered freemen in these little kingdoms, and in some places chiefs appeared who had risen from the ranks of the serfs. In 1848, Kohler notes that 'only a small proportion' of Bonny's people were freemen. Burton confirmed this in 1863. Hugh Goldie, writing as late as 1890, says 'slaves greatly outnumbered the freemen' in Calabar.

Although intermarriage between bond and free often brought manumission to the progeny, the stigma of slavery usually remained; soon, in the words of K. Onwuka Dike, 'the surviving free classes wielded power out of all proportion to their numbers.' To some extent this situation was caused by the fact that in post-Abolition 19th Century slaving, the Delta ports (plus Lagos occasionally) tended to surpass the Slave Coast, the Congo and Senegal put together as centers for the illegal traffic.

In many of these places strong monarchies had emerged, notably at Warri, Kalabari (known in Europe as New Calabar) and Ibani (known as Bonny). In places like Brass and Old Calabar there was a division of power among rival clans. The four communities of Old Calabar – Creek Town, Henshaw Town, Duke Town and Obutong – each had their own chiefs, united in their membership of the secret society of the freemen, Egbo. Whoever headed Egbo in a community was automatically its most powerful citizen.

The community itself would be divided into Houses, headed by men enriched in, first, slaving, then legitimate trade. The trader, his family and his domestic slaves formed the House. A small House might be as few as three hundred people. The royal-clan Houses numbered thousands. The famous missionary Hope Waddell notes that in 1847 King Eyo of Creek Town had 'many thousand slaves' and 'four hundred canoes with a captain and crew for each one.'

Houses were ruled with an iron hand. Count de Cardi, the trader, in an appendix to Mary Kingley's *West African Studies,* notes punishments inflicted on slaves: 'Ear cutting in its various stages, from clipping to total dismemberment; crucifixion round a large cask; extraction of teeth; suspension by the thumbs; chilli peppers pounded and stuffed up the nostrils, and forced into the eyes and ears; fastening the victim to a post driven into the beach at low water and leaving him there to be drowned with the rising tide, or to be eaten by the sharks or crocodiles peacemeal; heavily ironed and chained to a post in their master's compound, and reduced to living skeletons; impaling on stakes; forcing a long steel ramrod through the body until it appeared through the top of the skull.'

Onwuka Dike comments that 'terror and despotism were normal features of a system' that kept 'the masses in subjection', but that this pattern 'met the needs of the day'. He quotes Waddell as saying that 'Absolute authority on the one part, and entire subjection on the other, is the theory; but in practice both the authority and subjection are checked and limited in many ways'. Half a century later, the same analysis could perhaps have been made of colonial rule, an enlightened interpretation of similar imperatives.

Consul Hutchinson noted in the 'Sixties that slaves often exercised considerable power themselves and acquired much wealth. Miss Kingsley noted the opportunities for slaves to rise in the power hierarchy. There was thus a seed of democracy within these autocracies, and a King would usually avoid interfering in the affairs of a House unless obliged to, thus decentralizing power further.

These Atlantic kingdoms bought their produce mostly from up-country in the Delta, and were therefore themselves predominantly middlemen. The up-country farmers' secret society was Aro, ruled by the Aro Chukwu oracle, a source of dread to all Ibos and to most of their neighbors. Aro members had formerly used the oracle as an ingenious means of procuring slaves: villages which had 'offended the gods' were informed of this by sorcerers of the oracle, who would explain that Chukwu required sacrifices. The Aros received people for Chukwu to 'eat' — and these were in fact sold to the coastal middlemen, who traded them to the ships. Professor Onwuka Dike says: 'The dominant power of the Oracle was widely understood and rarely opposed, so that the slaves obtained by violence and kidnapping could not have greatly exceeded, and may even have been fewer than, those who surrendered to the dictates of the Oracle'.

As the oil trade developed, Bonny became the main trading state, its power dependent on its relatively powerfully armed war-canoes, which swept the Niger Main. The biggest boats carried one hundred and forty men and mounted a brass and iron cannon. Smaller craft carried less pretentious artillery, and about eighty musketeers. Even the lesser Bonny Houses could muster about ten canoes. This river power ensured Bonny's control of the inland, farming communities; the bonds were strengthened by exchanges of daughters in marriage and by inland families sending their sons to be 'adopted' by Bonny traders and trained in the art of trading.

Quarrels between the farming and trading communities were regulated by 'market laws', with rigid punishments, often strictly enforced. Murder was punished by public hanging. Laws specified the acceptability of the different manillas, the alpha-shaped 'coins' which are still found in West Africa and often mistaken by uninitiates for bracelets or anklets. Coastal kings frequently traveled to the interior to settle palavers, and the cost of this prevention of disturbance to trade was paid by the European traders: the tax was called 'comey', and in Cardi's time was a pound sterling for every eight tons of oil bought.

*

This, then, was the prevailing society which was to receive, a few generations later, the most ambitious imperial project in West Africa – the concept of Nigeria. By its religious beliefs and practices; the non-literate character and other limitations of its languages; its dwellings, its types of farming and methods of trading; its native weapons and other implements; its types of government, warrior systems and secret societies; its river craft, and its failure to affront the sea and explore the world, this society is strikingly similar to that of Ancient Britain at the time of the Roman invasions in the century before Christ. Its partners in the historical adventure about to begin were the children of the prevailing industrial revolution. The relatively smooth association between these dramatically contrasted cultures probably reflects credit on both sides.

British association with the area dated from 1553, when Richard Wyndham, who had sailed from Bristol on August 12, brought the *Primrose*, the *Lion* and the *Moone*, manned by 'men of the lustiest sort', into the Benin River to trade for pepper. On this occasion, an epidemic panicked the crews, who scuttled the *Lion* and abandoned some expeditioners upriver. Wyndham himself died in the Delta. Only forty of his one hundred and forty men returned to Bristol alive. But money was made and a voyage under John Locke was undertaken the following year. Mortality was less; the profit was 1,000 per cent, and therefore commensurate with the risks and the time involved.

A certain James Welsh had chartered ships in 1558 and 1559, buying pepper, ivory and palm oil. The trading association with the area developed faster during the slave trade. Then, as industrialism began to replace mercantilism, the Abolitionist humanitarians carried the day – and posed a dramatic problem to the people of the Niger Delta.

The first commodities sought to replace slaving were gold, ivory, timber, pepper, rice and gum, but finally the economy became almost exclusively one of palm oil and kernels. Palm was quickly developed as a market commodity by the traders of Liverpool – the most severely affected in Britain by Abolition. The Delta area became known as the Oil Rivers.

The changeover was not immediate. Bonny and Brass continued to slave, using mostly small creeks. In 1833, Superintendent Nicholls, at Fernando Póo, reported thirtysix slavers in the Delta at one time. Legitimate trade was stopped at Old Calabar that year when a French slaver anchored. In late 1835, legitimate trade ceased at Bonny while ten Spanish slavers shipped living cargo. The slave ships fought off opposition with violence, often killing legitimate traders. In revenge, captured slavers' crews were marooned on Delta islets, where they bleached in the sun.

Fernando Póo, from which prohibition was organized, had been taken over in 1827, the first superintendent being the cartographer-navigator Owen, who had recommended its lease from Spain. In 1828, noting that slaves frequently died on the voyage up the coast (after 'liberation') to the Court of Mixed Commission in Freetown, Owen landed two slave cargos at Port Clarence (now Santa Isabel) to help build the new community. They formed the nucleus of the population group now known as Fernandinos.

Owen's practical but high-handed action was opposed by Freetown – fearful that Port Clarence would supplant it as the main British 'capital' on the Coast. Freetown successfully opposed a Parliamentary Select Committee recommendation that the Court be moved to Fernando Póo. Spain's ownership of the island was the main reason why Britain did not allow traders to move their headquarters there; but ships from Britain, America and other countries were chandlered and repaired at Port Clarence.

Colonel Edward Nicholls, who succeeded Owen, naturally recommended acceptance of Spain's 1831 offer to sell the island for one hundred thousand pounds – a tiny fraction of the value of Delta trade. When the Colonial Secretary, Lord Goderich, succumbed to the Freetown lobby and turned down Spain's offer, British traders protested, noting that palm oil trade had increased in the area from 94,246 cwt in 1827 to 213,477 cwt in 1830.

The tussle between Freetown and Fernando Póo lasted several years. As early as 1828 Sierra Leone had allowed supplies on its faraway dependency to peter out, and Owen had depended for food on Ephraim Duke, the Old Calabar chief. Nicholls was bitter when Britain officially decided, in 1833, to withdraw from Fernando Póo. When Palmerston tried to revive the purchase offer in 1841, opinion in Madrid had changed.

But the brief occupancy of Fernando Póo, and its later use as a base for British Consuls, was to introduce a note of official control in an area in which Euro-African relations had been, for the most part, wildly anarchic. The Delta traders, or 'palm oil ruffians' as they were beginning to be known, were unashamed rascals who depended on laissez-faire. Mary Kingsley has shown that some of them, at least, were not an unattractive breed of men. That they were lawless, often cruel rogues was no doubt essential for survival. An American writer of the period, J. W. Russell, had noted that Delta trade 'ruins the health or takes the lives of nine-tenths who are concerned in it, and poisons the morals of most survivors.'

To remedy some of the anarchy, Colonel Nicolls, in his just over five years (1829–1835) on Fernando Póo, set about making treaties with the chiefs – frequently without permission from London. 'Fighting Nicholls', who had been a Marine under Nelson, had previously governed Ascension.

He was to become a general, and MacGregor Laird's father-in-law. When ordered to evacuate the island settlement in February, 1833, he prevaricated until April, 1835.

Nicholls' African ally was Ephraim Duke, whom the colonel describes as a 'man of great knowledge and humanity'. He was the first to sign an anti-slavery treaty, and Old Calabar frequently informed the Abolition Squadron of the movements of Delta slavers, by despatching canoes to Port Clarence. (The Chief's real name was Efium, and his title was of course just the British supercargoes' estimate of his rank: his abode became – and remains – known as Duke Town.)

*

For about forty years, activity in the Delta centered on Bonny. The powerful King Opubu died there in 1830, leaving the throne to his thirteen-year-old son William Dappa Pepple, under the regency of Chief Madu, an ex-slave whom Opubu had made head of the royal House. (The name of this House was Perekule, but Western historians have accepted the European version of the time – Pepple.) When Madu died, the headship and the regency passed to his eldest son Alali. Opposition to Madu, then to Alali, grouped around the boy King, who did not share his father's tolerance for ex-slaves. When Dappa Pepple came of age in 1835, Alali still usurped most of the powers. Alali's undoing was to come about when he challenged a greater power than his King.

In January 1836, the British warship *Trinculo* entered Bonny waters and seized four Spanish slavers. Alali was indignant, so the commander went ashore to explain that the seizure was legitimate under the terms of the Anglo-Spanish 'reciprocal search' pact of the previous year. A Spanish trader, Capsios, offered to read the treaty to Alali in Ibo, but when doing so completely changed the terms of the agreement.

Alali, according to the Foreign Office record, 'foaming with rage, struck the table'. He ordered the capture of Lt. Tryon, the *Trinculo*'s commander, the chief supercargo Jackson and the other Britons present. They were chained and confined. News of the seizing of the naval officers and British oil merchants led to several warships sailing into Bonny waters. Alali capitulated and signed a treaty guaranteeing British lives and property. This seems to have been the first time the six-ship squadron had been used on a major scale to protect merchants, its principal task being to intercept and capture slavers.

The following year, 1837, Rear-Admiral Sir Patrick Campbell, the new squadron commander, ordered Commander Craigie to Bonny with a plot to overthrow Alali and reinforce Dappa Pepple, who had been in contact with Fernando Póo. British official anti-slaving interests and British merchants were alike agreed on the overthrow of Alali, who was described in reports as savage, tyrannical, brutal and vindictive.

When Craigie landed on April 5 with an impressive entourage, he found the King awaiting him on the beach alone, the House chiefs having been afraid to come because Alali was opposed to the meeting; but at the King's house, Craigie met some House chiefs and other traders who formed a sort of 'party of the King'. Craigie later held a conference with the European supercargoes on board his ship.

On April 9, a show of naval force in the river obtained the presence of Alali and all Bonny society at a shore meeting. Before the assembled community, Craigie told Alali that in view of his insults to British officers, his oppressive, usurped role and 'conduct of affairs of trade', he was to be removed from all activities except those of a trader. Alali was soon cringing, and signed a sort of abdication document. Dappa assumed effective rule; aware that he could not resist Britain, as Alali had tried to do, he ensured a measure of independence for his kingdom by the arts of diplomacy. A new treaty was signed with Bonny, whose trade with Britain was then worth half a million sovereigns – seven and a half million dollars a year to the Ibo population. Lord Palmerston sent gifts to the King, who tried to clean up a permanent source of murder and intrigue in his realm by partially abolishing credit, then known as 'trust'.

*

The Bonny Treaty of 1837 prohibited slaving at the port – but was not observed, because of Britain's failure to pay the agreed subsidy, a point on which the Treasury overruled the more conscientious Palmerston. A Commander Tucker got a new treaty in 1841, but this raised Dappa's official bribe from two thousand to ten thousand South American dollars – which in turn raised the hackles of Lord Aberdeen, who had succeeded Palmerston and who refused to pay. The inconsistencies of British policy alienated the chiefs and exasperated the traders, who acted as advisors to the successive plenipotentiary naval officers.

In 1844, war broke out between the King and the merchants. Dappa captured some traders, threw them into prison and threatened to roast them alive. Ships were damaged and guns captured. At nearby Juju Town, Awanta, a fanatical witch-doctor, organized 'young hotheads, who patrolled the numerous creeks and killed or destroyed all the British men and property they could lay hands on,' writes Dike, who quotes incidents. Masked men raided ships at anchor. The Navy, which intervened, found that both the African and European traders were of like race and did not easily accept rules or treaties, except where these directly aided the serious business of making money.

The squadron Commodore, Sir Charles Hotham, recommended leaving the two parties to fight it out on their own terms in future; but by 1847, with Palmerston back at the Foreign Office, the sacrosanctity of British lives, property – and promises – was once again dogma. Having informed himself at the Board of Trade of the value of Bonny commerce, Palmerston asked the Admiralty to order Hotham to protect British interests, and to enforce payment of debts due to British traders. Hotham sent an officer sympathetic to Palmerston's views, Commander Birch, who captured Awanta by force. As the sorcerer was not a British subject, his trial posed problems; so, on Colonial Secretary Lord Grey's suggestion, the Navy set him ashore 'on the Coast of Africa as far as possible from the Bonny'. He was never heard of again.

To some extent, Awanta had successfully echoed a grass-roots feeling of xenophobia. Dappa now exploited this sentiment, too, in his dealings with the British: Awanta's hooligans were given the task of terrorizing the waters between New Calabar and Bonny, depriving the British of access to their trade and property on these channels, and seeking to force New Calabar into submission to the throne of Bonny. As a consequence, the 1848 treaty obliged Dappa to send guards on British ships trading to New Calabar and to 'afford every protection in our power to the persons and property of British subjects trading in the River'. The waterways would only be navigated by daylight. In this treaty, the King accepted his original subsidy of two thousand dollars. By then, British annual export trade to the Niger area was worth thirty million modern American dollars – and to Lagos, the Gold Coast, Gambia and Sierra Leone combined, nine million dollars.

Palmerston was convinced that trade in the Delta could not be protected sufficiently by occasional showings of the flag, and in 1849 he appointed a Consul. The partly Spanish Eurafrican trader, John Beecroft, who had on nine previous occasions aided the Navy in delicate negotiations with African chiefs, was the obvious choice.

Beecroft, the greatest figure in Delta history, had been in the area permanently since 1827; in 1829, Superintendent Nicholls had put him in charge of the Works Department on Fernando Póo. After evacuation of the Department in 1834, Beecroft became a partner of the trading firm Tennant and Company, which went bankrupt in 1837. Robert Jamieson of Glasgow then employed Beecroft on Niger exploration in the steamer *Ethiope*. He had already been up-river in 1836, and was on good terms with a number of back-country chiefs. When Spain reasserted its influence over Fernando Póo in 1841, the Spanish asked Beecroft to be their Governor there. Colonel Nicholls had said of him that he was 'highly respected, and possesses influence such as no man on the Coast has ever obtained (before)'.

Nevertheless, his consular appointment was contested by an economy-minded parliament which, in 1865, was to recommend British official withdrawal from all West Africa except Sierra Leone. Beecroft's salary was three hundred pounds (four thousand five hundred dollars) a year, and it was two years before he was given a clerk to help him. He traveled on naval ships. In 1853, some of his work burden was eased by the appointment of Benjamin Campbell as Consul to the Bight of Benin at Lagos.

The man who was himself the progeny of both Europe and Africa, and who stood like a colossus above his contemporary Europeans and Africans in the Delta, was proclaimed Her Britannic Majesty's Consul for the Bights of Benin and

Biafra on June 30, 1849. His competence then extended to Lagos and Dahomey. In the draft establishing the Consulate, a phrase stating that Britain had no territorial ambitions in the region was crossed out in Palmerston's own hand. The Nigerian historian Onwuka Dike writes: 'During this period Palmerston was the only Foreign Secretary who appeared to have an intelligent grasp of the meaning of events in the Bights of Benin and Biafra. He was convinced that with the growth of equitable traffic British interference could no longer be delayed. It was he who had attempted to purchase Fernando Póo . . . had urged the payment of abolition subsidies to Bonny, and two years after making his appointment of the first Consul to the Bights in 1849 had ordered the occupation of Lagos.'

In 1850, Beecroft led his unsuccessful mission to Abomey to try to establish trade relations and procure Abolition. He made missions to Liberia and Abeokuta, was instructed to open the Ogu to safe navigation and to assist a cotton plantation scheme.

Meanwhile, the palm market, the main justification for British interest, suffered fluctuations. Oil exports stood at 13,945 tons in 1834, had dropped to eleven thousand tons three years later, were up to twentyfive thousand tons in 1845 and down to eighteen thousand tons the following year. Revivals of the slave trade, usually blamed for the erratic nature of the palm market, were rarely the true reasons. The 1837 drop was caused by hinterland reaction to Alali; the northern Delta chiefs rallied to the King. The drop after 1845 was caused by Dappa's war on Andony, which he annexed.

When the price was good, as in 1845 (thirtyfour sovereigns a ton), Delta oil was worth seven hundred and fifty thousand pounds – nearly twelve million US dollars. By 1864, the Delta's twentysix thousand tons were worth eight hundred thousand pounds, out of a total African oil export value of one and a half million pounds. In contrast, the sums earned by ivory and timber together were less than fifty thousand pounds.

West African products were mostly still bought by barter. The export of British manufactured goods to West Africa rose from an average of less than two hundred and fifty thousand pounds in the 'Thirties to about double in the

'Forties. Cottons rose from seventyfive thousand pounds to two hundred and sixty thousand pounds, while liquor sales fell by about thirty per cent. Liverpool trade to the Delta averaged between twelve and fifteen thousand tons annually. Ships trading to Bonny in 1840 grossed 13,170 tons and employed nearly a thousand seamen.

Despite the attempts to abolish 'trust', as late as 1848 about six hundred thousand pounds-worth of goods were distributed to native middlemen in the Delta before oil began to arrive. The credit of individual African traders went as high as five thousand pounds (seventyfive thousand dollars of modern money). It was sometimes vastly higher for the Kings. Beecroft reported in 1851 that Old Calabar middlemen held seventy thousand pounds-worth of commodites on trust, and could easily seize another one hundred and thirty thousand pounds-worth from the barracoons if they had a mind to.

In 1855, Consul Lynslager reported the value of European goods and property in the River to be eight hundred thousand pounds – twelve million dollars. To some extent this was due to the impenetrability of the hinterland – a factor which only broke down in the 'Seventies but which, by the 'Forties, had already been attenuated on the Gold Coast, less hostile to white penetration.

Since the absence of a universally accepted currency made barter trade more or less inevitable – and since changing fashions and tastes made it unwise for middlemen to 'save' their commodity capital – everything earned was spent, thus perpetuating the credit system. The value standard was the 'bar'; all articles, from European manufactured goods to native produce, had a bar value; barter was based on this. At different ports the 'bar' had a different value when translated into the traders' sterling. Main barter goods were textiles, guns and gunpowder, with Bonny also taking beads, cutlery and brandy. Calabar also bought rum and salt.

The coastal middlemen's monopoly of Delta produce came from their supplies of guns; as Benin bronzes show, the musket had been a powerful factor in Nigerian politics since the days of the first Portuguese pioneers. Originally the most popular weapons came from Denmark, and their copies made in other countries were and still are called Dane guns.

Goods not paid in barter or reckoned in bars were paid or reckoned in South American doubloons or dollars – issued by the Sierra Leonean Government and worth, at that time, about the same as the contemporary American dollar. But despite its constant causing of trouble, the credit system was favored by most of the palm oil ruffians, since it gave them a control over native traders. The same people who had opposed naval convoys during the Napoleonic Wars – because they would have increased the number of ships in the Delta, and forced up the buying price of oil – also preferred greater risk and greater profits through the continuation of 'trust'.

New traders had to offer better terms than the veteran supercargoes, and many unscrupulous native traders took 'trust' both from their regular trading partners and from 'interlopers'. The veterans sometimes responded by 'chopping oil' – seizing puncheons intended for the newcomers. Fighting ensued, with the Africans regularly siding with the 'interlopers'. At times, however, the white trading community combined to bring prices down. But the native traders were just as effectively organized and equally unscrupulous; time was on their side, since the Europeans knew the dangers of a prolonged stay on the disease-ridden Coast, and the cost of delays.

*

Prosperity was already showing in terms of education. In the 'Forties, the Baptist Mission was founded on Fernando Póo, and Hope Waddell's Presbyterian Mission in Old Calabar. Schools had existed since the previous century in Old Calabar, where the science of literacy acquired by chiefs' sons who had been to London was passed on from generation to generation. Now more, better schools appeared. Nor was prosperity limited to the Nigerians. Some supercargos could earn fortunes for their employers and still turn a cool six thousand sovereigns (ninety thousand modern dollars) a year for themselves.

There were, of course, substantial risks – the main ones being non-payment by rascally middlemen, and disease. Profit margins were of course proportionally great; because trade goods were overvalued by the Europeans, Dappa tried – unsuccessfully – in 1841 to have his subsidy paid in cash. In

Kamerun, a subsidy of two thousand South American dollars was converted that year to mean: six muskets, one hundred bolts of cloth, two barrels of gunpowder, two puncheons of rum, a scarlet coat with epaulettes and a sword. There was, at the time, a habit of selling incredible articles of fancy dress – represented as being what the nobility wore in London. In 1842, King Eyo Honesty of Creek Town told the Navy he wanted 'proper Indian romorle (a sort of cloth). I no want fool things.'

In 1852, the British Government advertised for a shipping company to carry mails to West Africa. The contract went to the African Steamship Company (later, Elder Dempster) created for the purpose largely by MacGregor Laird. Three steamers, each of six hundred tons, undertook the service, at a speed of eight knots and a Government subsidy of £2,500 per sailing. Business rose considerably within a year or so, as small traders took advantage of the cheap freight rates offered by Laird.

The veterans had always worked on large profits and slow returns; the interlopers wanted quick, more modest profits. The big merchants offered to charter all Laird's steamers on their homeward journey to prevent the small traders or the African chiefs themselves shipping oil. Laird, who had a number of liberal principles, refused. With the assistance of the Rev. E. Jones, a Negro American who was Principal of Fourah Bay University (then, Institution) in the 'Fifties, he also encouraged the repatriation of Ibos from Sierra Leone. Other assistance for this scheme came from the Church Missionary Society. Laird's aim was to break both the ruffians and the coastal Kings and to open up the hinterland to direct trade.

The returning, Westernized, Sierra Leonean Ibos not unnaturally got a cold reception from both threatened groups in Bonny; but at Creek Town, King Eyo Honesty welcomed them. The new community at Old Calabar swiftly grew. By 1855, the middlemen and the Sierra Leoneans had joined in alliance, and were shipping oil direct to Britain before paying off the middlemen's outstanding 'trusts'. The Consul of the day, Lynslager, destroyed Old Town, in Old Calabar, by naval bombardment – theoretically to stamp out human sacrifices, but actually to press defaulting middlemen.

The following year, the supercargos announced to the new Consul, Hutchinson, that by 'trust' they had bought all the produce of Calabar River for thirty months ahead; in all they had purchased 9,030 tons. Meanwhile, more Sierra Leoneans had arrived, and trade friction led to fighting. Naturally, the veterans were active in collecting their debts. A typical case was that of a Captain Cuthbertson, who had seized sixteen puncheons of oil on Old Calabar beach, where it had been placed to await the packet. It had been bought by a Sierra Leonean, Peter Nicoll, but sold by King Eyo, who was indebted to Cuthbertson. Another Liverpudlian supercargo, Captain Davies, seized oil bought by a Sierra Leonean, Daniel Hedd.

These incidents, and more violent ones, occasioned greater assumption of powers by the Consuls. In 1857, Eyo, who owed oil for eighteen thousand pounds to his traditional trading partners, shipped oil direct to Liverpool aboard the packet – and went on to charter a brig, the *Olinda,* to take more. Consul Hutchinson 'interposed'. The same year, consular magisterial powers were increased – notably to prevent violent 'rough justice' by supercargoes.

Violence was worst at Old Calabar, where power was divided among the four Egbo cities, and in similarly fractured communities of the Wuri River (modern Kamerun), where the ruffians collected their debts by executing some of the more notorious debtors. The Kamerunian chief King Akwa complained to Burton, when he assumed the consulate, of the violence of British supercargos and of former Consul Hutchinson himself. Conditions were better at New Calabar and to some extent at Bonny.

New Calabar, under the royal clan of Amakiri (also written Amakree, and by the Germans Amachree) had never taken 'trust'. This fact, plus its distance from the open sea and gunboats, made 'Amakree the most independent King on the Coast', according to Consul Hutchinson. At Bonny, after clashes over trust, and British official failure to pay Abolition subsidies, the British merchants, says an historian, 'learned not only to act together in their own defense but to evolve a system of settling trade and other disputes between African and European merchants in a "Court of Equity" '. Attempts to create similar courts elsewhere were less successful. Burton urged one in Kamerun but reported to Lord Russell that although all the merchants in the Wuri signed the agreement, none of them adhered to it.

*

The dominant personality in the Delta was Beecroft. Onwuka Dike says of him: 'Until his appointment as Consul in 1849 British intervention in Nigerian politics was desultory. With the sole exception of 1837, when she interfered to restore to King Pepple (Dappa Pepple) the power he had lost to the regent – an action made imperative by the threat to British life and property in that quarter – Britain abstained totally from the domestic politics of the African states.

'Beecroft reversed this policy. Twenty years' experience of Delta life had taught him that European occupation of West Africa could not long be delayed, and from the date of his assumption of office his activities were guided by that awareness. In him Palmerston found an enthusiastic ally who launched a forward movement marked by bold intervention in the internal politics of the city-states. The period of his consulship, 1849–1854, saw the end of non-interference and the inauguration of empire building in Nigeria.'

Dike further notes that: 'Recognizing that the African chiefs stood in great dread of the warship, he invariably visited them in such a vessel and introduced the practice of settling the lengthy palavers on the spacious decks of the men-of-war instead of, as before, in the courts of the native potentates.'

Ephraim Duke, Eyamba, Eyo Honesty and Archibong were Beecroft's personal friends. Dike writes: 'When King Archibong died in 1852 Beecroft presided over the election of the new King and his right to do so was never questioned. He in turn reciprocated the confidence of the chiefs and allowed them to install a man of their choosing. The event ended in great rejoicing with the Consul inviting the new King and "his principals" to dinner on board a warship. They drank Her Majesty Queen Victoria's health and that of King Ephraim Duke, after which the latter and his suite "retired into their canoes".' In Kamerun, Beecroft deposed King Akwa, whom Beecroft said was 'a drunken imbecile, a liar and a great rogue', and installed someone described by the

186

Consul as 'Prince Jim'. In 1851, he had successfully supplanted the intransigent usurper of the Lagos throne, Kosoko, by more docile, legitimate King Akitoye. From then on, Beecroft concentrated his attention on Bonny, the sole remaining core of resistance to his authority.

At the end of August, 1852, the supercargoes in Bonny River reported to the Consul that Dappa Pepple had had, three months before, what was presumably a stroke. He was paralysed, 'in almost imbecile state, and quite unable to conduct the business of the country'. In his sickness, the King's hatred for the coterie of the ex-regent grew, and – rather than choose regents from that quarter – he appointed two favorites, Yanibo and Ishacco.

In February the following year, Beecroft despatched Palmerston saying these appointments were bringing the long Bonny feud to a head. Dappa Pepple had carefully associated the British traders with the appointments by asking for their presence at the meeting at which they were chosen; he thus hoped to ensure their support – and consequently Beecroft's – when, as expected, the two regents were challenged by Alali and his followers.

In November, the King was sufficiently recovered to resume control of affairs, but the feud had by then gone too far to be forgotten. To cut down the growing power of the ex-slave majority in commerce and politics, the King introduced laws prohibiting the amalgamation of Houses – since strong Houses could mean strong oppositions – and forbade Bonny merchants to trade in the interior unless they took trusts from the King. As this handicapped African traders, it hit the European merchants, who were also affected by the fact that most Bonny traders already held trusts from them which had not been redeemed.

Pepple sought to unite his kingdom around him by directing the discontent caused by his measures toward the white supercargos and their men. Warriors attacked Europeans on land and in the river, and warehouses were robbed. When the supercargoes urged meetings to settle the matters, the chiefs failed to attend. The merchants saw in their sufferings the hand of the King and of the successor to Awanta, a witch-doctor always referred to in English as Juju Peterside.

Pepple had another trick up his sleeve to rally the kingdom: nothing less than the conquest of New Calabar. In November, he told his chiefs to ready fortythree war canoes so that he could visit the Billa country, birthplace of his mother; since on recovery from a severe illness he was in honor bound to make sacrifices to his ancestors, the proposed journey was cloaked in an aura of legitimacy. Pepple then wrote to the supercargoes asking that two of them should accompany him as far as Calabar River, where he would invite King Amachree aboard his canoe 'and make him a small present'. If Amachree was reluctant to board Pepple's canoe, one of the supercargoes would be asked to go ashore as a hostage.

The 'small present' was presumably to be received by Amachree between the ribs. Pepple's main chiefs knew what Pepple intended, but most of the crews of the canoes genuinely thought their King was going to the Billa country for sacrifices. The Europeans guessed at once what was intended – a war, which meant a stoppage of trade. They tried to dissuade the King from his plans.

The canoecade reached Calabar River and was ordered to blockade the city, cutting it off from the area where the foreign merchants had their ships and warehouses. Over half the Bonny Navy deserted, returning home; there, they 'deposed the King' – according to the statement of the Alali party, written by the supercargos. Although the deposition was not yet an accomplished fact, it was clear Dappa Pepple had over-reached himself. A Court of Equity met, under Beecroft, and deposed him; but his loyal chiefs said it was not traditional for Bonny Ibo to depose a King, and that if he went his 'trusts' would not be paid by his former subjects. But Beecroft won; the King went, and the trusts were paid. A nephew of the ex-King, Dappo, was proclaimed in his place. British warships fired twentyone guns in his honor. Beecroft persuaded the former monarch to request asylum in Fernando Póo, and this was granted. Later he was exiled to Ascension.

Clearly some subterfuge was used to spirit Dappa Pepple away without a scene, for in November, 1855, he wrote to Lord Clarendon saying: 'Upon my embarkation from Bonny in H.M.S. *Antelope* for Fernando Póo it was rumored that I was forced away from my dominions by the voices of my

chiefs. This is at total variance with the truth, as is certified
by letters, which I still have in my possession, from the late
John Beecroft and other Englishmen, which distinctly state
that I left against the wishes of my chiefs and people . . .
who would not be pacified until assured by Mr. Beecroft that
I should return among them whenever I thought proper,
that I was going a free agent and not a prisoner.' But the
patience for 'palavering' of the better Europeans in Africa
was not reciprocated in London, and Dappa Pepple remained
in his island exile. He later went to London and was away,
in all, over seven years.

The main grievance against him, from the British point
of view, was his attempt to monopolize trusts. The Court of
Equity, in which British influence was paramount, forbade
the new King to trade: his income should come from customs and other taxes. The Court itself was to become the
supreme authority in matters of commerce. The new King
also lost the right to make war without the approval of the
Court – which was of course an unlikely permission to be
obtained. Meetings between African and European leaders
would in future be held at the Court, not at King's House.

Dappa Pepple's contemporaries show him to have been a
man of – in Dike's words – 'intelligence, arrogance and
duplicity'. Hope Waddell was not impressed by him. Dr W.
B. Baikie, the explorer, who saw him in exile at Fernando
Póo in 1854, found him shrewd, relatively well-informed.
The reporter Winwood Reade found him equivocal. All
described his brand of intelligence by the derogatory term
'cunning'. He was certainly very rich. Baikie says he made
as much from oil as any King ever made from slaving, and
put his annual income from 'shipping dues and other
sources' at between fifteen thousand and twenty thousand
pounds. Twenty thousand sovereigns would be three hundred
thousand dollars in modern money.

A new period was beginning – that of inland trade; but
Beecroft did not live to see it. He died the year of Pepple's
exile – 1854. Dike notes the great increase in trade from
this period, and traces what was to become colonial rule
largely from this point, adding: 'This is not to say that the
sole motive of British penetration of Nigeria was trade. The
men who led the great missionary movements of the time

were undoubtedly inspired by genuine idealism. Only a cynic could read the journals of the missionaries and explorers and remain unconvinced as to the sincerity of their motives. With trade expansion, however, economic and political issues dominated the Nigerian scene, both on the Coast and in the vast interior.'

In Bonny, Alali sought to recover his power over the throne, scheming to eliminate what remained of Dappa Pepple's party, and taking Yanibo prisoner. The English captains summoned the new Consul, Lynslager, to procure the release of the former co-regent. The Court of Equity ordered his liberation, but Alali swept out of the room, followed one by one by the chiefs, until only Dappo himself remained. There were incidents involving Europeans. Lynslager warned Alali 'to alter your ways, as long as you have yet time'. Dike notes: 'But Alali was an impetuous character, impatient of diplomatic processes, and where the exiled king would negotiate and reason he would act regardless of the consequences.' He had succeeded in making a mockery of the Court of Equity, and with Beecroft gone an era had come when mediocrity could triumph.

Dappo went to the interior in August, 1855, on the usual tour of the inland markets, was caught in several days of incessant rain, and died on his return to Bonny, presumably of pneumonia. He was attended by Dr. Stiles, an English doctor in the River, but from what accounts remain it looks as though the witch-doctors prevented the King using 'foreign' medicine. Alali preyed on the superstitions of his simple compatriots by assuring everyone Dappo had died of witchcraft effected by Yanibo and Ishacco – although at the time they had been away from Bonny. Alali's story was a clear attempt by the leader of the ex-slave class to remove the last major representatives of the freemen. The two victims took refuge aboard the ship of a Mr. Witt, who refused to give them up, even after the other supercargoes unanimously urged him to do so to ensure the restoration of peaceful trade.

Fighting began in the city, houses were burned and, as the sound of musketry was heard from all directions, the traders' ships dropped down the river to safety. In the massacre, most of the leading loyalists and freemen were killed – about three hundred people in all. Yanibo and

Ishacco settled at Fernando Póo, and the ex-slaves inherited the kingdom.

Consul Lynslager arrived in H.M.S. *Philomel* and found the defiant Alali ready for a showdown if need be. The trusts held, for eighty thousand pounds, gave the Bonny authorities a powerful bargaining point. Lynslager reported to Clarendon: 'On consulting with Commander Skene, we considered it advisable to open negotiations with the chiefs by letter, to be carried on shore with the Flag of Truce.' A supercargo, Captain Stowe, took the letter to Alali, who agreed to the *Philomel* anchoring off Bonny if a mission came ashore headed by a naval officer in full uniform. The Consul agreed.

A four-man council of regency – three of ex-slave caste, one freeman – was established to rule the kingdom. Alali was the effective ruler. The victory of the slave caste in Bonny was to be reciprocated elsewhere in the Delta, during the third quarter of the 19th Century.

Already from the slave ranks came, broadly speaking, the richest traders, some of the best warriors, and of course most of the labor of the agricultural Delta. Mission influence was also against privilege by birth. Then as now, religion and politics were closely interwoven, and political theories had to be imposed, as in modern times, as articles of semi-religious dogma. Waddell had preached for less cruelty toward the slaves, urging that slaves had 'heads and hearts, feelings and passions, like ourselves'. A Nigerian historian comments: 'These were strange doctrines to people used to the despotic laws of the Egbo code, which accorded the serf population neither justice nor rights.' The chiefs complained that Waddell wanted to go too fast, that 'black people had not laws like white people', that slaves wished to remain in slavery. But events proved Waddell knew the feelings of the Ibo slaves better than their Ibo masters.

*

In the Efik hinterland of Old Calabar lay food plantations worked by serfs. One area, on the thickly forested banks of the Kwa, had become from the 'Fifties onward an 'independent' haunt of runaway slaves, bound together as the 'Order of Blood Men' to fight Egbo terror. These men had tasted one another's blood and were thus linked in a compact

191

which only death could untie. The Blood Men rose in power just as Egbo was beginning to quake before the onslaught of new ideas brought by the missionaries and by palm oil prosperity.

In 1851, some Blood Men were arrested in Duke Town to be ordealed under Egbo. Their blood brothers ravaged the town's plantations and came into the place in force. The Egbo elders gave way and released the prisoners; many slave and half-slave families joined the new Order. The super-cargoes feared for their property and two warships steamed in, whereupon the victorious slaves withdrew in good order to the Kwa. Beecroft arranged a meeting between Egbo, Blood Men and himself. The Consul reported to Palmerston that after ten days' palaver 'we succeeded in conciliating the insurgents'.

The 'treaty' signed by both parties, and drafted by Bee-croft, leaned too heavily toward Egbo for Palmerston's demo-cratic taste, but Beecroft convinced him in a second despatch that 'the "Egbo" is at once the Legislature and Police Establish-ment of Old Calabar. At present no Government or order can exist in Old Calabar without Egbo in its present form.' Beecroft, obviously piqued at being doubted for once, by Palmerston, noted that his action 'saved the loss of an immense sum, two hundred thousand pounds, to English merchants, and allayed the storm in a manner which could have been done only by myself, for no one else knows so well how to deal with African character'.

History tends to confirm Beecroft's high opinion of him-self. Dike comments: 'The principle behind Beecroft's action must be grasped. In the Delta Britain was not ready to take over the responsibilities of Government. Yet the valuable trade carried on by her subjects in these parts needed peace, and it would have been bad politics to remove the sole pro-tection that trade enjoyed by destroying Egbo power.'

Egbo power persisted through the 'Fifties. In Bonny, in the hiatus caused by Dappa Pepple's exile, the chief of the four regents found his slave status affected his authority, and in 1858 he wrote to Consul Hutchinson asking for British backing in raising his social rank. His petition said: 'I savey very well English Queen want to do good for all Blackmen and I come for Man of War to ask you for give me book to make me free, and that no man can call me slave, for Queen of England make me free. I remain, Consul, you good friend and friend of all English men, Manila Pepple.'

Hutchinson issued a decree of manumission, forbidding reference to Manila's slave origins under pain of incurring the 'displeasure of Her Britannic Majesty's government and of suffering such penalty as Government may attach to such a step'. But Hutchinson also despatched Clarendon saying he did not think this white-man juju would do much for Manila; Egbo continued, in fact, to prevail in many ways, preserving the dying but still extant authority of the freemen. Bishop Crowther and others reported European merchants purchasing Egbo orders for as much as three hundred pounds, taking part in the dances and 'idolatrous rites' required of new members. The slave revolt had half worked, and the comparison with changes of power in some parts of Africa in modern times is inevitable: the authority was lacking, anarchy became unbearable, and Hutchinson reported a desire of Pepple's old enemies to see him back. The masters of the trading ships agreed in 1859 that to restore order to Bonny someone *amanyanabo* (of royal blood) was essential. In 1861, Britain agreed to restore the King, paying him £4,520 compensation for his troubles, and £3,003 legal expenses.

The kingdom was by then divided between the now pro-monarchist majority, led by an ex-slave, Oko Jumbo, and the diehards of Alali who feared the King's revenge. The King arrived in the river on August 18 and stayed aboard his chartered vessel, the *Bewley*, until October 15, trying to effect agreement between the two parties before he landed. But Alali refused to come aboard the *Bewley*, presumably fearing murder. There was an apparent attempt to capture him, and he fled. Shortly after, he had a stroke and died. The new Consul, Burton, believed he was poisoned.

But the returning King's problems were still not over. His great slaving and oil fortune had been sacked at his downfall, and strong anti-authoritarian feelings remained, among the slaves or ex-slaves. As Yanibo and Ishacco had fled, his 'trading house' had faded away. In such a materialistic society, a poor King was almost no King at all. He moved away from the center of his capital to Juju Town, where he died in 1866.

His son, King George, was a man ahead of his time. Educated in England during the exile there of his father, he spoke good English. The Count de Cardi, a noted Bonny trader, says he would have made a good monarch if the powers of the 'Thirties had still remained. Without these full powers, or a fortune, he became a puppet in the hands of his chiefs. A Christian and a Westerner, he was vulnerable to popular criticism on chauvinistic or xenophobic lines. Mary Kingsley noted that unless an educated native returned to 'all the pagan gods of his forefathers', political power and prosperity tended to elude him. There are, of course, some echos of this in modern times also.

*

The Delta was the only area of West Africa where Britain had not actually tried to reduce its commitments in the 'Sixties. London was influenced by costs, by the traders' desire for laissez-faire – balanced by not infrequent requests for official assistance or gunboats. But in the Niger the modest foretaste of an incipient imperial policy was now visible. The success of the Baikie expedition up the river in 1854, when nobody died, had led to MacGregor Laird getting his 1857 contract to maintain a subsidized steamer on the river for five years.

Dr Baikie again went up the river on this new steamer, the *Dayspring*. His Number Two, naval Lieutenant John Glover, was later to become Governor of Lagos. Baikie established a trading post and Consulate at Lokoja, on the Niger-Benue confluence, and fought the stranglehold on trade of the African middlemen and palm oil ruffians on the Coast. Before he died in 1864, Baikie had pioneered relations with King Masaba of Bida and established British presence as far North as Kano. Permanent trading stations at Aboh and Onitsha were added to that at Lokoja, where the Consulate was maintained for eight years after Baikie's death by Lt. Bourchier and Lyous McLeod.

At the river-mouth, black and white traders united against the threat; some reminded the newcomers that they had killed Lander for trying to breach the hinterland. Steamers going through narrow channels came under artillery fire mounted by Africans on the banks. War-canoes made boarding raids.

Warships made reprisal attacks. It became hard to recruit native crews for the trading steamers, and insurance grew prohibitive.

In 1860, when Laird had proved that inland trading could pay, the Admiralty at last bowed to his request for regular escorts for his convoys; but Commodore Edmonstone, commanding the African Station, resisted the order, pleading that escorts would be suicide. Laird's vessels were stymied for many months and his goods were auctioned in the Delta for poor prices. The interior trading posts were left without supplies and were overrun by hostile warriors.

Laird sued the Government for failure to honor its promises. He died the following year, a broken man. But historically, his battle was won. In 1861, Britain acquired Lagos from King Docemo by treaty of cession, and Lord Russell despatched Consul Brand that since the Niger was navigable for about six months in the year, 'permanent commercial intercourse by this route with the interior of Africa' was to be policy. Delta opposition was to be mastered. Baikie had shown that Lokoja opened the trade route to the Hausa heartland as well, and the opportunities were immense. No other river in West Africa had the same trade possibilities. But native hostility persisted, and the Lokoja Consulate had to be closed in 1869.

Five major trading companies were formed in the 'Sixties to exploit the Niger interior; the largest, the Company of African Merchants, with a capital of four hundred thousand pounds, asked for a government subsidy for pioneering the dangerous ground. The Liverpool traders, Coast monopolists, counter-attacked, and the subsidy agreed by Lord Russell was cancelled. Prominent among the Coast lobby was Charles Horsfall, whose company, Chas. Horsfall and Sons, had a monopoly of the Brass River, and whose agents – according to Foreign Office records – organized and armed the warriors that fired on British shipping trying to pass through the Brass on their way up to Lokoja. But eventually, the Coasters and their companies were to join in the scramble for inland trade themselves.

*

Meanwhile, at Bonny, Oko Jumbo and the leader of the

slave party, Ja Ja, were facing off for the city-state's greatest power battle. Of the two, Oko Jumbo was the more sophisticated, Ja Ja the wilier African politician. The latter had inherited the leadership of Alali's House. Born inland in 1821, he had been sold to a Bonny chief at twelve and – because he was headstrong – given away to Chief Madu as a gift.

Ja Ja rose in prestige and, when the succession to Alali was disputed after the ex-regent's death in 1861, he was the only candidate prepared to take on Alali's debts – in modern money, something like two hundred thousand dollars-worth of oil owed to supercargoes on 'trust'. Ja Ja was a good trader, respected by Europeans for his honesty.

The succession had been slow and it was not until December, 1863, that Ja Ja took over the House. Consul Burton commented that he was 'an unknown bushman', but 'energetic and decided'. Burton calls him 'the most influential man and the greatest trader in the River, and fifty thousand pounds, it is said, may annually pass through his hands'. That would be seven hundred and fifty thousand dollars in current values. Burton also noted that 'he lives much with Europeans, and he rides rough shod over young hands coming into Bonny. In a short time he will either be shot or he will beat down all his rivals.'

Ja Ja cultivated the inland chiefs and the supercargos, and based his policy on his understanding that Europe intended to master the inland trade. He raised a score of young ex-slaves to positions of trust, providing them with canoes and credit; thus he had a House led by men entirely loyal to him. He paid off Alali's debts in two years and, says de Cardi, 'from this date Ja Ja never looked back, becoming the most popular chief in Bonny and the idol of his own people'.

Power in Bonny was still divided between Ja Ja and Oko Jumbo, with the King little more than a figurehead and occasional arbitrator. Fighting between the two factions took place in 1867, and King George requested the presence of the Consul and a gunboat. Consul Livingstone, brother of the explorer, declined to interfere.

In 1868, there was a great fire in Bonny and Ja Ja's House suffered heavily. The royalist party challenged the weakened Ja Ja to conflict, but he evaded hostilities for a while. In September, 1869, the supercargos despatched Livingstone that a civil war was about to begin and that they had been given three days to slip down-river; 'But we cannot move the valuable property on the beach in three or even thirty days' time. Extensive preparations are being made in Bonny Town for fighting: heavy guns are in position all around and about the town and all the war canoes are afloat heavily armed with cannon.'

Ja Ja's ammunition store had gone up in the fire, and he was soon defeated. He craftily withdrew to outlying villages faithful to him and wrote Livingstone, as Chairman of the Court of Equity, offering his domains to Queen Victoria in return for a Protectorate Treaty. Oko Jumbo for his part was prepared to be generous toward Ja Ja if peace could be restored to Bonny. The supercargos arranged a truce, and in the ensuing talks backed Ja Ja because he was the most reliable and honest trader.

Consul Livingstone arrived at Bonny eight weeks after the outbreak of fighting and was surprised to learn that Ja Ja was entrenched in Andony Creek, where he had rallied his forces and seemed ready to blockade Bonny. He had drawn up an agreement with some chiefs loyal to him, establishing a new state with himself as King. By February, the new state was a reality.

Livingstone refused protection to traders going to Andony, but it was soon clear that the old order was finished and the new state was there to stay. Two major supercargos, the Count de Cardi and Archie McEachen, took their trade to Ja Ja; soon other masters anchored in the Ikomtoro River, defying the threats of the Bonny chiefs. Bonny war canoes fired on British merchantmen, but the Navy intervened to protect them.

After nine months of war which affected inland trade, Bonny was ready to capitulate and give Ja Ja both that kingdom, in all but name, and his own. In June, 1870, Livingstone paid his first visit to the Ikomtoro and found Ja Ja unprepared to come to terms. The ex-slave said he had fourteen House chiefs with him, while only four remained in Bonny. He had access to the oil markets, and would deny his enemies access to these markets 'for ever'. He had scented the desire for appeasement in Bonny, and was enough of a politician to know that appeasers are made to be destroyed.

Livingstone threatened force to open the markets to Bonny. He feared constant war if Bonny was blockaded, and noted in a despatch to Clarendon that seven British companies had shore establishments at Bonny that made it impossible for them to move their trading arrangements to the Ikomtoro. In August, Ja Ja again refused to lift his blockade, so Livingstone was obliged to call a warship, the *Pert,* into the Ikomtoro. The commander told the five English firms who had joined Ja Ja to put their shipping down-river. The traders, all on Ja Ja's side, were not happy: they petitioned Livingstone regretting that Kwa canoes had been fired on by the *Pert,* and that one of Ja Ja's tributary chiefs, the 'King of Encoro', had been turned back when his canoe reached Andony Creek. The masters warned against violence.

Two people lost their lives in the show of force, and after two days Ja Ja capitulated; but fighting soon began again, with British traders helping both sides. One Bonny super-cargo, a Mr Cheetham, brought a gunboat from England and was miffed to be informed by Livingstone that 'I could only regarded her English crew as pirates should they fire on their own countrymen'.

Such men as Cheetham had reason to be desperate. Ja Ja's drive for power had already cost the Bonny supercargos over one hundred thousand pounds. Gradually, Livingstone was obliged to swing his support to the Ikomtoro, since resistance to Ja Ja was too costly. On Christmas Day, 1870, Ja Ja and his European allies held a feast and proclaimed the 'official' foundation of Opobo – naming the new kingdom after the almost legendary Ibo king, Opubu.

Two years of conflict were to cost traders, finally, five hundred thousand pounds – seven and a half million dollars at modern values – render several firms bankrupt, and to break Livingstone, who died at Bonny in November, 1873, on his way to England and retirement. The previous year, a settlement between Ja Ja, Bonny and the British – aided by the presence of five warships during the talks – with the arbitration of neutral Delta chiefs, gave Ja Ja almost every-thing he wanted, including British recognition as King of Opobo. The war had had one other effect; because of the buccaneering role of many British supercargoes, an Order in Council, in 1872, gave the Consul the power to try and to

198

punish British subjects in the Bights; he could impose fines, imprisonment of up to twentyone days, and banishment from the Delta for up to one year.

*

While France was investigating the Western Sudan with military expeditions, Britain was pushing in from the Coast with traders – including sometimes armed traders, who sailed armored steamers up the Niger and its affluents to establish trading stations, 'tapping' the oil trade normally monopolized by the Delta. Even Ja Ja's monopoly was finally broken in the late 'Seventies.

The Navy also helped smash Delta resistance to inland trade, although the warriors would return to the attack in the dry season when the trading posts were unsupplied and unreachable by steamer. In 1879, H.M.S. *Pioneer* took off the fifty thousand pounds-worth of British trade goods in Onitsha Market (the largest of all African market places) and bombarded the city for three days. Punitive expeditions then went ashore and burned or destroyed both the riverside and inner towns. Consul Easton reported that 'our proceedings at Onitsha will have a most salutary effect up and down the Niger, and the Missionaries and Traders unanimously gave us their thanks for our promptness and decision'.

The smell of Empire was in the air, and a new and impressive figure had just appeared on the scene – Goldie Taubman, an officer in the Royal Engineers. The Taubmans were a Manx family which had made its money in previous generations through piracy. In 1877, Taubman and his brother set off up the Niger in a steam launch; they intended to go up the Benue, then strike across the continent to the Upper Nile, which Taubman had already explored. The Benue trip had to be abandoned as Taubman's brother became sick, but Taubman – who later became Sir George Dashwood Taubman Goldie – returned to England fired with the idea of empire-building in Nigeria.

Taubman noted that between the French coastal stations in Senegal and the British coastal posts on the Gulf of Guinea on the one hand, and the Mediterranean on the other, no power of any importance existed. Goldie's ambition was to take for Britain the Western Sudan – all of it. When he

199

realized the extent of France's ambitions in the same area, he concentrated on the problem of consolidating British interests in the Niger basin.

He first negotiated an end to the fratricidal struggle between British trading interests, uniting most companies into the United African Company in 1879. He later bought out French competitors and renamed his firm the National African Company. Two years later, he sought a charter for the company so that it could install an administration in the Niger territories. His objective, in an historian's words, was to 'assume practical control over the entire waterway and then present the British Government with a *fait accompli*'.

Goldie combined the Empire-building patriotism of the traditional gentleman, and the courage and taste for danger of a 19th Century officer, with the traditional Jewish instincts for trade – not on the buccaneering lines on which the Coasters conducted it, but by painstaking organization. He was endowed with a ruthless will. The family does not appear to have practised its religion and Goldie himself was an outspoken atheist. Like most patriots, he found his Government unworthy of his country; he enjoyed bullying ministers. Goldie established over a hundred riverside trading posts, employing fifteen hundred men. In three years of chugging up and down the mighty river in his rusting launch, he made treaties with thirtyseven chiefs. In the next two years, to 1887, he and his agents, notably David McIntosh, signed pacts with two hundred more, giving Goldie trade monopolies, the right to exclude foreigners, and sovereignty over the land. Twenty light-draft gunboats that could go up the stream in the dry season were built for Goldie's company, to police the trading beaches and 'pacify . . . robber chiefs . . . ever ready to plunder our factories' (the word then used for stores).

Goldie fought off French and German encroachments, notably when his agent Joseph Thomson secured treaties from the Sultans of Sokoto and Gwandu just before Edward Flegel, Bismark's envoy, got to those places. Goldie's 'police' and ammunition gifts helped the Emir of Nupe fight off rebels, and thus won another powerful ally. Goldie's main problems came from the French. He was to tell a reporter in 1889: 'The only stroke of fortune we have had was the reaction in France in 1884 against colonial enterprises, in consequence of those disasters at Tong King. . . . But for this reaction in France, which lasted until the Paris Exhibition this year, and which she has long and rightly deplored, we might have been pushed out of Nigeria.' The situation helps explain Goldie's high-handed interpretation of his limited charter. An equally frank Frenchman of the same period would have been able to say that, but for vacillations in London in the 'Sixties, 'Seventies and early 'Eighties, the French might have been pushed out of most of West Africa.

Dike says of Goldie that 'between 1879 and 1885 Goldie secured Nigeria for Britain by defeating the French, by unifying British trading interests, and by providing through the Government of the Company some sort of protection for interior trade'. (His work is examined in greater detail in Part 3 of this book, on colonization.)

Meanwhile, on the Niger coast, Ja Ja was moving his frontiers inland and forbidding trade to Europeans except through his warehouses in Opobo. His idea, of course, was to counter the growth of European inland trade, but historically his actions helped, like British inland expansion itself, to make colonization inevitable. In spite of his monopolistic tendencies, Ja Ja maintained good relations with London for a long time. He had sent a contingent to the Ashanti war in 1874, and received a sword from Queen Victoria. But his opposition to free trade was to lead to his over-reaching himself.

In February, 1882, the famous trader John Holt appealed to the Foreign Office to protect a Mr Watts, a trader in the Kwa Ibo river who was being persecuted by Ja Ja; the latter had burned villages and executed villagers who traded with Watts. Holt has given a graphic description of the engagement, noting that at dawn on the day in question Ja Ja 'suddenly invaded them with a force of about fifty fully manned canoes, armed with breech loading cannon and rifles, by means of which he bombarded seven of their villages, which he plundered and afterwards burned, destroying their crops and stores of food, and taking prisoners upward of a hundred people, whilst the natives of Qua Eboe, unable to protect themselves . . . took to the woods, where many of them greatly suffered from want and exposure.

'Ja Ja's canoes remained in the river several days, broke into Mr Watt's factory, scattered his goods about, and either took away or destroyed a number of barrels and hogsheads of oil belonging to him which were in the native homes that were looted. With their plunder and their prisoners, consisting chiefly of women and children, they returned at length to Opobo, where their unhappy victims were cruelly slaughtered, Ja Ja's own children being made to cut off the heads of some of the Qua Eboe children, to entitle them to wear the eagle plume (of) . . . those who have slain an enemy.'

Holt recommended that the Coast 'from Lagos to the Cameroons' be annexed. The cause of colonization dragged on, gaining support, and the following year Consul Hewett is also found recommending annexation, particularly in Kamerun. The middleman system, represented by Ja Ja and the other coastal potentates, had had its time, and French and German ambitions made the requests for government takeover more urgent still. In 1879 and 1881, Kings Akwa and Bell of the Dwala area of the Wuri were persuaded to write letters asking Queen Victoria to rule over them.

On May 16, 1884, Consul Hewett received instructions from the Foreign Office to secure a protectorate over the Niger area. By the end of August, he had the Coast 'in his pocket'. In September, he went up-river, where he found his task made easier by the fact that Goldie already had most of the chiefs bound by signature. Finally, in October, he worked on the sensitive Delta area just behind the Coast.

Britain's position at the Berlin Conference, which opened at the end of the year, owed more to Goldie and Hewett – and the departed figures of Beecroft and Laird – than to any other contemporaries. Characteristically enough, the British government had been less than co-operative with these stalwart benefactors who dropped an undeserved empire into Whitehall's lap. London's hesitancy and perfidy had driven Laird, a courageous explorer and philanthrope as much as a businessman, into his grave; Goldie had been left to organize his own 'army' and 'navy'; Hewett had been treated as an over-zealous nuisance of a pro-consul. Only the gigantic figure of Beecroft had managed to penetrate the cobwebs of official thinking – mainly due to the timely presence of Palmerston, himself an impatient despiser of mediocrity.

Still the dominant note was caution, and although officially colonialism in Black Africa dates from 1885, in practice it was established only gradually. Vice-Consul Johnston reported, a year after Berlin: 'So long as we keep other European nations out, we need not be in a hurry to go in.' Sealing off the Coast was thus the only immediate requirement. For some time, the Berlin treaty demarcated European spheres of influence but did not determine actual control, which had to be enforced. In Nigeria, this was to take fifteen years, until 1900.

But Johnston was soon to be forced to settle the long conflict with Ja Ja and his bid for a monopoly on oil in his area. Ja Ja had threatened to deal with the up-river tribes trading with Europeans as he had dealt with the Kwa Ibo. His spadassins had already attacked isolated Europeans. The Consul, in retaliation, forbade Ja Ja to collect 'comey' duties, since this unfairly increased the price of others' oil compared to his own. Ja Ja sent a delegation of chiefs to London. This 1887 mission was unsuccessful. Johnston gave Ja Ja an ultimatum: the trade war must be called off, or gunboats would enter Opobo. There were fresh reports of Ja Ja's excesses, and Johnston sailed up-river to find his passage blocked by a boom across the waterway. He cabled London for permission to deport Ja Ja. An affirmative reply which may have referred to another message was received, and Johnston acted quickly.

Returning to Opobo on H.M.S. *Goshawk* he invited Ja Ja to meet him at a British traders' 'beach', giving him an assurance he could go free, after the meeting, if he wished. But at the meeting Ja Ja was told that if he did not go to Accra to stand trial, Opobo would be bombarded. Ja Ja surrendered, was found guilty in Accra of not honoring his treaty, and deported to the West Indies on a pension of eight hundred pounds a year – at that time about the salary of a colonial Governor. He was allowed to return home in 1891, but died on the way.

Portugal and Atlantic Africa

ALL OF THIS LONG PART ON TRADERS AND EXPLORERS has dealt, so far, with those who 'worked' West Africa, the pioneers of what Africanists call the Coast, with a capital C. Closer to Europe, and to Europe's ambitions, favored by a past studded with tough, indigenous Tamerlanes and seasoned with ideas imported from Mecca and from Liverpool, both the West Africans and the Coasters provided a history that was perhaps to prove the most significant part of Africa's story for the future of the whole of the continent. Now the time has come to look South and East, to areas more remote from Europe and Islam, less populated, less able – in the ruthlessly aggressive 19th Century – to defend themselves from the onslaught of Europe's excess population. Here the actors in the drama are quite different from those in the earlier sections of this section on pre-colonialism: the Portuguese are a dominant force; a new and curious group, the Afrikaners, appear; the British are, more and more, quite different from John Holt and Beecroft and Charles Macarthy and Maclean. The Africans are different too. They speak a different group of tongues – reflecting a different culture and personality – grow different crops, follow entirely different customs; until comparatively late, even their *élite* was thrown back on itself, evolving within a sort of cultural vacuum. Almost no indigenous, non-Swahili African in eastern and southern Africa had made a fortune from slaving – or from anything else. The story of eastern and southern Africa is simpler, grimmer; unlike the story of the Coast, it tends to be a diversionary, contradictory cul-de-sac, rather than an inevitable chapter in the narrative of human progress.

*

To look at Portugal's rôle in Africa means turning back the centuries – to 1483, when Captain Diogo Cão, more than five meridians south of the Equator, found the reddish-brown silt of a great river flowing tens of miles out in the Atlantic. Cão had found the Zaïre, now known as the Congo. A landing party erected a small monument at the mouth, commemorating their arrival, established friendly relations with the neighboring tribesmen, and sent a party of four upriver with gifts for the paramount chief. Cão then sailed southward.

When he returned, he found his 'embassy' had been seized. Cão consequently took four natives as hostages, explained he would be back in a year or so, and sailed to Lisbon. Here, every effort was made to impress the captured Africans with the wealth and wisdom of Portugal. They were taught the language and Christianity, well housed, clothed as patricians and received at court. From frightened prisoners, they went home ardent apostles of Portuguese culture, and bearers of more gifts for King Nzinga Nkuwu. The hostages were exchanged. Cão sailed deeper into the South Atlantic, to a point near what is now Walvis Bay. When he returned, he went up the Congo to what is now Matadi. Halted by the great cataracts, he had carved on a rock: 'Here came the ships of the illustrious D. João of Portugal.'

The dauntless captain and a party proceeded inland to Mwanza, the Paramount's mud-hut capital; they found him delighted by their visit, and eager to copy his recently returned subjects by embracing Christianity. He asked for missionaries, builders and agricultural instructors, and selected some young favorites to go to Portugal and study.

Portugal's interest in this distant, primitive area, rather than in more accessible places further up the Coast, has always remained a mystery to historians. Lisbon, in the words of the leading authority on Portuguese Africa, James Duffy, 'believed – or wanted to believe – that it was dealing with a king of more sophistication and greater political power than was actually the case. . . . There is no evidence that the Manikongo's people enjoyed a civilization more advanced than they do today.'

Reports at the time, however, 'estimated' the population at 'two and a half million', and the borders of the kingdom as the Atlantic, the Congo, the Kwango and the Dande. Although any estimate of the population could only be absurd, under the circumstances, the exaggerated tribal frontiers were presumably those claimed by the Manikongo. Today, the Bakongo number about a million, and cover a very wide area, including land North of the Congo.

In 1490, a party of priests, skilled workers and returning natives, who had been tutored in a Portuguese monastery, reached Mwanza. A month later, the Manikongo was baptized, taking the name of his fellow-monarch João. A son and some elders copied his example. The new expedition leader, Rui de Sousa, helped the native King put down a small tribal rebellion.

Portugal also settled São Tomé, with religious exiles, criminals and adventurers. Since there was neither royal representative, trading post or fortress in the Congo lands, around the end of the century these castaways began to open trade with Mwanza. They bought mainly slaves for the incipient sugar plantations on the lush, green island, which later writers have claimed to be the most beautiful in Africa.

The son who succeeded Manikongo João, Afonso I, was a completely Westernized, medieval patrician by the time he ascended the ivory stool in 1505. But he failed to change his people, and the slave trade did not help the progress of Christianity. Afonso persisted, getting a fresh supply of over a dozen priests. In the climate, many fell sick. In the moral climate, others became slave-traders. One took a concubine and became a father with a small *f*. Others insisted on returning to Portugal. The last surviving priest of this group died in 1532.

To try to save what had begun as a promising alliance, Portugal's new King Manuel sent Simão da Silva to be Afonso's advisor, bearing a *regimento* of thirtyfour points to be applied in the conduct of the Congolese kingdom's affairs. Silva was to be in charge of the local Portuguese community. Those who abused the natives were to be repatriated. Fallen priests should also be sent home: their slaves should go to Lisbon – with the holy fathers paying the freight bill. Manuel himself hoped for slaves, copper and ivory: a royal factor was appointed. Finally, Silva was told to chart the Congo. In retrospect, it would seem that most of what Silva was supposed to do was technically impossible. In any case, he died within a few months of arrival.

The far-sighted but weak Afonso wrote again to Manuel, outlining the plots and disturbances caused in his kingdom by Portuguese slavers and buccaneers from São Tomé; naïvely, he asked for jurisdiction over the distant island. He asked for more priests to replace the recent arrivals, who had all set up house with the village belles.

In 1526, we find Afonso still fighting slavery, priestly venality and concupiscence – and pleading for fifty more missionaries, preferably including six from the order which had educated his son in Lisbon. This son, Henrique, had been appointed by the Pope, on Lisbon's insistence, Bishop of Utica and Vicar Apostolic of the Congo. He had returned home in 1521, after thirteen years in Europe, to find his European clergy a nest of scoundrels who despised both his piety and his theological ignorance. Says Duffy: 'In the middle 1530s, Henrique died, a useless product of Afonso's vanity and two nations' aborted hopes.' Power in the kingdom was by now largely in the hands of about two hundred resident Portuguese and their more numerous Eurafrican progeny. When Afonso died in the following decade, his son Pedro and Pedro's cousin Diogo bloodily disputed the stool.

In March, 1548, a Jesuit mission arrived. In four months they had baptized over two thousand persons and built three churches, one of which, São Salvador, gave the city the name it still bears today. But the local Portuguese community was equally vigorous in its evangelism, and soon one of the Society, Father Jorge Vaz, was looking for a buyer for the sixty slaves he had acquired. The Jesuits sided with Pedro, who had been deposed, and against Diogo, but the usurper won the dispute: in 1552, the Jesuits departed in disgrace. A second Jesuit mission, arriving the following year, fared no better.

When Diogo died in 1561, violent fighting again broke out over the succession. A bastard of Diogo's briefly took the stool, but was murdered by his brother Bernardo while at Mass. Bernardo took the stool, lived on reasonable terms with the white community and the Lisbon Crown, and died a few years later in tribal warfare.

In 1568, two cannibal tribes, the Jagas and Anzicos, captured São Salvador. Manikongo Alvaro, his chiefs and the whites fled to Hippopotamus Island in the river and the Paramount despatched King Sebastião for help. In 1570, Captain Francisco de Gouveia arrived with six hundred men and thrashed the cannibals. The grateful Alvaro declared his realm to be tributary to the kingdom of Portugal and began sending annual gifts of cowrie shells. In fact, however, the kingdom remained independent *de facto* until the 19th Century.

In 1596, São Salvador was proclaimed a Portuguese city and episcopal see, but by 1615 an expedition found that the whites had died, fled or been absorbed, and that Christianity was almost extinct. The Manikongo became more and more despotic, and vassal tribes rebelled. By 1690, São Salvador's twelve churches – which had given it the name of the 'city of bells' – its fortress and outer walls were all in ruins. When Stanley was there in the 1870s, he reported no trace of the rambling village's Lusitanian past.

*

Three or four hundred miles to the South, in the lands of the Ngola, the port of Luanda had been founded in 1576. The great figure of the time was the navigator Paulo Dias de Novaïs. By the end of the century, Angola had replaced the Congo in Lisbon's interest. In the absence of a strong chief, and in view of the promising development of the slave trade, the Portuguese decided early to impose direct rule in Luanda. Duffy notes that 'Angola still retains today some of the harsh frontier aggressiveness that has characterized its past and left its stamp upon the present; it is a quality which sets the province immediately apart from the more leisurely, perhaps more cosmopolitan, Moçambique.' From Angola, more than three million Negroes went to the Americas: their descendants today must outnumber present-day Angolans.

The Ngola, traditional head of the Kimbundu people, noted with envy the attention paid to the education of the Bakongo, and in 1519 asked for missionary teachers and merchants. The Ngola wisely backed his demand with a sample of Angolan silver, and Manuel took the bait. To lead the expedition he chose Manuel Pacheco and Baltasar de Castro. Pacheco was to collect a priest from São Tomé, explore the coast and land at the Kwanza, where he would take African hostages while Castro was away at the Ngola's *embala.*

At São Tomé, the Captain-General refused to give aid or a priest, looking upon Angola as his own source of slaving, not the King's. The Ngola appeared to have had a change of heart when Castro arrived and, despite his long stay with the native King, Castro eventually came away with nothing achieved and few precious minerals found. Long before, Pacheco, on learning by letter from Castro of the poor success of the mission, had sailed away without waiting for his comrade, and without carrying out the King's other instructions to trade to the South and to chart the coast. The Ngola kept Castro as hostage until a priest should be sent, and he was finally rescued by the despatch of a father from Mwanza. In 1526, after being away six years, Castro finally staggered into Mwanza.

The growth of interest in Angola angered the Portuguese community in Mwanza, who persuaded the Manikongo to raise an army in 1556 to attack the Ngola. Europeans fought on both sides. The Ngola won.

In 1560, Paulos Dias de Novaïs, who was a grandson of the great navigator Bartolomeu Dias, took a group of four Jesuits to Angola on a mainly ecclesiastic mission. While five months were wasted on the coast waiting for permission to come to the chief's *embala,* one of the priests died, but finally Father Gouveia, two lay brothers and Dias set off up-country, where they found the new Ngola, Mbandi, inhospitable. After suffering brutalities, the men were kept peaceably as hostages; Gouveia built a church in the sprawling city, which he says contained five thousand huts. Dias helped Mbandi crush a rebellious chief, and finally became so well-liked by the Ngola that he returned to Lisbon in 1565 with slaves, copper and ivory. Gouveia, for his part, was so popular he was not allowed to leave, even when he was sick; there was a ludicrous, only too final touch, as the distraught chieftain made his witch-doctors use every juju in the tribal lexicon to try, without success, to save the life of his beloved priest. In Lisbon, the captivity of Dias and Gouveia was held to warrant a military occupation.

In 1571, Dias was granted the *donatária* of Angola – a freehold title. He could exploit the territory and in return would bring it under the *aegis* of the Crown and Church. The *donatária* system dated from the previous century when it had been used by the Crown to ensure administration of lands captured from the Moors; (there are also traces of its being used in the 15th Century by Henry the Navigator in Madeira). The *prazo* in Moçambique was a later derivation.

Dias had the right to buy, sell, and raise taxes. Only slaves were royal trade: on these the feudal lord could only collect a fixed commission. The proprietor of a *donatária* could authorize other Portuguese to trade, in return for taxes. At his death, the *donatária* was to revert to the Crown, and to be administered by a Captain-General.

Dias built Luanda, and forts along the Kwanza. But many of his settlers returned home; others died; and his embroilment in tribal wars prevented any useful agricultural scheme from developing. He died on his conquest in 1589. The Jesuits had made little progress with evangelization and complained that Dias was tender-hearted in matters where the 'best sermon was a sword and an iron rod'. Slavers complained that warfare was frequently unfavorable to business, since there was no systematic capture of prisoners. Dias' attempt to find the silver country had been foiled by attacks from the Ngola's forces, and the murder by the Ngola of the score of European traders in his *embala*. Dias' heroism and the endurance of his troops have become historical fact, but the furthest he got inland was about a hundred miles up the Kwanza.

In 1592, Dom Francisco d'Almeida was appointed Governor-General, inaugurating the modest beginnings of a colonial system now over three and a half centuries old. Royal plans were ambitious, but they ran counter to entrenched interests. Notes Duffy: 'The Jesuits and the *conquistadores* refused to be despoiled of their hard-won gains. When d'Almeida fulminated against their arrogance, the priests promptly excommunicated him. The following year, 1593, he was forced to retire from Angola.'

In 1602, João Rodrigues Coutinho took over command with powers to confer royal honors on deserving citizens – notably those who helped him meet the royal demand for 4,250 slaves a year for the New World, and the exploitation of the silver mines at Kambambe. Coutinho brought eight hundred soldiers, plus horses and artillery, the largest Portuguese force yet sent to West Africa. Coutinho died of malaria on the march upriver; he was replaced by Manuel Cerveira Pereira, who reached Kambambe but found there was no silver in commercial quantities.

The next Governor, Manuel Pereira Forjaz, sent an expedition eastward to try to link up with the lands of the Monomotapa. The leader was Baltasar Rebelo de Aragão, builder of the fortress in Muxima. Rebelo de Aragão marched four hundred miles, and says in his account he would probably have completed his mission if he had not been called back to defend Kambambe. Pereira died in 1611, having achieved little.

In 1617, Cerveira Pereira, who had left Angola under a cloud, returned to found São Felipe de Benguela, later to become the Colony's main port. His brutality brought the project to the brink of disaster. Finally a Franciscan friar, an African priest and some other men took advantage of the Governor's illness to put him in a small boat with a ragged sail and a small container of water and float him out to sea. But Cerveira was tough as well as rough; in his unlikely craft, he cruised over three hundred miles to Luanda, where the Jesuits nursed him back to health.

He returned to Benguela in 1620 with the aid of forces sent out by King Felipe, and there were six more years of troubled gubernatorial rule until his death. Gradually the new Colony fell under the dominance of Luanda, until 1641, when it was briefly captured by the Dutch.

Duffy writes: 'The small group of outcasts in Benguela who withstood the lustful ambitions of Cerveira Pereira, the scheming neglect of Luanda and the Dutch occupation have a unique position in the early history of Angola. The combination of renegades from the Congo, exiles and convicts from Portugal, criminals from Brazil, with their wives and children, were the first genuine colonizers of Angola. Frustrated in their search for mineral wealth and unable to compete at first with the slave marts of the North, they were driven to gain an existence from the soil and the sea. The settlement of Benguela was from an early date the home of traders, farmers and fishermen, a strange contrast from the bustling mercantile center of Luanda. Only at Sofala after the decline of the gold trade may one find a parallel in Portuguese Africa to the situation in São Felipe de Benguela in the middle of the 17th Century. Benguela was no showplace of Lusitanian civilization and remained for the next several centuries a haven for undesirables and the extreme element of Portuguese society, but at the same time it became an almost self-sufficient agricultural and fishing community. On a very limited scale its pattern of existence exemplified the traditional Portuguese way of life better than other more flamboyant centers of expansion in Africa and the East.'

In 1617, Luis Mendes de Vasconcelos became Governor of Luanda and almost at once found himself at war with the Ngola. When João Correia de Sousa succeeded Mendes in 1621, the Ngola sent his sister, Jinga, and an 'embassy' to sue for peace. Jinga finally negotiated a full Kimbundu-Portuguese treaty, and capped a year in Luanda by being baptized in the cathedral with great pomp. She took the Governor's name, to become Dona Ana de Sousa.

Duffy notes that 'Christianity rested easily on the soul of this impressive virago. The year following, she adroitly poisoned her brother, who had been chased from his *kraal* by a Portuguese column after breaking the treaty his sister had signed with the Europeans. In a barbaric ceremony, Jinga declared herself Queen.' Allied with cannibals, she fought her own people, then the Portuguese. Tribal wars increased, says Duffy, 'with bloody monotony until 1636 when emissaries from Governor Francisco de Vasconcelos da Cunha prevailed upon Queen Jinga to make peace.'

In 1641, the Dutch Navy took São Tomé, Luanda and Benguela. In 1645, Brazil, alarmed at the loss of slave supplies, sent an army to help Portugal reconquer Angola but this force was massacred by Jaga cannibals. A second Brazilian army defeated the Dutch and their zealous new native ally – none other than Queen Jinga. But the Dutch were only finally driven out by Salvador Correia de Sá e Benavides, former Governor of Rio, who brought fifteen hundred men and fifteen ships, more Brazilian than Portuguese. The energetic new Governor, in three years, assured Crown control over about fifty thousand square miles of land, and generally got the territory 'moving'. He set a pattern for choosing top Angolan administrators from the Colony of Brazil.

Already the distant African domain was beginning to look, itself, like a Colony, and successive Governors had a hard time resisting the entrenched interests of permanent settlers – some second or third generation, some mulatto – and of the unscrupulous Jesuits, who had a finger in everything. The tribes were far from pacified, also. From 1665 to 1685 all the major ethnos rose against the Portuguese. Lusitania vigorously reacted. The Congo was conquered; the Manikongo, António I, died in battle. The Ngola was defeated by the twentythree-year-old Governor Francisco de Tavora. Even Queen Jinga was subdued in her tempestuous senility. The Jaga were scattered. Slaving posts were set up inland. A government charter was drawn up for the whole of 'Angola'.

*

For a century, Angola lived and even prospered on expedients. It was in 1765 that a new Governor, Francisco de Sousa Coutinho, arrived with ideas that went beyond the trade in slaves. He envisaged systematic occupation, the settling of colonists in the healthy highlands. Although most of his plans were never allowed to blossom, Portuguese historians still see him as Angola's best Governor. In 1819, another live-wire, Tovar de Albuquerque, also shook the sleepy Colony, and initiated the culture of coffee and cotton. He reformed fiscality, started a public works program and pioneered inland mails. He was deposed in the uprising which followed the independence of Brazil in 1822, and the subsequent troubles in Portugal.

By then, Angola at its highest society levels had a coffee-colored look which has since served Portuguese propaganda. Duffy points out: 'Miscegenation in Portuguese Africa, although admirably free from the sense of shame which accompanied it in English colonies, still must be considered primarily as erotic expediency; it has become colonial policy only in retrospect.'

Luanda rejected Brazil's offer for federation between Brazil, Moçambique and Angola, although Benguela was in favor. Disorders rent the Colony until the appointment of a Liberal Governor, Bernardo Vidal, in 1834. Lisbon policy vacillated,

but most legislative powers were still reserved to the metro-
politan parliament. The free populations of the overseas
territories became Portuguese citizens in name, in 1838. Some
lasting reforms were introduced, with which the name of
Prime Minister Sá de Bandeira are associated. He officially
abolished slavery in 1836, and removed Vidal in 1838 for
taking bribes to allow it to continue. The traffic still persisted, however, until 1845, when Governor Pedro Alexandre
da Cunha co-operated with Britain's Royal Navy in abolishing it.

ix

East Africa : the Zanj, Azania and the Portuguese

EXPLORATION OF THE EASTERN COAST OF AFRICA started earlier
than travels on the Western Coast, the Congo and Angola
excepted; but it has less of a history. Herodotus records a
supposed circumnavigation of Africa. Two generations before
Ptolemy, the *Periplus of the Erythrean Sea* was composed by
an unknown Greek navigator during the second half of the
1st Century AD. It shows some dimly recognizable portions
of the eastern coast of Africa. Ptolemy's own map is slightly
different. The *Periplus* notes that Arabian ships were then
common in the area. The Arabians were the first regular
visitors to what they called the Zanj, and the writer Abdul
Hassan ibn Hussein ibn Ali al-Masudi went down the coast
in the early part of the 10th Century aboard an Omani
trading vessel. Before dying in Cairo in 956, he wrote about
his voyage.

The Zanj – the Blacks, or the Land of the Blacks – was
probably a Persian word, and may date from the incursions
of the Shirazi. From early times, once ships were able to make
the voyage, the Zanj attracted attention. Nature had been
kinder to the Black Africans than to the Arabs. They had

ivory, gold and cattle, sorghum and honey. By the 12th Century, when Adrisi, protégé of Roger, the Norman King of Sicily, visited Africa, most of the coastal tribes of East Africa were reportedly smelting and exporting iron. The Zimbabwes may have been exporting it four centuries before. The polity of the area was mostly seated in divine kingships or chieftaincies.

The trade routes were the sea. A writer says: 'What the Sahara was to West Africa, one may emphasize the Indian Ocean was to East and South-East Africa. . . . Camels crossed the one, sailing ships the other.' Monsoon winds carried this Ocean's trade in the convenient directions – North-East and South-West. Numerous records exist of early commerce, with Arabians, Indians, Persians, Greeks and Chinese. The last four peoples, already well settled into civilizations, found the peoples of the East African coast quite anarchical. They describe them variously as 'savage', disunited, 'piratical'. For this reason, traders confined themselves largely to islands like Kilwa Kisiwani, Songo Mnara and Sanje ya Kati, where in recent years considerable quantities of Chinese porcelain, amber, topaz and cornelians have been found.

Elements of unity date from Arabian penetration; the Arabians helped this trend with their language which, bastardized and heavily infiltrated with Bantu words – and in more recent years with German and English words – became the tongue ki-Swahili; today, this is still an important lingua franca. Also under Arabian impulsion, new exports developed – tortoiseshell, frankincense, copper, rhinoceros horn and slaves. Slavery was then ethical throughout the Middle East, and the presence of a less sophisticated people to the South was an obvious temptation.

From the 15th Century, when East Africa was generically referred to as Azania, the great trading partners were the Chinese, who were builders of big ships with watertight bulkheads and inventors of the magnetic compass. They were also fine sailors. The Africans welcomed the contact. In 1414, Malindi sent envoys, in Chinese ships, to the Emperor of China with the gift of a giraffe. The main Chinese exports to Azania were silks, brocades, porcelain and lacquerwork. The origin of the name Azania is unclear, but it is obviously a European word.

By the end of the 15th Century, a great new commercial power appeared. In his voyage of 1487–88, Bartolomeu Dias rounded the Cape and initiated a period in which the Portuguese flag would be, for two centuries, the emblem of power in the Indian Ocean. The supremacy of the Portuguese in East African trade was to be momentarily defied by the Ottoman Empire, which occupied Egypt in 1517 and controlled the Red Sea. Ottoman power, however, soon became nominal in Egypt, and the challenge receded.

The trading islands were essentially Arab and Shirazi creations – a fact recorded in recent times, in one of them, Zanzibar, by the presence of an Afro-Shirazi Party. But as the African mainlanders became the plebeian majority of the populations, they imported their culture, style of dwellings and so on.

Vasco da Gama returned to the scene of Dias' exploit in early 1498. In March, he docked at Moçambique harbor. The sheikh of the island, an appointee of the Sultan of Kilwa, thought the Portuguese must be Muslim traders. They soon corrected this impression; negotiations broke down and the visitors departed, bombarding the little city from their ships. At Mombasa, da Gama sent two convicts ashore with beads for the local sheikh; but this parley also degenerated hastily. The Arabians tried unsuccessfully to scuttle the Portuguese ships. The convoy sailed North to Malindi, capturing a loaded dhow on the way. At Malindi, da Gama forced the ruler to give him an Indian Ocean pilot, and reached some sort of trading agreement. This alliance was to last for the remainder of the century. Elsewhere the navigator's high-handed manner cost him apparently needless animosities.

Portuguese contact with the Black African population, during the 16th and 17th Centuries, was to be limited to the hinterland of the shoreline from Sofala to Quelimane. Arabs or mulattos (who, with a few Arabized Negroes made up the Swahili) ruled the coast. At the time of da Gama's arrival, Kilwa was the main power, monopolizing Sofala's gold trade. There was general Arab hostility to the new competition, although the Portuguese were able to some extent to play rival sultans against each other.

In 1505, a fleet of twentythree ships was sent to India under Francisco d'Almeida. On the East African coast, d'Almeida attacked Kilwa and built and garrisoned the stone fort of Santiago. Mombasa was bombarded, burned and looted. By 1510, Portuguese authority was complete on the coast; but in 1512, the Arabians retook Kilwa, and there were challenges in Mombasa in 1528. The cannons roared regularly down the years, and the Portuguese captain at Malindi was never completely able to prevent the flow of Arab contraband into India. Smuggling also affected Sofala – some of it by Portuguese privateers.

Later in the century, wars in the interior seriously affected the gold trade, while Arabian challenges to Portuguese supremacy in Indian Ocean commerce led to naval and shore warfare on the coast. To increase its hold on commerce, and to cure the anarchy inland, the Portuguese pushed into the interior; by 1550, they had established an envoy at the Monomotapa's court – António Caiado, a trader at Great Zimbabwe who became the African King's advisor. Caiado was given by Lisbon the vice-regal appointment of Captain of the Gates.

In 1607, the then Monomotapa deeded to the Portuguese Crown the contents of his mines in return for military protection. The treaty says: 'I, the emperor Monomotapa . . . give to His Majesty . . . all the mines of gold, copper, iron, lead and tin which may be in my empire, so long as (he) . . . shall maintain me in my position.' Portugal also offered aid against a robber baron who was troubling the ruler. But the allies soon quarreled, and the quarrel rotted into conflict. In 1629, following defeat in war, the Monomotapa signed a further treaty accepting Portuguese overlordship, and agreeing to the presence of Christian missions. Portugal was to have a monopoly of trade.

Travels into the hinterland had begun in 1505 with António Fernandes – probably a convict left at Sofala by d'Almeida. He explored Manicaland and parts of Mashonaland – the eastern half of what is today Rhodesia. He recommended that a trade 'factory' be established up either the Lundi or Save rivers, whence gold could be brought from the Monomotapa. Finally, the Zambezi was preferred.

Moçambique became an important port of call of Portugal's globe-girdling mercantile empire, and some Portuguese were tempted to settle there. Essentially it was a trading post, with the Captain acting as royal commission agent and monopolist on certain trade items not reserved to the Crown. He was also, of course, administrator and commander. The Portuguese bought gold, ivory and ambergris, and sold beads and cloth. For most of the 16th Century, the Captain had little control beyond the coastline. The European population, beginning at about a hundred, reached about four times that number by the end of the century.

In 1531, the Captain at Moçambique established a market at Sena, on the Zambezi, and from here plantation and colonization schemes were to be initiated later. Tete, two hundred and sixty miles from the sea, was founded in the same decade.

Sebastião ascended the Portuguese throne in 1568, at the age of fourteen, and soon became interested in African empire-building. The following year he dispatched a volunteer army of one thousand men to Moçambique under Francisco Barreto, a former Governor-General of India, with instructions to obtain a harder treaty from the Monomotapa. In November, 1571, the force sailed up-river to Sena, where problems of feeding and hygiene were peremptorily semi-solved by butchering the Muslim community – in some cases by firing them from cannon.

An envoy sent to the Monomotapa drowned in the Zambezi, and six months were spent needlessly waiting for his return. Barreto exhausted his bored army on a rebellious local chief, finally made contact with the Monomotapa, presented his terms and returned downriver. When he came back to Sena in May, 1573, only one hundred and eighty men had survived. Barreto himself died of exhaustion and fever two weeks later. The expedition, in spite of encouragement from the Monomotapa, was withdrawn. A 1574 expedition under Vasco Fernandes Homem was more successful, getting somewhere near modern Umtali (Rhodesia), and making arrangements concerning mines with local chiefs. But a two-hundred-man garrison left behind at Chicoa was massacred after Homem's departure.

Portuguese rule soon became arbitrary and cruel, both on the coast and in those places where it occasionally existed up-country. To encourage the Portuguese to depart, some African chieftains closed their mines. The Nguni king tried to outwit the Portuguese by being even more barbarous than they: he had his own mineworkers massacred.

Lisbon decided to concentrate its East African operations on Moçambique, which was made a dependency of the vice-regal administration of India. Fort Jesus was built at Mombasa in 1593 to reinforce the limited coastal control of the Captains of Malindi and Moçambique. Portuguese trade between Africa and India flourished at the turn of the century – despite British and Dutch challenges to the far eastern empire, the capture of Fort Jesus by the Omanis in 1599, and the deaths of two thousand five hundred Portuguese, Indians, Arabs and Swahili at the post. But the Portuguese from then on tended to limit their attention to Moçambique; the coast North of Cape Delgado was recognized as an Arabian sphere.

By 1590, the importance of Sofala was diminishing. At Sena, trade continued, with the Portuguese paying tributes of cloth and beads to the embassy which the Monomotapa sent there every three years. Sena then had a fort, warehouses, a church, a population of about fifty Portuguese, and nearly one thousand Indians and mulattos. Tete was almost as large, and the Factor had a two thousand-man slave guard given by the Monomotapa. There were lesser establishments at Massapa, Luanza and Bukoto.

Portugal's continuing advantage over other European powers in the Indian Ocean area was assisted by Lisbon's enjoyment of a sort of corner in naval charts. At the time, English, French and Dutch competitors paid high prices for maps, and for the information available from Arab mariners. There was a considerable traffic in fake charts. But relatively little could be done by Portugal with its advantages. The possibilities were limited. Portugal's slaving interests in Africa were mainly confined to Angola, the principal source of supply for Brazil. In East Africa, although slaving gradually developed, Portugal sought principally to develop and protect Indian Ocean trade, and to extract gold and silver from the mines of Manicaland. A fresh Zambezi gold expedition was ordered by Felipe III in 1608, but ended in failure.

Also in this period began the growth of the *prazo,* or plantation system, spreading out from Sena and Tete. It was this which kept up the Lisbon court's hopes of genuine colonization. In 1643, João IV, the first King of the Braganza line,

219

opened Portugal-India trade to all Portuguese; 'India' then included, in the Portuguese expression, the small Indian Ocean stations in Africa. But this, and a further order in 1671 applying specifically to Zambézia, met heated objections from entrenched interests, and these decrees were never applied.

*

It was noted earlier in this book that when Catherine of Braganza married England's Charles II in 1661, England received Tangiers; another part of Catarina's dowry was Bombay, and the change of power brought many Portuguese Indians to Portuguese East Africa, where they established a foothold in trade. As the century drew to a close, slave-trading began to be a serious item in commerce, and was to grow steadily in the century that followed.

In the interior, the degenerating political situation had taken a dramatic turn for the better in 1628, when a rebellious new Monomotapa, Kapranzine, had been defeated in war and replaced by his pro-Portuguese nephew Manuza. Kapranzine had denounced agreements signed by his father, besieged Portuguese fortresses and blockaded trade. Manuza signed a new agreement pledging vassalage to the Portuguese Crown. To each new Captain at Moçambique, the Mono-motapa would send three pieces of gold in tribute. The Portuguese would enjoy free movement across the realm; the Arabs would be expelled, churches and missions built. All Kapranzine's claims were renounced. Manuza also converted, and took the Christian name Felipe.

By the end of the 17th Century, the gains had been lost, and were not to be fully recovered for two hundred years. Portugal's supremacy in the Far East was destroyed, principally by England; its empire there was reduced to a few enclaves like Macão and Goa. At the beginning of the 18th Century, the Sofala garrison was withdrawn. 'Portuguese subjects at Sena and Tete and on the surrounding estates,' writes Duffy, 'lived in barbarically splendid isolation, squabbling with each other and with the Africans, creating a half-caste community which recognized no law but its own.'

Zanzibar and the exploration of Capricorn Africa

EXPLORATION OF THE INTERIOR to the North came at first by way of the Nile. In a five-year trip, 1769–74, the Scots explorer James Bruce came up through Egypt to trace the source of the Blue Nile in Ethiopia. The East African coast, at this period, was still under Arabian influence. The Imam Seyyid Saïd, who ruled in Muscat from 1806 to 1856, built up a navy and reasserted Arab claims to the coastal ports, basing himself on Zanzibar and exacting tribute and customs. In Zanzibar, he pioneered the culture of cloves, with such success that, by the time the Imam died, the island and its neighbor Pemba were producing three-quarters of the world's supply.

Under Saïd, Zanzibar became the chief commercial center of the coast, the main chandler post for ships, the export market for the slaves and ivory of the mainland, the import market for beads, cloth, arms and hardware from India, Europe and America. Saïd spent more and more of his time there, and in 1840 made it his capital. A class of Arabian plantation-owners formed his court, while other Muscat and Oman Arabs arrived to pioneer the mainland market, borrowing money from Indian usurers and disappearing up-country for years at a time.

The trade routes of the interior from Lake Tanganyika to the coast had been pioneered by an African people, the wa-Nyamwezi. In the 1820s they pushed as far West as the Mulunda country – Katanga. They traded on their own account, and in conjunction with the Zanzibari and 'Swahili', into Buganda, Bunyoro and other Ugandan kingdoms. They were famous as bearers, for which work they trained their children from infancy. With the money they earned trading or bearing they bought slaves, who tilled their farms while they traveled.

Gradually, the Nyamwezi became bearers more than traders, as they were unable to compete with the greater capital and superior organization of the Zanzibari and other Arabic-speaking merchants. The latter carried more – and more varied – goods, including guns, which were gradually becoming the trade item most sought after by African chiefs. At places like Tabora in the Nyamwezi country, or Ujiji on Lake Tanganyika, the Arabs exercized political influence similar to that of Europeans at the West Coast trading stations. West of the Lake, Zanzibari or Swahili, in alliance with wa-Nyamwezi, sometimes overthrew local rulers and usurped small chieftaincies; but on the whole the Arabs used little force – except to capture slaves – and worked mainly through intrigue and negotiation.

In Uganda, by the 'Fifties or early 'Sixties, the Arabs of Khartum, referred to as 'Turks', began to challenge Zanzibari influence. Zanzibar, by then, had a long alliance with Britain, starting with Saïd's predecessor during the early part of the Napoleonic wars, and continued to the satisfaction of both parties since: Britain still welcomed any influence in the Indian Ocean which halted possible French advances. Thanks to Saïd, Britain saw the possibility of avoiding the anarchic multiplicity of power complexes with which London had to deal in the African West. This could be an advantage both for the development of legitimate trade, and for checking slaving.

In 1822, when Saïd still resided in Muscat, he agreed to sign a treaty with the British, limiting slaving to the Western half of the Indian Ocean. This prevented slavers importing 'flesh' into British India. When Saïd moved to Zanzibar in 1840, Britain's first East African Consulate was established at his court. In 1845, a further treaty limited slaving to the Sultan's personal African dominions. Naval Abolition squadrons now began to clean up the Indian Ocean just as they had swept the Eastern Atlantic for a generation.

In 1861, five years after the Sultan's death, one of his sons took Muscat and the other Zanzibar, thus dividing the kingdom. In 1873, Barghash, who had taken Zanzibar, agreed to abolish slave-trading altogether. A Christian cathedral was built on the site of Zanzibar's great slave market. But East African interests continued to slave, and to sell illicitly into

Zanzibar and Pemba. The status of slavery continued, of course, and was only to be slowly abolished on the islands in colonial times. The ivory trade grew, and to some extent this caused a continuance of slaving. Bearers for ivory coffles were often slaves, and the currency used to buy ivory – arms and ammunition – were in turn used for tribal wars, the reason or result of which was to procure human coin. In East Africa, there was no suitable substitute – like palm oil in the West – for the money to be made from slaving. Nyamwezi farmers, Swahili traders, clove-planters on Zanzibar and Pemba all needed a regular supply of slave labor. This sort of sleepy, semi-illegal, feudal, Arabized type of economy would probably have continued for some time, had Germany's ambitions in the sector not started a sudden colonial scramble for territory.

*

Two German missionaries, Johannes Ludwig Krapf and Johannes Rebmann, were the first Europeans to explore Central East Africa from the Ocean side. They brought back accounts of two snow-capped mountains, Kilimanjaro and Kenya. This and other aspects of their narrative fired their compatriots' imagination – despite widespread disbelief of their accounts – and between 1862 and 1869, Gerhard Rohlfs explored land to the North of the East African highlands.

From 1870 to 1874, Gustav Nachtigal and others explored the Sudan between Lake Chad and the Nile. Between 1860 and 1872, Karl Mauchs became the first European since the Renaissance Portuguese to explore the derelict former empire of the Monomotapas. German missions had preceded all these initiatives, but had been concentrated in Western, Southern and South-West Africa.

Krapf and Rebmann were followed into the 'eternal snows' area by a British Methodist missionary, Rev. Charles New, who climbed Kilimanjaro to the snowline and was later nearly killed by Masaï. To the South, Dr. David Livingstone had begun his endless journeyings as a missionary, doctor and geographer as early as 1842. He had married the daughter of another famous evangelist; Mary Moffat Livingstone died on the gospel trail, and Livingstone himself was to finish his life in Africa.

From 1842 to 1846, Livingstone had crossed the Kalahari twice and explored the upper reaches of the Zambezi. In 1852, he had set out from Cape Town, reached the upper stream of the Lualaba (the upper Congo), marched from the West coast to the East coast and sighted the famous cataract which he baptized Victoria Falls. In 1858, he had been appointed Her Majesty's Consul for the East Coast and the Unexplored Interior. He had led an expedition to investigate the navigability of the lower Zambezi, a task which occupied him until 1864.

In 1866, the dour, hardy Scottish doctor had set off again to explore the land between Lakes Nyasa and Tanganyika. The Church in Nyasaland – now Malawi – traces its origins to Livingstone, and the country's main city, Blantyre, is named after Livingstone's Scottish birthplace. On his trip, he joined an Arab slave-trading party. Livingstone's tests of endurance were among the most difficult to which Africa's great discoverers were exposed; he covered enormous distances in conditions of pain, sickness and great fatigue. It was during this monumental journey that he disappeared from contact with the outside world for years, until he was finally discovered by the *New York Herald* reporter, Henry Stanley, on November 10, 1871 (Livingtone's diary says October 28, but appears to be at fault).

Stanley brought Livingstone news of the defeat of France at Sedan, the laying of the trans-Atlantic cable, and much else that had happened while the wanderer had been 'lost' in the uncharted brush. The two explorers marched from their meeting point, Ujiji, up the lake to a point about ten miles South of the present Murundi capital of Usumbura, where they parted – Stanley to return to the coast, Livingstone to explore the Lualaba, which he thought was the Nile. When Livingstone died in 1873, his faithful bearers smoked his body and brought it down to the coast.

Verney Lovett Cameron, who came out to join Livingstone and help him with his researches, arrived in Zanzibar in December, 1872. He learned of Livingstone's death while on the trek up-country. He continued westward, reaching Benguela in 1875, thus possibly becoming the first white man to cross Africa from East to West.

Stanley's own journeys are perhaps the most well known

of any African explorer's. In 1869, James Gordon Bennett Jr., owner of the *Herald*, told Stanley in Paris that he wanted him to cover the Suez Canal inauguration, continue from there to India, and then on to Africa to find Dr Livingstone. Carrying out this fantastic assignment brought Stanley to Zanzibar in January, 1871, where he stayed with the British Consul and prepared his trip. The following month, he crossed to Bagamoyo, on the mainland. From here he set out with a British seaman and an American called Goodhue, who was living on Zanzibar, plus a great retinue of porters.

It was one of the best-equipped expeditions ever seen, and Stanley upheld the traditions of his profession by taking with him choice foods and wines. In the traditional phrase, no expense was spared, and it was several months before this very far-flung reporter began to file despatches. His white companions died en route, and most of his porters succumbed or deserted. Bedraggled, weary and with only a small clutch of bearers left, he reached Livingstone's *boma* at Ujiji at the end of the year.

Upon his return to Europe and America, Stanley was urged to return to Africa, on behalf of the *New York Herald* and the London *Daily Telegraph*, to follow the Lualaba to the sea. He again set out from Bagamoyo, and in a journey that took nine hundred and ninetynine days, cost the life of his European companions and scores of his followers, this eternally lonely and bitter Welsh orphan accomplished the best-known journey of exploration of all time. The trip, which showed that the Lualaba was the Congo, and that the Congo had sixty waterfalls impeding its navigation, inspired King Leopold of the Belgians to press for the Berlin Conference of 1884–85.

The saga of the incredible passage from Bagamoyo to Boma on the South Atlantic probably has no parallel for sheer individual greatness in the history of Black Africa. In intellectual terms, Stanley's journey does not compare to Barth's in the Western Sudan; academically, it was a cartographical feat and a military reconnaissance, little more. But the human mind still boggles that one man could survive so much.

Stanley, three European assistants and two hundred and

twentyfour bearers left Zanzibar for the mainland port on November 12, 1874. The march began five days later. The 'property' of the expedition, listed by the explorer, consisted of: seventytwo bales of cloth, thirtysix sacks of beads, four headloads of wire, fourteen boxes of assorted stores, twenty-three boxes of ammunition, two headloads of photographic material, three loads of 'Europeans personal baggage', a dismantled river-boat carried in twelve headloads, six loads of pontoons, one box of pharmaceuticals, one load of cooking utensils and 'twelve other miscellaneous loads'.

By January, 1875, this immense caravan found itself in dense forest, cutting a passage through the bush, climbing terrible hills, besieged by warriors and decimated by death, desertions and disease. Only its Snyders and Stanley's indomitable will kept the suffering column pointed forward. On January 24, a major battle was fought at Vinyata, in Ituru; one of Stanley's four 'military detachments' was annihilated, while only five members of another survived; but the attackers were repulsed.

By the end of February, the expedition reached Lake Victoria; one European assistant, Edward Pocock, had died near the coast, and a second, Frederick Barker, was soon to follow. The *Lady Alice*, twentyfour feet long and six feet wide, was floated at Kagehyi, and Stanley and ten sailors set off around the lake, leaving Frank Pocock (Edward's brother), and Barker with the train of the column.

After Ripon Falls, where the Nile leaves the lake, Stanley came to Usavara on April 4, and was at first much impressed by the Kabaka of Buganda, Mtesa. 'I see in him the light that shall lighten the darkness of this benighted region, a prince well worth the most hearty sympathies and evangelical teaching which Europe can give him. I see in him the fruition of Livingstone's hopes, for with his aid the civilization and enlightenment of a vast portion of Central Africa becomes most possible.' Stanley rejoined his 'base camp' at Kagehyi on May 5 and learned of Barker's death and other misfortunes.

The force then moved down from Lake Victoria to Lake Tanganyika, fighting several battles with the bellicose islanders. Stanley always believed in punishing his attackers if he could, and his daring reprisal raid on Bumbireh Island with two

226

hundred and fifty men in six large canoes, procured locally, is typical. With his own men, he was just but severe, frequently keeping discipline by allowing the most loyal followers to chose punishments for captured deserters. On August 23, Stanley rejoined Mtesa at Jinja.

He was received with 'such state as is not to be found in Africa out of Egypt'. There was an honor guard of thousands. Mtesa wanted trade with Europe and offered Stanley an army for the journey to what is now called Lake Edward.

Stanley first followed Mtesa to war against the Wavuma – estimating the Baganda force at one hundred and fifty thousand warriors, fifty thousand women, fifty thousand slaves and boys, led by the Katikiro (Vizier) and the King himself. Four hundred canoes carried a ten thousand man navy, and there were four hundred women warriors. The Wavuma navy proved better at first, but with Stanley as an unexpected strategic advisor the Baganda gradually edged toward victory.

To fill the spare time between battles, Stanley began translating the Scriptures for Mtesa. The Baganda won a lake engagement on September 21, but the following day were decisively thrashed. Stanley's early high opinion of Mtesa wavered, and he wrote: 'Mtesa is like a child. It is useless to advise him; any of his slaves or chiefs who will flatter him makes him oblivious of all counsel tending to his honor. The Wavuma deserve all praise for their hardihood and courage, while the Waganda to me make themselves objects of contempt.' The following day, the explorer noted: 'I have written well of Mtesa, but I begin to think I was too premature in my praise.'

On October 12, Mtesa converted to Christianity. Two days later, the Wavuma surrendered. On the morrow, before dawn, Mtesa burned Nakaranga and set out for his old capital at Ulagalla. Stanley recovered his admiration for the Kabaka, writing on November 8, 1875: 'Mtesa is the most intelligent African, who owes his intelligence to his own natural capacity, in or out of Africa I ever saw. His faculties are of a very high order. He is not adverse to flattery, and herein is one weak fault: he is also too fond of women.' Stanley was deeply impressed by his power: 'When he blows his nose, the three greatest chiefs rush down on their knees, and implore the honor of brushing or drying the mucus with a napkin. If he smiles, the whole court smiles. If he frowns, instantly all wear submissive, patient looks. If he storms, all fall prone to the ground, and swear to clutch the moon for him should he desire. Often, they have caught full-grown lions, leopards, crocodiles, boa constrictors alive for him.'

Mtesa supplied about two thousand men as an escort for Stanley when his columns left friendly Buganda for hostile Bunyoro on January 2, 1876. But on January 12, encamped on a bluff over Lake Edward, the force was surrounded by hostile tribesmen and the Baganda had to fight their way back toward Buganda. Stanley and his men left later, heading South-West toward Lake Tanganyika. He halted at Kafurro, capital of the friendly King of Karagwe, then under threat from the expanding kingdom of Rwanda. Stanley left Kafurro on March 1, now suffering repeatedly from fevers, still heading for Lake Tanganyika: on April 10, he noted that 'the watershed at which the Nile and the Congo are born is hardly two miles wide from base to base' – an indication that he already felt that the Lualaba was the Congo.

On the 21st, while at Sesombo, Stanley noted the arrival of Mirambo, the famous African robber-baron and slaver. Musketry was fired in greeting of the dread figure, and hundreds of women ululated; the following day, Stanley was presented to the notorious chief, a tall, lithe, handsome man of about his own age – thirtyfive. Stanley was impressed by the simplicity and healthy look of the Ruga-Ruga leader, who had been a thorn in the side of the Arabs and who had become the chief central African dealer in ivory. The two men took a blood oath of brotherhood that night. The next day, Stanley left with five of Mirambo's men to ensure safe-conduct. Mirambo also sent bullocks, cattle and calves after his new brother, now advancing into hostile, savage country. There were nearly two hundred miles to go before Stanley once again found himself in Ujiji, where he had overtaken Livingstone five and a half years earlier.

On June 11, Stanley began sailing around Lake Tanganyika, discovering the depredations of the Ndereh tribesmen. On June 20, he went through a village where all except fifty huts were burned, dead men lay speared in the streets and skulls and broken calabashes rolled underfoot. 'Blood, dried and black' stained the remaining walls. It was a warning of what lay in store for the expedition. Stanley's men looted the abandoned town. Stanley found the lake to be rising and to have no effluent. On June 29, he floated three feet over the roofs of a submerged village.

Serious fighting began again on July 27, when unfriendly tribesmen who had refused to sell grain followed the canoe-cade, shaking spears. Stanley answered them with six shots of his Winchester repeating rifle, killing four of the expedition's tormentors. Some of the party seized canoes, fish and nets. An eight hundred and ten-mile circuit of the lake was completed in fiftyone days, with the return to Ujiji on July 31.

The exhausting and dangerous two years which Stanley had survived was to prove but a practice run for the final year of horror that was about to start. The worst part of the long journey began when Stanley left Ujiji on August 25, 1876, into land unexplored by Livingstone or Cameron – whose furthest point heading due West had been Nyangwe, eightyseven miles West of the lake. It was there that, on October 18, Stanley met the most notorious of the Arab slave traders in Central Africa, Hamed bin Mohammed, better known to history by his *nom de guerre,* Tippu Tib. Stanley reached an agreement with him to escort the expedition through the rain forest that lay around them and particularly on the expedition's route to the West. From here, Stanley's task was to follow the Lualaba to the sea and discover whether it was the Congo or, as Livingstone had thought, the Nile.

The entry for November 5, 1876, says: 'Start from Nyangwe North-north-east to Nakasimbi, district of Nyangwe. Marched nine and a half miles for three and a half hours.

'Hamed bin Mohammed *alias* Mtibula, or Tippu-Tib, accompanied by nearly five hundred souls and over two hundred fighting men which, added to our party, make a list of about seven hundred souls. Muini Kibwana and several young Arabs accompany him. Tippu-Tib is the most dashing and adventurous Arab that has ever entered Africa and to ensure success in this exploration I could not have done better than to have secured his aid in exploring a dangerous country. Few tribes will care to dispute our passage now. I

229

look forward in strong hopes to do valuable explorations. From Nyangwe we travelled over a fine rolling plain-like country – crossed one stream going East.'

Stanley found that a slave was worth only a twelfth of an elephant's tusk, or a twelfth to a sixth of a sheep, in these parts; most slaves were taken by force, for nothing. The Arabs and their mulatto offspring had succeeded in by-passing not only the African 'coast middlemen' but also the simple up-country slave-catcher. In addition, the slavers had upwards of a hundred women each, Stanley recorded, from whom they bred warriors and slaves.

Thick forest was encountered; carrying the loads proved a killing task. From time to time, the Lualaba could be seen, but tribes thirty miles from the great river did not know of its existence, 'imprisoned for generations in their woods'. The outlook from hilltops offered no relief, and Tippu Tib became refractory. By November 19, Stanley was having his first brushes with the Wagenya. He and the more intrepid of his followers began to coast down the dangerous river by canoe, while Tippu Tib and the rest of the expedition marched on by land.

By now, the great human train found itself among people so wild that they had to be captured even to be questioned. To feed the great column in this hostile area, the expedition, although equipped to pay in the usual trade goods, often had to plunder. Goats, corn and cassava formed most of their diet, but there were periods of near-famine. Passage down-river was about four miles a day. The land party went more slowly. Smallpox attacked the joint camp in mid-December. Finally, the unnerved Arabs and their wa-Nyamwezi legion had to be released from their contract and allowed to return to Nyangwe. Canoes were purchased and the whole remainder of the expedition was made waterborne.

Fighting began again on the river on January 2; within a few days it became necessary for the expedition to fight for its life almost every day. Whirlpools, cataracts, rapids and the usual bouts of sickness, death and occasional desertion also beset the party. On January 31, describing an engagement with Divari Island tribesmen, Stanley begins: 'Today I thought I would try to pass one day without fighting, but....'

Fighting was heavier on the morrow. Twentythree canoes

attacked from one side, twentyone from the other, 'about 10 of which were enormous things containing probably 500 men.' Later, came 'a magnificent war canoe . . . probably . . . the King's canoe, containing about 100 men. About 6 were perched on a platform at the bow, hideously painted and garnished with head-dresses of feathers, while one stalked backwards and forwards with a crown of feathers. There were probably about 60 paddlers and each paddle was decorated with an ivory ball handle and the staff was wound about with copper and iron wire.' The wire was a sign that trade goods had reached these parts, through Arab slavers.

On February 7, the day's entry in the diary begins laconically: 'River called Ikuta Yacongo' (actually Ikutu ya Kongo: river Congo). The tremendous discovery of the Lualaba's real identity then draws one brief comment: 'Thank God.' There followed days of battle and endurance, hope and despair. On March 15, he camped at what became Stanley Pool – the western narrows of which are now fringed by Kinshasa and Brazzaville. There Stanley entertained four (for once) friendly chiefs. From here, another series of cataracts had to be negotiated, including the terrible canoe-trap which he descriptively called The Cauldron. Stanley lost his young gun-bearer, Kalulu, after whom he named the falls and nearby island that marked the scene of the capsized canoe. Other expedition members had hair-raising escapes. One was even rescued from the waters and enslaved, then released on the strength of rumors of Stanley's spirit of revenge; he even managed to find his way back to the expedition with two others given up for lost, by scudding through rapids in an unguided canoe.

At places the boats had to be carried over hills; at others, the party clung to branches to slow the glide down-stream. Most of April, 1877, was occupied with these perilous exercises; most of the rapids were successfully shot, but at a growing cost in life and goods as some canoes failed to make the passage. This life and death atmosphere did not prevent the disciplinarian Stanley from noticing, on April 17th, that one sack of Blue Matoonda beads was missing. The next day he recovered part of the stolen loot, and flogged five men. On April 26, the six remaining vessels of the expedition were carried over a mountain; carrying the boats continued for several days. It was May 2 before the travelers reached the river again. Then some new canoes had to be made.

On May 20, news was received of European traders down-river. Two days later, a new, speedy, fiftyfour-foot canoe was launched, capable of carrying about sixty people. Progress began again on May 25: Pocock and others who were sick went by water, Stanley and the van of the expedition by land.

June 3 was a 'black woeful day'. In his long Journal entry for that date, Stanley painstakingly describes the terrible state of the river, which had to be descended mainly by roping the expedition's embarkations to bankside trees. Finally, after much preamble, Stanley tells us that 'In the afternoon I sat on the rocks of Zinga looking up river with fieldglass in hand, and after a long waiting I saw a canoe upset with eight heads above water. Kacheche and Wadi Rehani were at once sent along the rocks to render any possible aid. Meanwhile I watched the men in the water, as they were borne into the basin of Bolo-Bolo by the spreading current. I saw their struggles to right her, I saw them raise themselves on the keel of the canoe and paddling. Finally I saw them land, but the canoe was swept down river over the Zinga Falls, then over the Lugulufi Falls, then away out of sight.

'Bad news travels fast. I soon heard the names of the saved and those of the drowned. Among the latter was Frank Pocock.'

Stanley's grief, his attempts to put his feelings into the awkward, sonorous rhetoric he obviously felt was due, are painful to read. Pocock had apparently tried to move down the midstream to avoid the slow progress in the choppy waters near the bank, where however ropes could be used.

Without Pocock, life became a nightmare, since both camp and the rear party of canoes, as well as messengers between the two, needed superintending: the wa-Ngwana bearers were becoming fractious and slow and there was a rash of thieving. If Pocock had died up-river, Stanley would almost certainly never have completed his odyssey. Mean-while, stores were diminishing, local tribes were threatening again and the tormented Stanley publicly prayed for death. Behind his despair, however, the reader scents his unconquer-able ego, and this seems to have restored his equilibrium. On June 12, we find him saying: 'My people anger me, oh so much, and yet I pity and love them. The greatest feeling they provoke in me is astonishment of their apathy.'

By the next month, Stanley was near his goal. On July 17, he noted that in the course of the final lap of the journey the expedition had 'destroyed 28 large towns and three or four score villages, fought 32 battles on land and water, contended with 52 falls and rapids, constructed about 30 miles of tramway work through forests, hauled our canoes and boat up a mountain 1,500 feet high, then over the mountains 6 miles, then lowered them down the slope to the river, lifted by rough mechanical skill our canoes up gigantic boulders 12, 15 and 20 feet high, then formed a tramway over these boulders to pass the falls of Massassa, Nzabi, and Zinga. All this since leaving Nyangwe' (eight months before). The canoes referred to were, of course, not light craft, but hollowed-out tree trunks. The fiftyfour-foot one must have weighed over three tons.

'We obtained as booty in wars,' Stanley adds, 'over $50,000 worth of ivory, 133 tusks and pieces . . . but with the loss of 12 canoes and . . .13 lives, we lost nearly the whole of (it).'

On August 7, Stanley reached Nlamba Nlamba. Kacheche, who had been sent on ahead with three others, without loads, to get supplies from Boma, arrived with five gallons of rum, sacks of rice, potatoes, fish and tobacco, and delicacies for Stanley – tea, sugar, jam, bread, ale and other things. 'The skeletonized men began to revive. . . . The long war against famine is over.'

The next day the column marched five miles to Nsafu and on the ninth another five miles brought them to Boma where Stanley was greeted by Portuguese and British merchants. Here the proud column rested; it was fêted and photographed.

The wa-Ngwana were sent home to Zanzibar by ship. Stanley sailed for Britain and America.

*

Stanley's third journey to Africa, starting this time from the West, was in the service of the Belgian King; a vast and predominantly military initiative, it led to the establishment of the Congo Free State. (In 1961, the present author had the good fortune to discover, in two remote villages of the

233

Mukongo country, three men in their eighties and nineties who had served Stanley and his immediate associates as youthful porters on that expedition.)

Stanley returned to Africa a fourth time, in 1888, to rescue the romantic German figure, Emin Pasha; as Dr Schnitzer, Emin had served with General Gordon in the Sudan, and had been dismissed at the time of Gordon's death. Stanley found him on the borders of modern Uganda and Sudan – and most unwilling to be rescued. (Emin died later in mysterious circumstances, without achieving his cherished objective of a German empire around the headwaters of the Nile.) Stanley retired to England, where he recovered British citizenship, married and became an undistinguished member of parliament.

Earlier, valuable geographical research had been carried out to the North by Richard Burton – later to distinguish himself as Consul to the Bights – and his companion John Speke, an Indian Army officer. Speke accompanied Burton on his Somali expedition in 1854. The following year he fought in the Crimean War. In December, 1856, Burton and Speke were in Zanzibar, whence they set out to explore the lake country.

Halted by fever, they returned to the coast and set out again in June, 1857. Speke's *What Led to the Discovery of the Source of the Nile,* published in 1864, gives the first description of the snowcapped Mountains of the Moon, as the Ruhenzori ridge between the Nile and the Congo watersheds is popularly known. The first major discovery of the explorers was that no river ran North from Lake Tanganyika. Burton fell ill, and Speke went on alone to find Lake Ukerewe, which he renamed Lake Victoria, at the end of July, 1858. He was told a great river which could only be the Nile flowed out of the lake at Jinja, and he assumed the lake to be the Nile's source – an understandable mistake often repeated in modern literature; actually the source is to the South of the lake, in a pebbly spring, at a spot called Bururi, in Burundi.

Speke's discovery of the lake and of a great river which must be the Nile issuing from it was of enormous geographical consequence – although on his return to Britain he was to be met by the usual disbelief of the armchair explorers, who had similarly doubted Krapf's snowy peaks. His account of the great discovery falls a little flat: 'I no longer felt any doubt,' he writes stiffly, 'that the lake at my feet gave birth to that interesting river, the source of which has been the subject of so much speculation, and the object of so many explorers.' Burton, miffed at missing out on the main point of the expedition, also permitted himself to doubt that Speke had found the Nile.

*

Speke had returned to Africa in 1860 with a fellow Indian Army officer, James Grant. They made their difficult way up-country. Again, Speke withstood sickness better than his companion, and reached the court of Mtese (or Mtesa, or Mutesa), the Kabaka of Buganda, alone, in February, 1862. His account of the court is one of the most picturesque in explorer literature, and is perhaps best-known for his measurings of the Kabaka's monstrous, fatted queens.

There was great joy when, at the Kabaka's bidding, Speke shot a sitting bird and a loping vulture on the wing, with 'the king jumping frantically in the air, clapping his hands above his head and singing out "Woh, woh, woh! What wonders!"' (The schoolboyish rendering of Luganda is the explorer's.) Speke was able to observe the pomp and ceremony of the court. Grant rejoined him at the Kabaka's but had again fallen sick by the time Speke went on to see the Nile flowing from the Victoria Nyanza. 'Most beautiful was the scene, nothing could surpass it!' says Speke, always oddly inadequate at such moments. Crocodiles, hippopotami and fishermen's huts dotted the island-strewn river, only half a mile wide at this point. 'I told my men they ought to shave their heads and bathe in the holy river, the cradle of Moses,' Speke tells us in his *Journal of the Discovery of the Source of the Nile*.

Another beautiful cataract he called Ripon Falls, after Lord Ripon of the Royal Geographical Society. He baptized an arm of water from which the Nile flowed the Napoleon Channel, in thanks for France's gold medal the previous year – a reward for his discovery of the lake.

Samuel White Baker, a rich adventurer-explorer who left Cairo on April 15, 1861, to explore the White Nile, had the

235

added eccentricity to take his wife. Mrs Baker's great courage was rewarded by survival. The Bakers were delayed in Khartum by the Egyptian authorities; they finally set off South from there on January 7, 1863, with swimmers tying ropes to clumps of grass in the river in order to haul their vessel along against the southern wind. They met Speke and Grant at Gondokoro. On March 26, 1863, after misadventures with slave-traders, Baker and his men set off with camels for the Victoria Nyanza, with Mrs Baker – after experimenting with the 'ship of the desert' – either walking or riding wild oxen.

They reached what is now called the Victoria Nile in an exhausted condition. Baker gives an interesting description of Bunyoro (the kingdom which has figured in the violent 'lost counties' issue in recent Ugandan history). Their porters deserted them. Mrs Baker collapsed in delirium. But their growing depression was momentarily cured by the discovery of a large lake which they named the Albert Nyanza. Baker writes: 'The zigzag path . . . to the lake was . . . steep. I led the way, grasping a stout bamboo. My wife in extreme weakness tottered down the pass, supporting herself upon my shoulder, and stopping to rest every twenty paces. After a toilsome descent of about two hours, weak with years of fever, but for the moment strengthened by success, we gained the level plain below the cliff. A walk of about a mile . . . brought us to the water's edge. . . . I rushed into the lake and, thirsty with heat and fatigue, with a heart full of gratitude, drank deeply from the Sources of the Nile.'

The Bakers canoed along the lake and up the Victoria Nile, and 'wintered' in Bunyoro, finally making their way back to Gondokoro, on their way to Cairo and England. At Gondokoro, Baker was besieged by the same doubts of nearly all the great explorers:

'As I sat beneath a tree and looked down upon the glorious Nile that flowed a few yards beneath my feet, I pondered upon the value of my toil. I had traced the river to its great Albert source, and as the mighty stream glided before me, the mystery that had ever shrouded its origin was dissolved. I no longer looked upon its waters with a feeling approaching to awe for I knew its home, and had visited its cradle. Had I over-rated the importance of the discovery? and had I wasted some of the best years of my life to obtain a shadow?

I recalled the practical question of Commoro, the chief of Latooka – "Suppose you get to the great lake, what will you do with it? If you find that the large river does flow from it, what then?" '

Baker later returned to the area to head the Khedive's military expedition into the Sudan. The plan was to carry the Egyptian frontier southward, from Gondokoro into what is now northern Uganda. When General Gordon followed Baker as Governor of Egypt's Equatorial Province, he realized it was more accessible from the Indian Ocean than from the North. On Gordon's advice, the Khedive Ismail sent a sea-borne force to occupy the port of Kismayu, but since this was in the Sultan of Zanzibar's territory British diplomatic pressure on the Khedive brought about a withdrawal. From the North, the lines of communication were too long, and Gordon's attempt to bring Buganda and Bunyoro under Cairo rule failed. The project was abandoned in 1877. In 1881, the rising of the Mahdi in the Sudan put an end to Egyptian rule of the Sudan as a whole, and of course to Gordon.

An English contemporary of Baker's, Joseph Thomson, led a long expedition to the lakes at the age of twentytwo. Like many travelers of the period, he had trouble with the warlike Masaï. Thomson recounts his misfortunes with the same light humor which characterized most of the English explorers, and which may have been their principal weapon of survival.

Emin Pasha and Gaëtano Casati were two high-class swashbucklers, from Germany and Italy respectively, who showed enormous courage and great gifts of observation in their travels through East and Central Africa; they have left a valuable book to prove these qualities. The German was a considerable naturalist. Stanley's last expedition, as mentioned earlier, was to rescue Emin (and Casati) although when he finally found them on April 23, 1888, he was in worse state than they were. The German's death, shortly after, is believed by some researchers to have been suicide.

Count Samuel Teleki von Szek of Hungary and Lieutenant Ludwig von Hohnel of Austria explored what is now Northern Kenya in 1887 and 1888 and discovered Lakes Rudolf and Stefanie.

Government and exploration went hand in hand with the travels of Frederick Dealtry Lugard, later Lord Lugard, who foresaw the possibilities of settlement and development in East Africa. Lugard wrote gruffly in 1893: 'I am convinced that the firm hand is the merciful one . . . and that a resolute and decided course at first saves a great deal of loss of life. . . .' Most foreign and indigenous historians of Africa would agree with Lugard today, although most would resent some of his blunt phraseology. Lugard believed in swift and decisive force in anarchical, 19th Century Capricorn Africa, in the imposition of a 'Pax Britannica'.

In the early 'Nineties, the young officer wandered extensively for two years through modern Kenya and Uganda with Sudanese and local levies. He traveled extensively among the Kikuyu, and took a great liking to Uganda. Lugard made treaties with kings and chieftains, built forts, and prepared the terrain for occupation. By then, Britain was seriously contemplating African extensions to its imperial fiefs. Lugard's fortunes and experiences reflect the evolving policy of the period.

*

Fred Lugard was born in Madras in 1858, the son of an East India Company chaplain; his father died in 1865, a year after his return to Britain to take a rural rectory. After a lonely childhood dominated by his mother, Lugard failed the Indian Civil Service examination but passed the Army test in 1877. He saw service at Peshawar, on the North-West Frontier, then in Egypt after Gordon's death, then in Burma. It was an unfortunate love affair that began in Lucknow that pushed him, after a period of numbness and despair, to become the man of action which history remembers. Bored with garrison duty, he had himself put on half-pay and indefinite sick leave; then, in his own words, 'with fifty sovereigns in my belt, and . . . practically no outfit . . . except my favorite . . . rifle, I got on board the first passing ship, as a second-class passenger, and sailed I knew not whither'.

He was rebuffed, both in Rome and at Massawa, in attempts to join the Italian forces fighting in Ethiopia. He sailed on to Zanzibar, where Consul John Kirk had only recently succeeded in 'abolishing' the slave trade: Lugard saw many examples of the continuance of the traffic.

Lugard's first job in East Africa was for the African Lakes Company, which asked him to protect their Lake Nyasa posts from slave-raiders. He canoed up the Kwakwa River from Quelimane to Mopea, whence he continued up the Zambezi with a Polish fellow-agent of the Company. He eventually reached Blantyre, where the Company's local manager, John Moir, persuaded Lugard to lead a raid against the slavers.

The scene of Lugard's first exploits, Lake Nyasa, is part of the Great Rift. A deep, steep-banked lake, given to violent storms, it was and is rich in fish and temperamental dangers for those who travel on its surface. Lugard's expedition went on the Scottish Free Church Mission boat *Ilala*.

The adventurers Lugard had to work with were quarrelsome, and little if any better than the Arab slavers. The 'troops' were of mixed quality. Lugard had misgivings about the expedition. At the initial action, at Karonga, he was badly injured and his party driven off. The single bullet that felled him went through his right arm, part of his chest, and his left wrist. Skilful surgery by a Dr Cross saved his right arm from amputation and restored movement to his left hand, despite the tearing of all the tendons; but this hand was to give him pain for the rest of his life.

The ill-fated expedition suffered fresh tragedy on its return down Lake Nyasa: a spark from the engine fired a gunpowder bag strung around the neck of a sick or wounded African soldier, lying in a steel barge of casualties being towed by the *Ilala*. As most of the soldiers carried their powder in this way, an explosion rocked the whole barge, burning and killing most of the occupants. The whole thing happened, literally, in a flash and the officers aboard the *Ilala* noticed nothing. The convoy continued, in what seemed – to the survivors in the barge – sublime callousness.

Mutiny brewed among the troops at Karonga, and to add to the burned men's troubles the doctor was by now ill himself, and in a raving delirium. Before long, every European in the party was down with fever. Lugard himself was still bedridden from his wounds. Shortly after, he nearly died in a boating accident, but finally reached Blantyre where he recovered. Then he set off back to Karonga to deal with the slave traffic. This time he had some initial successes, routing the slavers and shattering the self-confidence of their ally, Chief Mlozi. He pulled the rowdy Europeans together, won the respect of his men, and stamped out as much of the trade as was possible with his limited means; 1889 found him back in England on leave.

At the end of the year, Britain declared a protectorate over Nyasaland, but Harry Johnston was preferred to Lugard as first Commissioner. Lugard's next job was to be for the East Africa Company, which asked him to lead an expedition up the Sabakhi, establishing trading posts on a trail leading from Mombasa to Machako's, three hundred and fifty miles inland; the ultimate Company aim was the legendary kingdom of Buganda, further West. Mtesa's realm was then a theatre for warring white interests – the Protestant missionaries, known as the *wa-Ingleza*; the Catholics, called *wa-Fransa*; emissaries of Gordon like Linant de Bellefonds; Henry Stanley, and representatives of Consul Kirk, acting in this case for the Sultan of Zanzibar.

In 1884, Mtesa died and his eighteen-year-old son, Mwanga, who succeeded him, began a bitter repression of the Christians. The Anglican bishop, Hannington, was killed as he approached the kingdom by the Busoga trail – the route by which, according to an ancient legend, a conqueror would arrive. The legend held, for it was by this road that the Company's first representative, Frederick Jackson, and later Fred Lugard himself, entered Buganda. Baganda Christians, including a number of children, allowed themselves to be massacred with surpassing courage rather than renounce their faith. (Twentytwo Baganda martyrs were canonized in 1964).

Mwanga was finally driven from the throne, replaced briefly by his brother Kiwewa, then another brother, Kalema, an avowed Muslim. Kalema recommenced the repression of Christians and expelled the handful of Europeans in the country. In 1889, Mwanga was restored, this time with Christian support against the predominantly Muslim forces of his brother. But Protestants and Catholics continued to intrigue against each other, and Mwanga's throne remained insecure. A week before Christmas, 1890, Lugard marched into Mengo, the King's abode, as emissary of the Imperial British East Africa Company.

Lugard was accompanied by two hundred and seventy porters and about fifty Sudanese and Somali soldiers, some of whom had served with Baker, Gordon, Emin Pasha or Stanley. He met Mwanga in some state. After a few days of parleys in the divided court, and in constant fear of assassination, Lugard got the King's signature on a treaty with the Company. But intrigues continued with the *wa-Fransa*, and the camp on Kampala hill, which Mwanga gave Lugard as a residence, lived uneasily until a fort was completed and a hundred soldiers installed in it, under a French-, Turkish- and Arabic-speaking captain called Williams.

After three months, Lugard was ready to attack the Muslims, led by Mwanga's uncle, Mbogo, who was under the protection of the Kabarega of Bunyoro, a neighboring kingdom. Mwanga's Katikiro, or Chief Minister, himself a Protestant, organized the Muganda army. Finally, six hundred and fifty men marched away to war, led by three of the seven white officers.

There was an impressive send-off, with war-drums and frantic dances before the Kabaka. Lugard's own force, with Williams and the two other Europeans, one a doctor, followed a week later. Its armament included a Maxim gun. In fifteen days, the combined force was massed at the frontiers of Bunyoro, and parleying began. After delays and betrayals, Lugard and the Baganda finally attacked, routing the enemy.

Most of the force then returned to Mengo. Lugard and a small party went on to Ankole, another principality, to make a treaty with the ruler, King Nkali. In an exotic ceremony, he became blood brother to Nkali's son. Reinforced, he pushed on through Toro and the Bahima country. He also searched for Emin Pasha, who was once again missing and who finally disappeared for ever in the Congo, reportedly trying to cross the continent to Kamerun.

For Lugard, 1891 was a year of marches, battles, more disputes with death, and effective repression of the slave trade. He built forts, and took the King of Toro, Kasagama, under British protection. Gradually, he pacified unruly Bunyoro. By then, he had a good fighting force of impressive endurance: his crossing of the turbulent Semliki River is a classic of determination. He made a new ally of Selim Bey, the Khedive of Egypt's representative. His caravan grew to number over four thousand soldiers, porters and camp followers, and the group stretched out over seven miles when on the march.

Lugard was famous for his fair dealing. He avoided fighting when possible, forbade his men to wreak exactions on local tribes, and judged disputes with rare impartiality. This, plus his great powers of leadership and his endurance under repeated bouts of fever made him a legendary trail boss. The unwieldy numbers of the caravan diminished as he garrisoned the forts which he built.

It was Lugard's reputation for humane dealing which, more than anything else, brought allegiance from the peoples of the Ugandan kingdoms, as he went about his task of bridging rivers, mapping the country and opening it to the trade of his employer, the Company. In six months, he covered seven hundred miles, 'signing' to the Company all the country west of Buganda as far as the borders of the now-established Congo Free State, and along the Ruwenzori chain to Lake Albert in the North. The expedition also brought back much ivory and salt – all, on Lugard's strict instructions, paid for.

At the height of his triumph, a letter arrived from the Coast with new instructions from the Company: he should withdraw to the Coast; the occupation of Uganda was to be postponed. Heartbroken, Lugard decided to resist; Williams offered to quit his regular Army service and support him. Both men were convinced war would break out all over, and that the Protestants would be massacred, if the British force withdrew. The missions were aroused also, and raised funds to back the hesitant Company in its Uganda venture. The Company agreed to stay on until the end of 1892. Shortly after, the acquittal by Mwanga of a Catholic who had murdered a Protestant led to a fierce outbreak of fighting between the now religiously divided Baganda people.

Mwanga was forced to take refuge on an island in Lake Victoria. He refused Lugard's request to return, so Williams and a Protestant force drove him and his ally, the Catholic bishop, to a more remote island. Mwanga finally agreed to a second treaty. An honest attempt was made to divide the land, especially the strategic lake islands, between Baganda Protestants and Catholics.

With pacification more or less complete, Lugard returned to Britain: Gladstone sent out a commission of enquiry. The end result of this was the establishment of the Protectorate, which took administration out of the wavering Company's hands and entrusted it to Colonial officials. Mwanga was replaced by his small son, Daüdi Chua – father of the present Kabaka Mtesa II, independent Uganda's first Governor-General, then President.

Lugard's third African employer was the British West Charterland Company, which had a mineral-search concession around Lake Ngami, lying to the North of the Kalahari Desert. On the expedition which he had been asked to lead, he was able to take his younger brother, Edward Lugard. His other companions, when he arrived in Cape Town in 1896, were a doctor, an army engineers sergeant and an American mining engineer known as 'Colorado' Browne. At Mafeking, Earl Grey, the newly appointed administrator of Rhodesia, tried to persuade him to join an expedition against the Matabele; but Lugard pushed on with the Company quest, leaving the town in May. He now had ten Europeans, twentyseven Africans, and several mule wagons. Then Browne had a nervous breakdown. Lugard cabled for a replacement, but soldiered on, through country ravaged by rindepest.

At Palapye, Lugard met, and at once unreservedly admired, Paramount Chief Khama of the Ngwato (or Bamangwato), an enlightened ruler, with whom he stayed two weeks. Then he went on, through largely waterless, sandy country, finally reaching Nakalechwe, where Sekgoma, chief of the Batwana, had his capital. Here he found two Europeans, a German and an English trader, and left with them an ailing member of his team. Sekgoma finally signed an agreement, and Lugard began the search for what would be the mining engineer's headquarters, when a new engineer finally overtook the party. Rindepest, locusts and fever beset the group. A German mining engineer arrived, and Lugard sent his brother back to the Cape for fresh supplies.

One of the European party had already died, and now the overseer committed suicide. Fever grew worse; another

European died; yet another set off back to civilization – and died in his tracks. Meanwhile, unknown to Lugard, a supply team sent by Khama was battling gallantly through some of the worst terrain in the world to relieve the British expedition.

Edward returned from the Cape in 1897, bringing with him a resolute wife and their small baby. But Lugard began to lose heart for the gruelling job, and news of growing animosity between Briton and Boer in South Africa, and of the ambitions of Cecil Rhodes, whom he mistrusted and disliked, helped to persuade him to resign, which he did on his thirtyninth birthday.

Lugard wrote to the Foreign Office asking for an appointment in East Africa, but was rebuffed by the bureaucracy of the day. Shortly after, however, the Colonial Secretary, Joseph Chamberlain, offered him command of a proposed West African military force to occupy the hinterland of the Niger and the Gold Coast, and repel the French.

Lugard's next African task, Nigeria, belongs in Part 3 of this book – the colonial section. This task, too, was to be a story of wounds, fevers, betrayals, constant bad luck and a superhuman attachment to honest principles – sometimes under conditions which made this attachment almost tragic-comic.

Lugard set off back through the lunar, South-West African desert at a pace that left most of his followers behind, and brought on agonies of thirst and suffering: his speed caused him to miss the relieving party sent by Khama, until his journey was nearly over.

Lugard's posting to West Africa was fortuitous, for all the caste attitudes he resented and despised most in white relations with black were about to become the rule in the East, Central and Southern parts of the continent. The gnarled, moustachioed warrior, who married a London *Times* lady reporter after a whirlwind courtship, and took her with him to Nigeria, retired in 1919 and became the colonial expert of the House of Lords. He still had the thin, nervous figure that once led him to tell a supposed cannibal chief: 'You wouldn't get a bowl of soup out of me!' In his influential, elder-statesman days, Lugard used his voice to oppose the more ruthless aspects of imperialism, and to put his now

244

famous case for a 'dual mandate' in Africa – Government, and preparing Africans to govern themselves. His loyalties were greater than just patriotism; they went to rigid standards of justice, to the Africans who trusted him, and to hundreds of his compatriots who found their graves in East and West Africa, hoping to help Lugard build the sort of empire worth building. With more Lugards, colonialism might have been less resented, and more successful.

Ethiopia

THE HISTORY OF ETHIOPIA is unique in Africa. One of the mountain kingdom's earliest rulers, Queen Makeda, governed from Axum a territory roughly equivalent to most of modern Ethiopia, plus parts of modern Yemen, across the Red Sea. It was from Axum that this famous 'Queen of Sheba' journeyed northward to Jerusalem to test the wisdom of Solomon who, legend has it, tricked her into sleeping with him by a ruse. From this brief union, the modern Kings of Ethiopia (falsely) claim descent.

The Bible bears witness to Makeda and her journey to Solomon, who is supposed to have made his visitor promise her favors if ever she should take anything in the palace not offered to her. Rising in the night, after a spicy dinner, to drink some unproffered water, she was supposedly held to account by the Jewish monarch, who had spent the earlier part of the night sleeping with Makeda's Negro maidservant. Both women bore children at close dates, the legend says. Makeda made her and Solomon's son, Menelik I, King in her own lifetime, and Ethiopian Emperors still take the title 'Conquering Lion of the Tribe of Judah'. Nothing remains of Axum's early fame, today, but the towering stone obelisks, carved from single hunks of the omnipresent mountains.

Having been influenced early by Judaism, Ethiopia, not

surprisingly, became Christian in the 4th Century AD, thanks to Byzantine missionaries, and remains today a Coptic stronghold. The rise of Islam in the region passed Ethiopia by; isolated in its eyrie, it neither suffered permanent invasion, nor progressed. A brooding country of awe-inspiring mountains and green, fertile valleys thick with lion and birds, its history was a panorama of strangely patterned anarchy, so bloody and spectacular that little remains in the records, in Ge'ez or Amharic – both written tongues – while even less is preserved in the modern extracts. 'Robber barons' of sanguine intransigence divided the lofty realm between them for centuries – until 1855, when the Emperor Theodore's demented genius for leadership and terror sealed much of the kingdom into a bloody bond that was never again completely fractured.

*

The first Europeans to reach Ethiopia were the Greek captains of Ptolemy II and Ptolemy III of Egypt, in the 3rd Century BC. They established coastal trading stations.

Except for Makeda's mention in the Bible, and some 4th Century AD inscriptions in Axum referring to a contemporary king, Aëizanas, son of Ella Amida, little but legend remains of the beginnings of the Ethiopian Dynasty. This inscription, in Ge'ez, Greek and Sabaean (the language of Yemen) bears witness to the real or theoretical extensiveness of the realm (including Yemen) and to the Byzantine conversion of Ethiopia to Christianity.

In the 6th Century, the 'Kings of Habashat and Axum', as the early monarchs were styled, are recorded as making expeditions to Lake Tsana every alternate year to trade cattle, salt and iron for gold by dumb barter. The Axumite caravan went armed because of marauders. Its outward passage was slowed by the cattle, but it habitually returned to Axum in haste, pursued by the seasonal rains.

Also in the 6th Century, Justinian sent an ambassador, Julian, to the Ethiopian court to develop trade. Julian recorded that the King appeared bare-chested and bare-legged, with a gold embroidered linen cloth about his loins, leather halters set with pearls across his back, a gold-embroidered linen turban, gold bracelets and a gold collar. In public, he

246

rode a four-wheeled, gold-plated chariot hauled by four elephants — a trade item sought by Egyptians and Romans as cavalry mounts. He carried a gilded shield and gilt spears. Flutes played during Julian's audience.

The original Ethiopian Church, with a nucleus of Roman trader converts, used Greek, but Ge'ez was used from the 5th Century. The Catholicus of Ethiopia was, until very recent years, subject to the Coptic Patriarch of Alexandria. The Ethiopian Copts still observe the long Coptic fasts, including ten extra days for Lent, and follow the liturgy of St. Mark. As in England, the Church embraced and 'canonized' earlier pagan rituals, including the sacrifice of an ox, a ewe and a nanny-goat at the dedication of a church. Drumming and dancing were absorbed into the liturgy. The Ethiopian Copts follow Jewish dietary superstitions concerning meat, and observe Saturday as holy, as well as Sunday.

Ethiopian contact with the outside world was interrupted in the 8th Century by Arab occupancy of the shoreline and Red Sea islands. It was not restored for some centuries.

In about 1270, the Zagwe dynasty was overthrown by a pretender claiming descent from Solomon and Makeda; he launched a cultural renaissance. Two centuries later, Zar'a Yakob (1434–68) undertook to stamp out paganism altogether. Every Ethiopian was ordered to wear on his brow an amulet inscribed in Ge'ez 'I belong to the Father, the Son and the Holy Ghost.' Amulets worn on the arms were marked 'I deny the Devil in Christ the God' and 'I deny Dasek the accursed. I am the servant of Mary, mother of the World's Creator.' Resisters were despoiled and executed. Spies sought out idolaters, under orders from an Inquisitor called the Keeper of the Hour. These monkish agents lived in celibate reclusion, leaving their hair uncut for fear magicians would use their clipped locks to cast spells. In the latter part of Zar'a Yakob's reign, some of the terror was eased, and the Ethiopian Coptic Church was reconciled with the Vatican. Zar'a Yakob also reformed the Axumite administration.

The Vatican envoy, a Frank, was probably the first Western European to enter the Ethiopian highlands. Ethiopian records say that he was put to shame, in theological argument, by the Coptic elders.

In the 16th Century, a Venetian painter, Nicolo

247

Brancaleone, arrived and collected many royal commissions, particularly for church murals. The distinctive style of Ethiopian painting and manuscript illumination stems from Brancaleone – who was so popular, he was not allowed to leave the country, where he died after forty years of exile.

Medieval Europe contained many legends about 'Prester John', a name which it seems reasonable to identify with the King of Ethiopia. He was seen as a possible Christian ally against the rise of Islamic power. When first-hand accounts of Ethiopia reached the outside world through Portugal, it was learned that the King was in fact an Emperor of several small kingdoms and bore the title Negusa Nagast, or King of Kings. Usually the Emperor would seek to retain the loyalty of the vassal kingdoms by marrying the daughters of subject kings, then having his whole polygamous household baptized Christian.

Military control was entrusted to imperial forces, each commanded by a *ras* or *shum*. Alvarez, the chaplain of a Portuguese embassy sent to Ethiopia in 1520, records the arrival of tribute from the kingdom of Gojjam – three thousand horses, as many mules, three thousand blankets, as many cotton cloths, and thirty thousand *ouquias* of gold. The tribute procession took ten days to file past the imperial palace. The Emperor's revenue greatly exceeded his expenditure, and was bulky because no currency of any kind existed.

Maintaining his court was the King's only permanent expenditure. Occasionally he made gifts to valiant officers or subject kings, but these were usually reciprocated. Lavish gifts were also expected by the Patriarch of Alexandria, who appointed the *abuna* or Ethiopian Coptic archbishop, and by the Sultan of Egypt. The monarch also endowed monasteries and churches; but most of the royal treasure was hoarded in caves, pits or fortresses.

The Emperor lived simply, but surrounded by the trappings of power. He was accompanied on travels by four chained lions; he rode on a mule, behind curtains held on poles, preceded by six pages. He was rarely seen by any except courtiers and high officials. Justice was centralized on provincial lines and rigid, although there was a channel for appeal to provincial Governors in major cases. The royal law-court, according to Alvarez, was in a tent. Thirteen empty chairs symbolized justice and the assessors of justice. The judges themselves squatted in two groups on the ground. The plaintiff presented his case, then the defendant. The doorkeeper, a simple and uneducated man, gave his version of what the judgement should be; then each judge gave a judgement; finally the chief judge summed up and gave the real judgement. Prisoners awaited trial in chains, and punishments were as terrible as those in Europe at the time, although in the case of patricians the floggings were often more a humiliation than a torture: the four whip-men, after staking the prisoner to the ground, flogged the earth and not the man himself. This was also the usual penalty for chief judges who became guilty, in the King's eyes, of poor justice.

Although the King lived in quasi-isolation, all his male relatives – his potential rivals for power – lived an even more secluded life. They were relegated to guarded forts, with their families. In contrast, women and girls of the royal line enjoyed complete freedom.

Alvarez found great religious curiosity; like his Frankish predecessor, he was unable to compete with the Ethiopian priests in theological knowledge. They were fascinated by his vestments and way of saying Mass, however. He, for his part, was shocked by the carnival of nude bathing with which the Ethiopians marked the Epiphany.

The Portuguese embassy was well received; the visit resulted in the Emperor's submission to the Holy See and the cession of Massawa as a naval base to Portugal, as well as two other bases. In return, the King asked for artisans and doctors, and for lead to roof his churches. All this was contained in a stylized letter from King Lebna Dengel to King Manuel, with versions in Amharic, Arabic and Portuguese.

Lebna Dengel needed an ally such as Portugal. In 1516, the Ottoman Sultan, Selim, had conquered Egypt and had received the surrender of the Hedjaz. Fear of Islamic imperialism had conditioned the Ethiopian-Portuguese discussions; but in 1527, when the embassy returned to Lisbon, neither Portugal nor Ethiopia were ready for the attack, which came from a small, well-disciplined force under Ahmed ibn Ibrahim al-Ghazi.

Ethiopia's forces were dispersed, and the treasures of the

fortress *ambas* looted, together with those of churches and monasteries. Princes of the so-called Solomonian line were put to death. Most Ethiopians hurriedly embraced Islam, although the King and a small force of loyalists continued resistance in the mountains. In 1535, he smuggled out a certain Bermudez, a Portuguese hostage, who reached Lisbon and convinced his King to send a relieving force from Portuguese India.

The Portuguese moved slowly and received a fresh setback when the Ottomans seized Yemen, Aden and other strategic points on the Red Sea and its approaches. It was 1541 before a son of Vasco da Gama's broke the blockade and landed four hundred men at Massawa. Lebna Dengel had died the previous year and had been succeeded by his son Claudius. The Portuguese force fought its way up from the coast, made contact with royalist forces and resisted two attacks by much more numerous Turkish armies near Lake Tsana. This harrying however delayed da Gama until the rains, and frustrated his attempt to reach Claudius' camp.

Ahmed got reinforcements from the Pasha of Zabid and finally routed the Portuguese, killing their valiant general. The resourceful Ahmed now faced serious resistance only from Claudius' personal force and from a high *amba* controlled by the remnants of the Portuguese force and a royal party led by the Queen Mother. Claudius managed to rejoin this *amba* with his followers. Soon there were eight thousand infantry and five hundred cavalry there, and a Portuguese survivor managed to manufacture gunpowder from locally discovered sulphur and saltpeter. This force marched boldly on Lake Tsana and, in a memorable battle, killed Ahmed himself. The Somali levies from Zabid broke in terror and the outnumbered Turks fought on until only forty remained. These were overrun.

The King of Portugal ordered the hundred or so surviving Portuguese to remain in Ethiopia, which they did, marrying into the population and establishing a military caste which completely rid the inland areas of the realm of its Muslim invaders, and also subdued the pagan Gallas. A religious and cultural revival was launched. But the Turks reoccupied Massawa, and Ethiopia was once more cut off from the outside world.

At this point begins Ethiopia's famous and unfortunate adventure with the Jesuits. It started when Bermudez – the hostage who had saved Ethiopia by getting aid from Portugal – returned with the da Gama party; Bermudez informed Claudius that Lebna Dengel's *abuna,* Mark, had – on his death-bed – named him (Bermudez) Patriarch of Ethiopia. Claudius knew Bermudez was an impostor, but to placate his urgently needed Portuguese allies he submitted to the spiritual authority of the pseudo-Catholicus.

Bermudez insisted on the Ethiopian Church becoming Roman, and all the Coptic clergy being re-ordained. Conflict between Claudius and his Lusitanian allies reached flashpoint; then the King awarded the Portuguese, including Bermudez, posts in the distant provinces, and secured a new *abuna* from Alexandria. Soon, a genuine Papal mission was to arrive, and the 'Patriach' Bermudez slipped off home to Lisbon.

The real Jesuit mission had greater initial success. Ignatius of Loyola volunteered to be the evangelist of Ethiopia, but the Pope vetoed this and appointed instead a certain Nuñez Barreto as Patriarch, with Melchior Carneiro and a certain de Oviedo as bishops. Nuñez Barreto stayed in India, but the others arrived at Claudius' court, where they found the Emperor less attracted by Romanism than his father Lebna Dengel had been, but well informed for theological discussion.

When Claudius died in 1559 and was succeeded by his brother Minas things became harder for the Portuguese priests. Claudius had allowed the Ethiopian wives and slaves of the Portuguese military to convert to Romanism, but Minas forbade this. In an argument, he was only just restrained from strangling the obstinate Oviedo, who bravely resisted years of intimidation. The Jesuits had less difficulties with Minas' son, Sarsa Dengel (1563–97) who remained a Copt but allowed Oviedo – who succeeded to the Catholic 'Patriarchate' on Nuñez' death in India in 1562 – to settle the mission at Fremona, near Axum. Here Oviedo died in 1577.

Because of the Ottomans at Massawa, the Fremona mission could not easily be reinforced. A Maronite was detected and captured in 1595, on his way to Fremona; but in 1596 a

Goan, Father Melchior de Sylva, made the journey, followed in 1603 by Fr. Pedro Paez of Spain. The resourceful Paez, after seven years' captivity in Yemen, had settled at Diu, in India, where he became the friend of a Turk who was *aga* to the Pasha of Swakim on the Red Sea coast. Paez said he was an Armenian who wished to return home; the *aga* promised to arrange safe passage through the Ottoman dominions. Paez said he also wanted to stop off at Massawa, and collect the property of friends who had died up-country in Ethiopia. Thanks to the *aga*, Paez reached Fremona.

A brilliant linguist, Paez swiftly learned Amharic and Ge'ez, which had become the tongue of religion. With patience and humility, he satisfied himself at first with running a school. After Sarsa Dengel's death, there had been a disputed succession, finally won by Za Dengel, who heard of Paez' work in Tigre province and summoned him to court. Paez appeared with two Ethiopian Catholic pupils who won a theological discussion with Coptic clergy. Paez then delivered a sermon in perfect Ge'ez which started the King on the road to conversion.

Against Paez' advice, the royal proselyte tried over-zealously to change the country's Christian system overnight, thus inevitably causing much discontent. Za Dengel wrote to Philip III of Spain (then the ruler of Portugal also), suggesting a marriage alliance (his son and a Spanish princess) and the loan of troops, ostensibly to fight the pagan Gallas. Philip did not react.

The nobles rose and the *abuna* took the exceptional step of releasing the faithful from their oath of royal allegiance. Most of the army changed sides. In the ensuing fighting, Za Dengel was killed. After another confused interregnum, a relative, Sisinius, was proclaimed King in 1607. The star of the Portuguese colony – and of Father Paez – rose again; the new King embraced the Catholic faith. Like his predecessor, he tried to abolish observance of Saturday as a second Sabbath; there was a further rebellion, but this was put down. In 1622, Sisinius publicly proclaimed his adhesion to Catholicism, and denounced the depravity of the *abuna* and his predecessors. Then, just as the King needed his sagacious counsel most, Paez died.

His successor was as bigoted as Paez had been intelligent.

Alfonso Mendez, a Spanish Jesuit like Paez, began by making the King reluctantly kneel to him in public, as a gesture of submission to the Vatican. Mendez then undertook a massive reorganization of the Ethiopian Church, beginning with the re-ordination of all priests and (theoretically) the re-baptism of the entire population. Churches were re-consecrated. Circumcision was forbidden, but graven images, held to be idolatrous by the pious Ethiopians, were introduced. Calendar and litany were standardized on Rome's.

A woman was tried for witchcraft – a conception in which the Ethiopians no longer believed – and the body of a saintly abbot was removed from under a church on the grounds that he had been a Copt and therefore a schismatic. There was violent resistance to all this – and violent counter-measures. Still, Mendez would not let the King compromise with his people. Finally in 1632, while remaining a Catholic himself, Sisinius restored the Ethiopian Coptic Church and abdicated in favour of his son Basilides.

A Catholic resistance then developed around the now imprisoned Jesuits and certain nobles, who looked to Portugal for military aid. The Jesuits escaped, were sheltered by a Catholic prince – then sold by him to the Pasha of Swakim, who got a ransom for them out of Spain. Some who failed to get out of the country in time were captured and executed. Basilides executed or dispossessed the Catholic noblemen.

Rome correctly blamed the apostasy of Ethiopia on Mendez and decided to replace the Jesuits by six French Capuchins. Four were killed and the other two turned back at Massawa. Basilides instructed the coastal pashas to execute all Catholic priests on arrival. Three more Capuchins arrived in 1648 and were beheaded by the Pasha of Massawa, who skinned the heads and sent the skins to Basilides as witness of his loyalty.

*

A report written by envoys of Sisinius who roved the country in 1614 reveals the curious customs still prevailing then in up-country Ethiopia. In Gingiro, a pagan kingdom, the monarch would refuse to do any business of state if the sun rose before he did. If he became sick, he was at once executed. When a King died, adult males of the royal family scattered across the district and hid themselves; a body of Electors, accompanied by a bird of prey, then tracked down the concealed men: the first to be found inherited the throne. He would resist coronation, then submit, in a time-honored ritual. A patrician family would contest, with the Electors, the right to enthrone the King: if they could wrest the new monarch from the Electors' hands in battle, they would perform the rites themselves.

A cow was slaughtered and the late king was wrapped in its hide and dragged around the kingdom to 'fertilize' the soil. The body was then laid in a pit and covered in the blood of scores of slaughtered cattle. Then his house, property, family and friends were ceremoniously burned. In contrast, during the age of Catholic Emperors, custom at the imperial palace was simplified, and more in keeping with the age. Isolation descended on Ethiopia again with the end of the Catholic chapter, and the next monarch of note was King Jesus the Great (1680–1704), who left his mark by his military powers in pacifying the Ethiopian Empire, and by his reform of administrative abuses.

During Jesus' reign, Louis XIV, on Jesuit advice, instructed his Consul in Cairo, a certain M. de Maillet, to go to the Ethiopian court and suggest an exchange of embassies; Louis also proposed the sending to Versailles of patrician Ethiopian youths and maidens, for education. Maillet, pretexting ill-health, sent instead to Gondar a French pharmacist in Cairo, Poncet; this man treated the King, successfully, for a skin complaint, and thus established friendly relations.

Jesus was reluctant to send students through Ottoman territory, where they would certainly be enslaved, but he sent a French-speaking subject – a Muslim Armenian named Murad – with Poncet, on an embassy to Louis. Between Massawa and Cairo, an elephant intended as a gift for the *Roi Soleil* died at sea; at Jidda, the Sharif of Mecca seized some slaves – another royal gift. When they proceeded further, a cargo of precious cloth was swept overboard in a Red Sea storm, leaving them with only one gift for Versailles – a solitary slave.

In Cairo, Maillet demanded Jesus' letter to Louis; Poncet haughtily replied that *he* was the ambassador to Ethiopia, and the despatches he carried would only be produced in

Versailles. In spite, Maillet persuaded the Pasha to impound the letters. Poncet rightly complained to Versailles; the Sublime Porte, the Ottoman Government, apologetically ordered a commission of enquiry. Maillet was ordered to pay the expenses of the commission when it held him responsible for the quaint international scandal. Maillet paid – then childishly arranged for Louis' last remaining Ethiopian slave to be confiscated.

Maillet's odd *mesquineries* were still not over. Poncet found himself, in France, the victim of a campaign of doubt inspired by the Cairo Consul's venomous letters to friends at court. Poncet's extremely interesting book on Ethiopia was denounced as being fanciful; armchair geographers poured such scorn on the work that suspicion became widespread that Poncet had never been to Ethiopia at all.

Because of the confusion created by Maillet, a fresh embassy was decided on and the Consul himself was once more instructed to proceed to Ethiopia. Once again, he evaded his duty, sending the Vice-Consul at Damietta, a M. du Roule. This man, says an historian, 'had all the Gallic contempt for anything that was not French'. After a number of gross gaffes, including presenting the royal princesses with a set of distorting mirrors, he and his party were murdered one day in the streets of Sennaar.

Shortly after, King Jesus himself was assassinated by one of his sons, Takla Haymanot, who took the throne, only to be killed off in his turn in a palace revolution and replaced by an uncle who died in 1709. A revolution followed and the so-called Solomonic line was superseded on the throne by the Governor of Tigre, Justus. Five years later, during an illness of the King, the army revolted and enthroned David, one of the several sons of Jesus. He began his reign by executing some Catholic priests whom Justus had allowed to return.

After five years, David was poisoned and a brother, 'Asma Giorgis, was enthroned by the army. Known as Bakaffa, 'the inexorable', the new King broke the power of the nobility, crushed several conspiracies and filled all major offices with men whom he could trust. Once he pretended to have died; when his enemies had shown their hand, he 'resurrected' himself and dealt harshly with them. He wandered about the country in disguise, learning the views of his subjects. On one journey of this sort he fell sick in a village near Sennaar and was nursed to health by the daughter of his host. He made her his Queen – and also remained monogamous. He found a chief minister by the same method, after a conversation beside a stream.

On another trip, he consulted an old fortune-teller who was tossing oracular sticks into a mountain pool. The old man, now knowing he was talking to the King himself, said the King would have a son but that when the monarch died a certain Wallata Giorgis, who was no kin, would succeed him for thirty years. Bakaffa began systematically killing off people with this common Ethiopian name. When he had a son, he told his wife the prophecy and she surprised him by revealing that Wallata Giorgis had been her own baptismal name.

Bakaffa died in 1729, after ten years' reign; his son, Jesus II, was proclaimed King, and the infant's mother, Wallata Giorgis, reigned as regent, putting Galla relatives in posts of power and confidence; the discontent this caused weakened the power of her son, who reigned 1729–1753. The driving force in the empire became Michael Suhul, Governor of Tigre, who personally controlled all the country's frontier districts.

*

During the reign that followed, the rarely-visited sanctuary of what was still, to Europe, the domain of 'Prester John', was violated by a courageous Scots explorer, James Bruce. A loud, tall, bulky giant with ruddy hair and an overweening self-confidence; horseman, marksman, linguist, tycoon and boor, Bruce was one of those over-lifesize persons whom fate compels to fulfil their boasts. After a frustrating and unhappy early life, Bruce found an outlet for his aggressive energies as George III's Consul in Algiers in the 1760s. At this time, the Barbary Coast was still largely a pirate's lair, and Algiers the fief of a cruel, depraved Turkish bey. Within a few weeks of arriving at his post, Bruce saw the French Consul flung into chains, his own assistant threatened with flogging and a court official strangled during his audience with the dyspeptic monarch. Often a prisoner in his house, Bruce survived two years and then struck out for the East, finally reaching Cairo in 1768 after several violent adventures. He was now thirty-eight; he had picked up an Italian 'trouble-shooter' called Luigi Balugani, had taken to dressing as a dervish and had decided to go up the Nile to Ethiopia and find the river's source.

Bruce visited Adowa, the ruined township of Axum, and Gondar, which then served as a sort of capital. He met Takla Haymanot, the new King, and Ras Michael, his terrible vizier, who bestowed on Bruce such titles as cavalry commander and provincial Governor, to secure him safe-conduct. In a country where life was frighteningly cheap, his impressive presence and iron confidence earned him his survival. He checked an outbreak of smallpox in the Queen Mother's palace, flirted with her daughter, Ozoro Esther, and accompanied the royal levies in putting down a rebel chief. Then he resumed his travels. On November 4, 1770, he discovered a spring at the head of the Little Abbai Valley, and concluded that it was the source of the Nile.

He wrote: 'It is easier to guess than to describe the situation of my mind at that moment, standing in that spot which had baffled the genius, industry and inquiry of both ancients and moderns, for the course of near three thousand years.' Having apparently triumphed, the thought of the weary journey home raised doubts in his mind as to the usefulness of his great purpose. 'I found a despondency gaining ground fast upon me, and blasting the crown of laurels I had woven for myself.'

Bruce was an engaging and precise observer, but he had made one grossly wrong conjecture; the Blue Nile was not the source of the river, which lay at Bururi, over a thousand miles to the South; he was not even at the source of the Blue Nile either – which is at Lake Tsana, near Bahardar. Nor was Bruce, as he thought, the first European to cross the Blue Nile highlands. Father Paez had been there, a century and a half before. But Bruce returned to Europe with a remarkable and unique contribution to the sum of man's knowledge – the most complete and observant account of Ethiopia that had been written. He brought back witness of a country where people wore rings in their lips and smeared themselves in the warm blood of living cattle, cut steaks from living

257

cows and dressed the gaping wound with clay, engaged in unlimited and humorless debauchery; he was to tell about safaris in which the prey was men, of mothers less than ten years old, of an interplay of treachery and brutality, of medieval horrors and endless, purposeless, lawless war.

When he first met the royal pair who ruled the kingdom, they were busy putting out the eyes of prisoners. Bruce saw debtors who lived for years in narrow cages, and victorious armies entering villages bearing on spears the testicles of their enemies, led by Ras Michael, a whitebearded homicidal tyrant clad in black velvet, waving a silver wand. When the torrential rains blackened the skies, he watched Ethiopian officers and women gather in foetid huts to hack meat from cattle roaring with pain, to drink themselves unconscious with mead, to fornicate noisily where they lay without exciting the interest of their companions. Bruce survived the diet of raw meat and honey, the bloodthirstiness and the license, and suffered only one bad attack of malaria and a painful onslaught of guinea worm.

By Bruce's time, Ethiopia's military problems were exclusively internal. The Somalis were no longer a power; the extensive Ottoman empire was a leprous ruin. The monarchy in Gondar was weak, but still kept up a brave appearance of power. The King went everywhere on horseback, dismounting only inside the palace. The exception to this rule was church, which he visited on foot, walking through streets cleared specially for the occasion. He was veiled at audiences, and his wishes were expressed through a spokesman called the King's Voice. He was much sought after as a judge, as were all provincial nobles – including Bruce, when he became one.

The King, seated behind a grill, controlled councils of state, pretending to govern what had become a warring shambles of an Empire. Even the army had reverted from archery to spears; but forces could still be raised among the peasantry by the issuing of three royal proclamations. The first said: 'Buy your mules, make ready your provisions and pay your servants, for after (such and such a day) they that seek me here shall not find me.' The second was still more curious: 'Cut down the thorns in the four quarters of the world, for I know not where I am going.' The third was more explicit: 'I am encamped at. . . . Him that does not join me here shall I chastise for seven years.'

On the way out of Ethiopia, Bruce found the monument-strewn town of Shendy and rightly guessed that it was ancient Meroë. At Berber, he bought more camels, and rested for the crossing of the desert – four hundred miles, to Aswan. On this ordeal of heat and thirst, one of his men went mad and had to be cast off to perish. All his camels died, and he had to abandon his luggage, including his navigational quadrant. The party was constantly attacked by marauders. He finally staggered into Aswan, whence he sailed to Cairo. A month later, ragged, in pain and ill, he reached the great city.

He recuperated in Marseille and Rome, then returned to Marseille, travelled up to Paris with the famous naturalist Buffon, and was received by Louis XVI, to whom he gave seeds of rare tropical plants. He was honored by French scholars.

Britain was different. On his return there, Bruce's monstrous frame and gigantic achievement, the fruit of ten years' effort, ran full tilt into a frenzied chorus of sedentary pedants. They seemed to crawl out of the woodwork and from under stones to mock the fantastic tales which he had to tell. Some who challenged Bruce's reports had traveled no further than Tooting Bec in the interests of geography. None had ever been to Ethiopia. Bruce, a morbidly sensitive boor in any case, was deeply depressed by the onslaught of doubt of the academic Establishment.

*

It was almost a hundred years before another explorer, Samuel Baker, penetrated Ethiopia. The bearded, wealthy Englishman and his undauntable wife covered many of the same tracks as Bruce. They found the country just as wild and violent (indeed it is still inadvisable, even today, to travel across Ethiopia without a gun). In the dry season, the portly Baker and his suffering wife were forced to keep away from villages, since at that time (Baker tells us) there was 'a season of anarchy along the whole frontier'.

We are in the 1860s. The Suez Canal was being built and Britain was becoming concerned with the political forces in the Red Sea and beyond, down the East African coast.

The political agent at Aden was a key figure. Whether the powers controlling the coast were Muslim or not, it was essential they should not pose a threat to the flood of British shipping which would use the Canal on its way to and from Britain's vast oriental empire. Unexpectedly, the political challenge, such as it was, came from the only Christian monarch ruling in this part of the world. Like power itself, the whole incident is at loggerheads with logic. It is rooted in a basic inconsequence of political life.

An incurable, mental collapse signals the end of any man's career. An occupation, however modest, is closed to those whose brains have become completely unhinged. But there is apparently one exception to this rule, and that is politics: history is replete with examples of people who were mentally incapable of any responsibility, but who have maintained their power regardless of a mental breakdown – and even in some cases enhanced their status. Neither in the past or today has there been a time when some country or countries were not in the power of a lunatic. King Teodros of Ethiopia, from whom the modern Ethiopian Empire dates its development, had one determining characteristic more apparent than any other: he was that standby of vaudeville – a totally insane, literally raving, roaring maniac.

Teodros – or Theodore, as he was usually known in English – was swarthy and slim, with a proud bearing. He wore a small beard and his hair in ringlets. It has been said that if he had been round-backed he would have resembled Jesus Christ – and his portrait seems to agree with Josephus' description of the Messiah. By 1853, he had conquered Amhara, and two years later most of the neighboring chieftaincies. He was then thirtyseven. He changed his name from Kassa and declared himself Teodros III of Ethiopia. Britain appointed a Consul, Walter G. Plowden, an Ethiopian resident, to sign a treaty of friendship with him. Plowden's friend, an engineer named Bell, acted at the time as a sort of court secretary. Britain had reason to believe its relation with the monarch was close; and so it was – while Plowden and Bell lived.

In 1860, Plowden was traveling up-country when he was killed by tribesmen. Theodore led a personal punitive expedition, killing and castrating two thousand people. During the fighting, Bell was killed rushing to the assistance of the

Emperor. As Consul, Britain now sent an Anglo-Indian civil servant, Captain Charles D. Cameron.

Theodore was badly shaken by the death of his two British friends. Then his wife Tavavich died. His new wife, Teru-Work, who was twelve years old, bored him and he soon became a profligate. He also took to drinking.

When Cameron arrived at Gondar in 1862 with a pair of silver-stocked pistols from Queen Victoria, he suggested Theodore send envoys to Britain for a formal treaty. The King addressed Victoria a letter complaining that since the Turks had re-occupied the coast he could not send envoys by that route. ('See how Islam oppresses the Christian,' he wrote). He asked Victoria to open up a route whereby an embassy, conducted by Cameron, could come to England. This letter found its way to London, where the Foreign Office, never a haunt of professionalism, forgot to answer it. To this grave inefficiency was added a major error of judgement. The FO instructed Cameron to proceed to Kassala in the Sudan, there to investigate slaving and the prospects of growing cotton. Cotton prices had quadrupled since the American Civil War had cut off supplies to Europe, and the Sudanese might be persuaded to give up slavery in return for guaranteed purchases of a cotton crop.

When Theodore, who thought Cameron had gone to England, learned that he was sojourning with his enemies, he raged and sulked. He not unnaturally connected Cameron's apparently strange behaviour with the genuinely mysterious absence of a reply to his letter to Victoria. In a country in which treachery was as common as bread, Theodore naturally concluded that Britain was plotting to invade Ethiopia from the Sudan. The German evangelists in Ethiopia, whose mission was aided by British funds, were at once thrown into chains; when Cameron returned in January, 1864, he too was fettered and even tortured. Then, a young assistant for Cameron called Kerans arrived with messages from the FO for Theodore, but still no royal reply to the forgotten letter; Kerans was of course jailed also.

Cameron got a message through to Colonel Merewether, the British Political Agent at Aden, and even got a letter to the *Times* of London. He insisted on the necessity for Theodore's letter to be found and answered. Since Theodore's prisoners could be executed on a moment's whim, London sent a carefully mollifying reply. Victoria addressed it to 'Our Good Friend Theodore, King of Abyssinia'. The Queen would welcome an Ethiopian embassy to England. Her Majesty had learned with regret that Theodore had withdrawn his favor from 'Our servant, Cameron. We trust, however, that these accounts have originated in false representations on the part of persons ill-disposed to your Majesty, and who may desire to produce an alteration in our feelings toward you.' Safe-conduct for Cameron and the other white prisoners was requested. The message was brought by Merewether's collaborator, an astute Iraqi Christian called Hormuzd Rassam. As assistants he was given a Dr Henry Blanc and a Lieutenant Prideaux of the Indian Army.

Merewether had got Cameron's message in April; the Queen had sent her letter in May and by July Rassam was in Massawa, then Egyptian territory. Rassam sent messengers to Theodore asking for a safe-conduct to Gondar, and letters and money to Cameron. No reply came until early 1865.

By then, about thirty European families, in some cases Europeans with Ethiopian wives and Eurafrican children, were under arrest – either in Magdala fortress, like Cameron, or with Theodore in the field near Lake Tsana. Rassam sent two more letters to Theodore but got no reply; but fairly regular correspondence with Cameron began. Cameron suggested Rassam take a firmer tone, adding: 'But for God's sake, do not come up here; he will cage you, sure as a gun, as he thinks that while he has us in his hands he is safe from attack, and, of course, with a swell like you in addition, matters would only be better for him.'

It was in August, 1865, that Rassam got a letter from Theodore stating – untruthfully – that Cameron had been released from his chains. Theodore inveighed against Cameron, but said he would receive Rassam: since Tigre was in revolt, he should come by Metemma. Rassam wrote that for various physical reasons this was impossible: he would go to Cairo and await the end of the rains.

In Cairo, Rassam bought gifts for Theodore – chandeliers, mirrors, glassware, liquor – and cabled London for instructions. These were that he should hand over the mission to a diplomat already in Cairo, William Palgrave. Rassam got this last order countermanded, and returned to Massawa, whence he set off with a coffle of camels through land pestered with cholera. In just over a month they reached Metemma, and Rassam sent off messages. Cameron replied that he and his comrades were now chained hand and foot. Theodore sent an escort of fourteen hundred irregulars, who took Rassam across wild, medieval country and through peoples exactly of the type Bruce had described a century before. By the time they reached Theodore's camp on Lake Tsana, the escort had swollen to ten thousand men.

The first two audiences with the King were mostly a long exposal of Theodore's persecution complex. The Queen's letter was delivered, and the sumptuous gifts; Theodore, in an answer to the British Sovereign, asked Victoria's pardon of 'an ignorant Ethiopian', adding: 'Advise me but do not blame me, O Queen.'

Rassam and his party then accompanied the King on another of his military expeditions, with ninety thousand people and their herds following the mad monarch across the cloudscraping pinnacles. As much as thirty miles a day were covered, and Moorehead notes Theodore's 'great skill in keeping order among his rabble'. Villages were plundered to feed each night's camp of twenty thousand tents. Theodore showed great hospitality to Rassam.

On February 6, 1866, Rassam's party was sent across the lake to a series of resthouses prepared for them and Theodore went up the shore to set up a military base. Theodore sent assurances that escorts had gone to Magdala to bring the captives, and gave Rassam two lion cubs.

The awaited prisoners consisted of Cameron and four other consular staff, German, French and Swiss missionaries and their families, and seven workmen, mostly Germans, who were free to move about Theodore's camp but who also sought to leave the country.

Toward the end of the month, the missionaries Mr. and Mrs. Flad arrived. They had been under house arrest at Debra Tabor, not imprisonment. The next month came the artisans and their Ethiopian wives. On March 10, the rest of the Debra Tabor group and the Magdala prisoners, including Cameron, rejoined the party. Most were weak from two years in chains. Then, on various pretexts, Theodore kept

263

the party waiting for permission to go, apparently afraid that his conduct would bring reprisals from outside once he no longer had hostages. The sudden arrival on the Ethiopian border of a British lawyer, Beke, who had persuaded prisoners' relatives to send him out to Ethiopia, complicated affairs and enraged the royal psychopath. Finally, permission was given for the prisoners to depart, and Rassam, Blanc and Prideaux were invited to Theodore's camp to take leave of him. When they reached the camp, they found Theodore had been drunk for three days already; his mood was black; warriors caught up with Cameron's party on the opposite shore, and everyone was thrown in chains.

On April 15, a mad trial was held in public, at which all sorts of charges were brought against Rassam and his party. But Rassam himself was invited to sit with the King, who stroked his victim's beard and called him 'my beloved'. Then, suddenly, the Emperor turned on the envoy and insulted him. The audience was over.

The next day, the plethora of charges recommenced, to be interrupted by Theodore crying out 'For Christ's sake, forgive me!' – whereupon the whole assembly knelt in prayer. After this, the distraught prince had a new idea. Flad was despatched to Metemma with an escort and two letters to Victoria. One offered to release everybody except Rassam, who was to be the new hostage. The other asked for British artisans. Flad had to leave without his wife, and the European party settled down to wait.

At first, most of the prisoners had the freedom of the camp, and Rassam and his two assistants were showered with gifts. When the Emperor learned that May 24 was Victoria's birthday, he called for a twentyone gun salute, and much raw beef and *tej* (mead) for everyone. He later took the prisoners hunting, and took part himself in a pageant for them. But at night the anxious Europeans heard ominous sounds – Ethiopians who had fallen out of favor with the demented tyrant being flogged and tortured to death.

Cholera caused a retreat to Gaffat near Debra Tabor, higher and healthier than the lake. A long policy of trying to humor Theodore got under way. Moorehead compares Rassam – a trim bearded figure who resembled Sigmund Freud – to a favorite dog who is alternately patted and kicked. Soon the prisoners fell foul of a new Theodorian mood of sadism and were confined to dark cells in Debra Tabor itself. The Emperor took to visiting them in the middle of the night with a lantern and a jug of *tej*. Rassam would be on hand to soothe the lunatic's whims. The Emperor told him: 'I used to hear that I was called a madman for my acts, but I never believed it; now, however . . . I have come to the conclusion I am really so. But as Christians we ought always to be ready to forgive each other.' Insanely egocentric, the worse Theodore behaved, the more he felt sorry for himself.

After this confession of dementia, Theodore disappeared on campaign for a year and nine months of rapine and terror across Ethiopia. The prisoners waited helplessly in their sodden jail. Back in England, incredible as it may seem, a group of volunteer artisans was found to buy off Theodore's raving wrath. They were presumably told nothing of the man or of what was going on in Ethiopia, and one may suppose they did not read *The Times*. Flad, who was to lead them, had a new letter from Victoria, signed at Balmoral on October 4, 1886. It expressed distress at Theodore's behavior and particularly at his treacherous arrest of Rassam, but in carefully sensitized language. Victoria added, however: 'Your Majesty must be aware that it is the sacred duty of Sovereigns scrupulously to fulfil engagements into which they may have entered . . . and we invite your Majesty to prove to the world that you rightly understand your position among Sovereigns.' The Queen added that gifts and the workmen would be sent to Massawa, there to be exchanged for the prisoners.

Flad reached Theodore in December, 1866. The Emperor told Rassam, as the Queen's envoy, that he wanted to see the workmen first; then he would be released. Theodore's treachery was crystal-clear, but Rassam considered they might all die if he recommended refusal of the Emperor's request. On the coast, however, it was decided to send the workmen home. In July, 1867, all the prisoners at Debra Tabor were moved to Magdala – and all, including Rassam and his assistants, were chained.

Later, some comfort was introduced. Each group of prisoners got a separate hut with beds, chair and table, and a central fire. They had their Ethiopian servants and ate copious meals. *Tej*, arak and coffee could now be bought. With seeds sent from Aden, they grew vegetables. They exchanged letters with Aden, received visits from sympathetic Ethiopians, and concubines were provided for the bachelors. The prisoners often quarreled, but Rassam's leadership was accepted.

At this time, the Emperor was building up Magdala into his capital, although it was in unfriendly Muslim, Galla country. The arrival of Rassam's group, and of hundreds of Ethiopian political prisoners, was part of this development. By then, Theodore's policy for controlling Ethiopia was insanely simple: he was seeking to kill as many Ethiopians as possible. He razed Gondar, his old capital. In the field, he immolated hundreds of prisoners at a time. Soon some of his hundred thousand-man army, hitherto disciplined into terrified obedience, began to desert. Rebellions grew stronger, especially that in Tigre under Chief Kassaï. Rassam's news of Theodore's military reverses reached Merewether and London. In August, 1867, Lord Derby sent Theodore an ultimatum demanding release of the prisoners. There was no reply, and war was declared.

*

British public opinion was appalled at the idea of invading a country of mountains and ravines, with no roads or bridges. And might not the very rescue operation cause the murder of the hostages? The Government confided the chivalrous task to the Indian Army – which was used to frontier warfare and was relatively close at hand – and the command to General Napier (later Field-Marshal Lord Napier), a dashing, much wounded fiftyseven-year-old widower who had just taken an eighteen-year-old bride.

Napier's requirements, which turned out to be too modest, were: twelve thousand combat troops, twentyfive thousand servicemen, twenty thousand mules and two hundred and eighty ships, both sail and steam. The campaign could begin in December, Napier thought, at the onset of the dry season, and could be concluded in six months. Pack animals were bought all over the Mediterranean world, and fortyfour trained elephants were to be shipped in from India to carry the heavy artillery. Two condensers were to convert sea-water into potable, and telegraph communications were to be run between coast and front. There were to be hospital ships with ice-making machines; a railroad would be built to the foothills; half a million special Maria Theresa dollars were ordered from Vienna.

Each officer got a servant and each horse a groom. Salaries ranged from five hundred and eighty pounds a month for Napier himself to one pound a month for mahouts, slightly less for ordinary Indian soldiers. Merewether came from Aden to run an intelligence service, which included the explorer Major James Grant, the explorer-missionary Johannes Krapf, and a Captain Speedy, who knew Amharic. Historians have naturally been impressed with the 'modern-ness' of this campaign compared with Napoleon's Egyptian venture only seventy years before; but one element perhaps borrowed from Napoleon was the decision to take a British Museum representative, a geographer and a zoologist.

There were observers from the armies of France, Prussia, Italy, Holland, Austria and Spain. The *New York Herald* detached Henry Stanley from his immense Asian-African assignment, and the novelist G. A. Henty covered the campaign for the London *Standard*.

Napier ended up with thirteen thousand combat troops, (including four thousand Europeans), twentynine thousand service men, fiftyfive thousand animals and half a million pounds sterling (in hire value) of shipping. The elephants required two ships, which were flooded with vomit and nearly sank in a cyclone off Calcutta.

Napier had been wise in not underestimating the obstacles which had saved Ethiopia from any successful previous invasion. But he soon learned that Theodore was so bedevilled with rebellions that he would stake all on resistance at Magdala, four hundred miles from the coast.

In October, the engineers arrived and began building a jetty-port, a railroad and a shantytown. Soon the normally deserted spot was humming with activity, with 'laborers from two continents and soldiers from three,' with animals in thousands, hospitals, bazaars, and condensers producing sixty tons of water a day. A further million tons had been shipped from Aden.

The water produced was for human consumption.

Meanwhile hundreds of animals died and rotted; others broke free and roamed in search of the wherewithal to slake their thirst; all the wells had dried in a drought. Flies arrived by the million.

An advance camp under Merewether was established at Senafe, forty miles from the sea, where the nights were cool and water abundant. The engineers began to hack a pass up to the plateau eight thousand feet above. Merewether was in contact with Kassaï, through whose friendly territory the British army would pass, and there were messages from the prisoners at Magdala saying all were well.

Merewether then sent off Napier's ultimatum to Theodore. This said, in part: 'My Sovereign has no desire to deprive you of any part of your dominions, nor to subvert your authority, although it is obvious that such would in all probability be the result of hostilities. Your Majesty might avert this danger by immediate surrender of the prisoners. But should they not be delivered safely into my hands, should they suffer a continuance of ill-treatment, or should any injury befall them, your Majesty will be held personally responsible, and no hope of further condonation need be entertained.'

This missive fell into rebel hands and was delivered to Rassam, who destroyed it, fearing it would anger the Emperor. Later, Napier's message to the Ethiopian people got wide distribution. It said notably: 'All who befriend the prisoners or assist in their liberation shall be rewarded, but those who may injure them shall be severely punished. . . .

'The Queen of England has no unfriendly feeling toward you, and no design against your country or your liberty. Your religious establishments, your persons and your property shall be carefully protected. All supplies required for my soldiers shall be paid for; no peaceable inhabitants shall be molested.

'The sole object for which the British force has been sent to Abyssinia is the liberation of Her Majesty's servants and others unjustly detained as captives, and as soon as that object is effected it will be withdrawn. There is no intention to occupy permanently any portion of the Abyssinian territory, or to interfere with the Government of the country.'

Napier himself arrived on January 2, 1868. There was a

suitable parade, with martial music, and the elephants followed him ashore. The road to Senafe was open. Magdala
was to be taken by an *élite* of five thousand men; the rest
were to hold open the lines of communication. Numbers
and supplies were cut: each officer would share a bell-tent, a
cook, a batman and a grass-cutter with two others. There
would be only one baggage mule each. On January 25,
Napier reached Senafe and the march was on.

Since Theodore's aim was no longer to govern Ethiopia
but to crush it, he was hysterically delighted by the news of
Napier's approach. He told some of his German workmen:
'I welcome the day when I shall see a disciplined European
army.' Theodore probably also hoped that once Napier had
conquered him, he would assist his defeated enemy in conquering the country. There seems no doubt that he looked
with glee on the prospect of seeing the British artillery
mowing down his levies. So as not to give too bad an account
of himself, Theodore had the Germans build a huge bell-
shaped mortar, which five hundred men dragged up the slope
to Magdala.

Theodore began to send messages to Rassam, announcing
the arrival of the royal host at the fortress. 'O my friend, do
not think that I bear any hatred toward you,' he wrote to his
chained captive. 'I have placed you in your present position
in order that I may come to know the people of your country.'
Almost daily, Rassam began receiving messages from the
Emperor and from Merewether with the advance party of
the British force. Both were approaching Magdala. It was,
writes Moorehead, 'just a question as to whether or not
Rassam would receive Theodore's maniac embrace before the
friendly British guns arrived'. Soon, all Theodore's European
hostages, and his main Ethiopian prisoners, were gathered
at Magdala, where the traditional custom was to throw
prisoners over the precipice.

The red and green cavalry, led by silver-helmeted officers,
were the vanguard of the British march through the wild
country of forests, mountains and white-draped villagers.
Many of the European infantry had beards. Some of the
Indians wore red and green tunics, and green turbans around
red fezzes. Others wore sky blue and silver uniforms, or scarlet jackets and white turbans. Some European officers had

designed their own accoutrements for this unusual campaign, and Stanley wrote of 'one young lordling' who wore kid gloves and a green veil.

The baggage train was seven and a half miles long, attended by Indians, Turks, Persians, Egyptians and Arabs. Tame elephants, with Indians squatting on their necks and cannon resting on their backs, stupified the population. The official history claims there was no plundering and that 'no swarthy damsel was subjected to any rude gallantry on the part of the redcoats' – presumably meaning that there were no complaints, an unsolicited tribute to Ethiopian womanhood's awe-inspiring sexual appetite.

The great legion trundled down thousands of feet into ravines. The sappers would build a bridge across the stream, and the army would crawl slowly up the other side. It was arduous, deliberate work. At night, camp was made. Napier's tent was laid with oriental rugs and the officers ate great Victorian heavy dinners. But the dry season was wearing on, and Napier had to lighten the march. Camp-followers were sent back to the coast, luggage allowances were cut (seventy-five pounds for officers, twentyfive for men), the officers had to rely on soldiers or each other for 'bat' services. The rum ration was cut to a dram a day. Gradually, the roasts and partridges disappeared, and *tej* replaced port.

The British and Tigrean armies – allies against Theodore – met in some state, with Kassaï riding a white mule and his courtiers bearing a crimson umbrella. Behind him, came kettledrums and four thousand warriors. Napier and his aides rode up on elephants. Kassaï, in a lionskin cape and silk robe, his hair plaited, was a handsome man in his thirties, dark like Theodore. In Napier's tent, he was presented with an Arab stallion, a rifle and Bohemian glassware. Port was served – from the hospital stores. Then Napier deployed his guns, drilled his infantry, staged a mock cavalry charge. Kassaï, impressed, offered every assistance to the British force.

In Kassaï's tent, Ethiopian girls plied the British general staff with bullocks' horns of *tej*, and pitchers of bread and curry. Minstrels and singers entertained. Napier was draped in a lion cape, given a sword, a shield, a spear and a white mule, and rode back to his lines.

Napier had been intrigued to see that all Kassaï's men had rifles. He feared – wrongly – that this might mean most of Theodore's had firearms also; they might deploy in the bush that stretched for two hundred more mountainous miles to Magdala, and harass the march. The high passes were now nine thousand feet above sea level; the animals were getting tired, and the guns seemed ever heavier; the men were weary and feverish from thunderstorms and freezing nights. The dry season was clearly drawing to a close.

Theodore, still approaching Magdala from the West, sent orders for Rassam's chains to be removed, apparently so that his 'friend' could come out and see, in the valley distance, the tents of the approaching Ethiopian horde. The royal treasure began to appear in Magdala, and on March 27 the Emperor himself arrived, prayed at the church and set up his throne outside the palace. He received the cowed Magdala chiefs, accusing them of treason, then returned to his camp in the valley. The black mood was on again: new, more brutal guards were placed on the European prisoners.

But when Theodore returned to the mountain fortress a few days later, he sent for Rassam. He was now in good humor, agreed that Prideaux and Blanc should be released from their chains, and only darkened when Cameron's name was mentioned. The Emperor was in one of his confessional moods. He said to the Iraqi: 'How can I show these ragged soldiers of mine to your well-dressed troops? . . . Were I as powerful as I was once, I should certainly have gone down to the coast to meet your people on landing; or I would have sent and asked them what they wanted in my country. As it is, I have lost all Ethiopia but this rock!'

Despite Theodore's childish satisfaction at having forced an army of such size and modernity to come across the world to Magdala, he seemed to realize that he was in fact being attacked and was about to be defeated. But he insisted his great mortar was to be used, not against the British, but against Ethiopians. To close the long monologue, he ordered that all the prisoners should be unchained.

Napier, below, found himself facing three flat-topped peaks of nine thousand feet, plus the fortress peak itself. Theodore was to be lured to give battle on plain or plateau, then Magdala was to be taken by climbers and scaling

271

ladders. The Galla tribesmen were to be asked to surround the fortress and cut down Theodore and his men if they sought to retreat. Theodore appeared to have about seven thousand men, artillery, rifles and the giant mortar. Napier sent a final ultimatum for the release of the prisoners.

The last forced marches were in a heat wave, followed each night by cold, hail and thunderstorms. The elephants began to slither and collapse. The food train got thirtysix hours behind. But at last the enemy was in sight. The legion crossed the Bascillo on the morning of April 10 – Good Friday – filling its water-bottles in the river, then began the five-mile ascent to the Aroge plateau.

On the Wednesday, Theodore had addressed his troops. They were, he told them, to meet an army far superior to themselves, riding on elephants. He took a twisted pleasure in demoralizing his own soldiers.

'Are you ready to fight, and enrich yourselves with the spoils of these white slaves, or will you disgrace me by running away?' he roared.

An old warrior called back loyally that they would cut the foreigners to pieces.

'What are you saying, you old fool?' screamed the Emperor. 'Have you ever seen an English soldier? Before you know where you are, your belly will be riddled with bullets.' There was more in this vein. Not unnaturally, when Rassam suggested negotiations with Napier, he dismissed the idea.

That evening he saw through his telescope the elephants arriving on the plateau and he became exalted – so happy that he released some of his prisoners (all the Europeans, thirtyseven chiefs, and some Ethiopian women and children). On the morrow, he declared a general amnesty, but later changed his mind and had one hundred and ninetyseven Ethiopian prisoners thrown over the precipice. One man, who had been chained for years for assaulting one of Theodore's concubines, was released, but his two innocent sons, who had been chained with him, were hurled to their death.

Theodore spent Thursday night in drunken prayer, crying for forgiveness for the massacre he had just committed. When a gray, wet dawn broke, most of the fortress population had gone down to the plateau, preferring the battle to Theodore's homicidal caprices. There remained on the pinnacle about fifty courtiers and guards, the European prisoners, and the staggering, screaming, weeping King.

Moorehead calls Theodore 'a Caliban with power. . . . He was caught in the African predicament – the imperative need of the intelligent man to emerge from sloth and ignorance – and it was too big for him. . . . He saw shadows and treacheries everywhere, and hatred instead of the thing he yearned for – love.'

Moorehead goes on: 'And so to settle an issue of pride, one man's against a nation's, we have now the extraordinary spectacle of two armies advancing against one another high up in this remote eyrie in the Ethiopian mountains. The armies are ignorant beyond dreams; they know nothing of one another's language, politics or way of life. They have no real hatred of one another, and no real interest in the quarrel. Yet someone orders them to fight and off they go, Christians and Muhammedans, blacks and whites, Sikhs, Hindus and Ethiopian tribesmen, believing implicitly that the action to which they are committed – the killing of one another – is absolutely inevitable and right.'

The battle, which was a massacre, was fought Good Friday afternoon in pouring rain. The Ethiopians charged ceaselessly and with enormous courage, mostly with spears against rifles. Fearing that his men would get lost in the darkness, Napier broke off the pursuit at sundown. In the morning, the casualties were counted: seven hundred Ethiopian dead, twelve hundred wounded. The British had twenty wounded, two mortally. The great Ethiopian mortar had burst on use.

Rassam had been awoken just before midnight, after the battle, by a messenger from Theodore. The Emperor was apparently well satisfied with the drubbing that his men had received, and was now prepared to talk of truce. Rassam sent the German missionary Flad, who had brought the Emperor's message, back to the royal tent with a suggestion that a dawn party, including Prideaux, be sent across to Napier to sue for peace. When Flad returned to Theodore's presence, he found him in a drunken fury. Theodore no longer wanted a truce, but war. He ordered Flad back to his tent. But at 4 a.m., he sent for him again and told him to go off with Prideaux and Dejatch Alami – Theodore's son-in-law – to the British lines.

At dawn that Easter Saturday, the group, bearing a white flag, reached the British camp with a verbal message from the Emperor saying he wanted a 'reconciliation'. Napier was magnanimous. In his response, he congratulated Theodore on the bravery of his warriors, and said if the prisoners were handed over he would guarantee 'honorable treatment for yourself . . . and your family.' At the same time, the Dejatch was shown the elephants and the heavy artillery which the British had not had time to deploy on the previous day. Verbally, the Dejatch was told that if Theodore did not surrender, these guns would be used. Unless Alami and his fellow princes restrained Theodore from further atrocities, they would be held in equal guilt.

Theodore, when he received Napier's message, quibbled. He still had enough men to go on fighting. What was 'honorable treatment'? Was he now a prisoner or an ally? He sent back a typically Theodorian response. There was no mention of the prisoners or of surrender. He abused his own 'cowardly' people, and finished on an *outre-tombe* note: 'In my city there are multitudes whom I have fed: maidens protected and unprotected; women yesterday made widows; aged parents with no children. God has given you the power. See that you forsake not these people. It is a heathen land.'

Theodore explained to the British general that his ambition had been to conquer the world, or die if he failed. 'Since the day of my birth till now no man has dared to lay hand on me.' Now, he wished defeat on the British, for robbing him of his ambition to 'lead my army against Jerusalem, and expel from it the Turks.'

A war council was called and many chiefs suggested he murder the European prisoners and renew hostilities. Curiously, in the face of impulsiveness from others, Theodore became sober. Executions, he reasoned, would invite reprisals. The prisoners would have to be released. On Saturday afternoon, a group of chiefs was sent from Theodore's camp on the plateau to bring the prisoners down from Magdala. Again, there was the Theodorian about-face: while the chiefs were away on their mission, he seized a double-barreled pistol and, weeping with rage, thrust it into his mouth and pulled the trigger; there was no explosion. One of his men grabbed the gun away; in the scuffle it went off, grazing

Theodore's ear. He covered his bloodied head in a cloth and lay on the ground.

When the prisoners came he asked to see Rassam alone, and there was another of the wierd cat-and-mouse scenes, with Theodore saying 'Unless you befriend me, I shall either kill myself or become a monk.' That night, Rassam and his party were sent safely to the British lines. Flad and Prideaux, on their way to Theodore with a fresh Napier ultimatum, turned back.

On the Sunday, Napier received another message from Theodore saying God had spared him from suicide, and asking for the body of Gabry, a dead warrior chief. Flad went off with a litter to bring down his wife, who had been too ill to come down with Rassam, and on the way through Theodore's camp they handed over Gabry's body. That evening, the sick prisoners, save for a French missionary called Bardel who could not be moved, were brought down to Napier's camp. Theodore sent a thousand cows and five hundred sheep – all he possessed – to Napier, who was informed that if he accepted them he was bound, by Ethiopian custom, to conclude peace. At this point, Napier could obviously accept nothing short of surrender, so he had the animals driven back.

Theodore assumed this decision to be his sentence of death. Taking two thousand men, he went back up to the citadel, whence he apparently intended to cut out for Lake Tana. But the vanguard of his party turned back when they realized that the Galla were lying in wait all around. Bitter arguments followed, with Theodore as usual scolding his men for cowardice. The chiefs were against abandoning their families and possessions: they should, they said, surrender or fight. They decided among themselves on surrender. In view of Dejatch Alami's account of Napier's warning, they also decreed that if Theodore attempted any more executions, they would put the King in chains. By now, as a result of the battle, there were several thousand people in the fortress, and during the night thousands came down to the British camp.

In the morning, Theodore left the citadel with an *élite* guard of fifty men to rescue some artillery from the plain below. The group was surprised, dragging the pieces up the cliff, by British cavalry. On horseback, Theodore rode up and down, firing his rifle in the air, challenging the British officers to take him on personally. The Emperor's men persuaded him to withdraw up to Magdala. Still, the British waited patiently for him to surrender.

During the night, there was a rumor that he had escaped. Napier offered a reward of fifty thousand Maria Theresa dollars to the Gallas, for his capture dead or alive. Light artillery and three thousand men were mustered for an assault on the fortress.

On the Tuesday morning, the roofed gate to the fortress was taken by rockets, scaling ladders and direct infantry assault – in the roar of thunder and gunpowder, under pouring rain. Ethiopians poured forward to surrender, and, from the camp below, the remaining soldiers saw the Union Jack go up on the ramparts. Theodore's body was found near a second gate. He had led the defence of the first gate, then had rushed back to the second to tell his followers to try to escape. Then, he had turned to face the invaders and, putting one of Queen Victoria's pistols in his mouth, had blown his brains out. The victorious Anglo-Indian army was allowed to loot the palace.

Empress Teru-Work said it had been her husband's wish that his son, Alamayo, should be educated in England, and that she would like to go with him. Napier agreed, but he ignored Theodore's plea for the British to take over Ethiopia. His instructions from London were clear, and the rescue of the prisoners had already cost a fortune. He abandoned Ethiopia to anarchy. The Queen of the Galla was installed as ruler of Magdala, and the wider issue of Ethiopian kingship was left for the Ethiopians to forge in further blood. Some of the elephants brought down the treasures, and everything of Magdala except the churches was mined and blown. The guns and armories went up in a deafening roar.

Teru-Work grew frail and died on the march to the coast. (Alamayo went on, was educated at Rugby School, but died at nineteen and was buried at Windsor.) At Senafe, leave was taken of Kassaï, who was given prodigious gifts of military hardware, making him the most powerful chieftain in Ethiopia.

*

276

But eventually it was an Amharic, John IV, not Kassaï, who began to restore the Kingdom's central authority. An old rival of Theodore's, Menelik, still controlled Shoa and, with arms bought from French hucksters – including the poet Arthur Rimbaud – Menelik subjugated the Galla country. In 1882, John and Menelik shared the empire: John remained Emperor; Menelik would succeed him, and meanwhile would govern Harar, Kaffa and the Galla country. The uneasy bond was thinly sealed by the marriage of John's twelve-year-old son and Menelik's seven-year-old daughter Zaüditu. Menelik became Emperor in 1889.

The chief problem of Menelik's reign was to be Italy. In 1869, an Italian company had bought a trading station on the Horn called Assab. The port became Italian Government property in 1882, and Rome began negotiations with Menelik in Shoa for a trade treaty. In 1884, Britain briefly occupied the Eritrean coast to evacuate Egyptian garrisons marooned in the Sudan by the Mahdist rising. The British sought Menelik's help by promising him Massawa and the formerly Egyptian territory, at the same time encouraging Italy to occupy Massawa and other points on the Red Sea coast.

Early in 1885, Italian expeditions landed at Massawa and pushed inland, coming into conflict with Ethiopian forces. On January 26, 1887, an Italian force was practically exterminated by twenty thousand Ethiopian warriors, at Dogali. Italian posts up-country were evacuated and Italy proposed military assistance to Menelik in his rivalry with John IV. In return, Italy asked Menelik to recognize Italian rights to Asmara and the neighboring upland territory. Menelik accepted Italian gifts of munitions – but did nothing to help the Italians occupy the terrain they coveted.

In 1889, John was killed by a Mahdist bullet in the war with the Dervishes. Anarchy followed – to the advantage of both Menelik and Rome. The Italians occupied Asmara and helped Menelik become the Negusa Nagast. By the ambiguous treaty of Ucciali, Menelik conceded to Italy certain protectorate rights over the whole empire.

The Negus sent his nephew, Ras Makonnen, to Rome to negotiate a loan mortgaged against the principality of Harar. In addition to the loan, King Umberto gave Makonnen twentyeight cannon and thirtyeight thousand rifles, as a gift.

Another power which evinced interest in Ethiopia was Tsarist Russia. In the 'Eighties, a group of about two hundred Russians, men and women, arrived in the country under the monk Païssi and the Cossack Achinor. The party included soldiers, engineers, craftsmen and priests. Exploiting the links between Eastern Orthodoxy and the Copts, the Russians established a monastery. Aware that Russia now sought a Colony in Africa, the Italians made extensive reports on all the Russian initiatives.

In 1890, French and Russian envoys made a bid to secure for their countries the position of most favoured power in Ethiopia. Italy protested, and grew more and more troublesome. Menelik repaid the Italian loan and denounced the Treaty of Ucciali. But it was the French who successfully intrigued to have the Russians expelled – although a small Russian community remained, after representation by the Tsar to Menelik. In modern times also, Ethiopia was the first African country in which Russia showed a deep interest.

Meanwhile, in 1885, Italy had secured a second foothold to Eritrea, further South, by the seizure of land around the Juba River mouth. In 1888, the Sultan at Obbia signed a protectorate treaty and the proto-colony of Somalia came into being. The hold on the Somali coast was extended in 1891. In 1893, an Italian chartered company was empowered to administer the territory.

Menelik's relations with Britain, now established at Berbera, and with France – perched on the little enclave of Jibuti – were good; but Italy became, more and more, an impatient thorn thrusting into the Emperor's side. Menelik now sought to recover most of the coast himself, and to push South as far as the Nyanza (Lake Victoria). Meanwhile, he maintained friendly links with London and, in 1894, gave a French syndicate concession rights to build a railroad from Jibuti.

Menelik's chief rival for power, Ras Mangasha of Tigre, had, in 1891, signed a treaty with Italy. Rome promised him assistance for a Tigrean rebellion. But in 1895, Mangasha rallied to Menelik: the two princes, together, marched North to Italian-held territory. The national cause achieved quasi-unanimous support, and Italy, hastily mobilizing, faced

Menelik's Shoan warriors, Makonnen's Harar levies, Mangasha's Tigreans, the forces of Gojjam and the Galla horsemen, all at once.

Italy's General Baratieri chose to fight at Adowa, on March 1, 1896. Using the arms and ammunition given to Ethiopia by Italy itself, plus the arms obtained from French dealers, and the great superiority of numbers – and taking advantage of a serious error in the Italian map of the country, which caused a fatal split-up of the attacking forces – the Ethiopians, under Makonnen, scored a decisive victory. Out of fourteen thousand five hundred soldiers, about eight thousand Europeans and four thousand native troops were killed. By a new treaty, in October, Italy accepted its humiliation, recognized Ethiopian sovereignty and agreed to be satisfied with Eritrea.

Until his death in 1908, Menelik expanded his empire and made a modest start at modernizing its administration. In 1883, he had founded a new capital, Addis Ababa ('New Flower') to please his Empress; after Adowa, numerous embassies arrived there, bearing gifts for the Emperor, who went from strength to strength in the constant internal battle for power. French interests finally defeated British ones over the railroad project, although Menelik forbade building to start when the French government took up a large part of the investment in 1902. Permission was finally given in 1906; Britain and Italy were authorized to extend the line beyond Addis Ababa, but have never done so. Trains did not run from Jibuti until 1918.

Britain secured a treaty fixing the limits of its colony Somaliland, and pastoral rights, but failed to overcome Ras Makonnen's Anglophobia. The main clause of the 1902 pact, from London's point of view, was the assurance that Ethiopia would not divert the waters of the Nile – necessary for the survival of Britain's protégé, Egypt. Menelik signed many private treaties which he did not take seriously; some gave the same concessions to different countries or companies; he pocketed the often substantial bribes offered to him for these privileges. Of the many business negotiations, the only two of importance that finally led to anything were those concerning the French railroad and a British 'Bank of Abyssinia'. Menelik drove a hard bargain in all cases, and exacted often exorbitant percentages. He lent money at astronomical rates of interest to new investing companies, using these profits to improve his army.

Madagascar

MADAGASCAR, whose place in a volume of African history is due only to its geographical propinquity, is culturally a piece of Asia – as Indonesia's apparently improbable claim to the island, in recent times, signifies. Cut off from the African mainland about five hundred million years ago – and later (but still before Peking Man) separated from the Asian-Australasian land mass – Madagascar has developed its own flora and fauna. The ancient coelecanth lives in its waters. Eggs of the horse-sized, wingless Aepyornis bird, which disappeared at the hands of hunters probably in the 19th Century, are still found: they measure three feet in circumference and hold a gallon of albumen. Incredible lizards, and chicken-sized butterflies, still lure zoologists.

Polynesian people from the Malayo-Indonesian archipelago arrived in Madagascar about two thousand years ago, by either land or sea routes or both: they brought with them their Polynesian language (with links to Maori, Indonesian and above all Malay), rice cultivation, outrigger canoes and Polynesian legends which still haunt the country, whose tall, well-built farmhouses, yoked oxen, irrigated paddy-fields and delicate manners and mores are still markedly non-African. The last immigration waves arrived around the end of the 15th Century.

Mention of a great island in the West of the Indian Ocean appears in Egyptian, Greek and Roman records. It was sometimes confused with Ceylon. The present name comes from Marco Polo's appellation Madeigascar – possibly due to his confusing the place (which he never saw) with Mogadishu.

The name, has, at all costs, been preserved in the Malagasy language, as Madekase. The island was put on the map in 1500 when one of Vasco da Gama's captains, blown off course, made landfall there. In the ensuing centuries, the four Indian Ocean powers – Portugal, Britain, Holland and France – did little about the island. Tentative settlements succumbed to sickness or violence from earlier (Polynesian) settlers.

The island was an important pirates' lair at the turn of the 17th–18th centuries. Diego Suarez became briefly "The International Republic of Libertalia', run by a three-man, tri-national pirate committee 'representing' England, France and Italy. The Republic had a constitution, an international language and communal farms, and the tri-piratate enjoyed diplomatic relations with Sweden, Russia and Turkey.

An American merchantman which traded with the Diego Suarez pirates in 1699 took back Malagasy rice to Carolina, thus starting rice in North America. But England and France had cleared the island's coves of pirates fairly thoroughly by 1724. Around 1750, a marooned French corporal married a minor Malagasy coastal queen and persuaded her to cede her realm to France – a treaty never in fact revoked. A friend of Voltaire's decided to convert Madagascar into Utopia in 1768 and use it as a base for Abolition; but he left three years later – with a cargo of slaves for the French West Indies.

A Polish-Hungarian, Bardo de Benyowski, was commissioned to take over the island by the French court, in 1774. When royal inspectors exposed his glowing despatches of pacification and development as fiction, and withdrew French support, Benyowski proclaimed himself Emperor and offered his empire to Britain, Austro-Hungary and the infant United States. Only in the U.S. did he find some support, when slave-dealers in Baltimore offered him a ship and a cash advance in exchange for a slave monopoly in Madagascar. In 1785, he returned to his domains, but the following year he was ousted and killed by French forces.

The Europeans, from the Portuguese to the French, only settled minor coastal stretches. In the highland interior, substantial kingdoms existed among the Merina (pronounced Merin), a Polynesian people untouched by the Arab, African and Indian influences found on the coast. News of this culture, harsh but orientally exquisite, finally reached European ears in 1771. The kingdoms appear to date from about eight hundred years ago, perhaps longer, and to have controlled the heart of the island by the 15th Century. The present island capital, Antananarivo, meaning 'city of a thousand warriors', refers to a siege by rebels survived by a Merina king in the 17th Century. The Merina remain, today, the upper caste of the island, and form about a quarter of the population; they are noted for their long names: one 17th Century King was called Andriatsimitoviaminandriadehibe.

The best-known of the Merina kings, Andrianampoinimerina, who ruled from 1787 to 1810, united and civically disciplined the realm, conquering the minor Polynesian and mixed-blood kingdoms in Betsileo and on the coast, introducing capital punishment for theft, and slavery for idleness – which he poetically defined as 'theft of time'. He made the kingship sacred, its inviolability signified by a red parasol. He banned tobacco and alcohol and refused entry to the kingdom to Europeans, with whom his only contact was to trade slaves for firearms. He forged the links with his former rebel enemies by marrying twelve daughters of twelve chieftains. To avoid assassination, the two beds in his chamber – one for the King, one for all twelve wives together – were raised ten feet from the floor. His death was an occasion for island-wide weeping, and he was buried, wrapped in eighty silken robes, in a silver canoe.

His successor, Radama I, selected by Andrianampoinimerina from among his twentyfour surviving sons, engaged British political and military advisors, and Malagasies began to go to Oxford. Today, after three generations of French influence, there as still as many Protestants as Catholics, in Madagascar. Radama encouraged European traders and English Protestant missionaries. At one point his fifteen thousand-strong army was commanded by three sergeants, all promoted general: one was an illiterate Jamaican mulatto, one a French deserter, one a Scot; the latter brought to the island the horse, the wheel and (of course) barley, the grain from which whisky is made. These men taught the use of modern weapons, and introduced western discipline: Radama added to this by decreeing that deserters should be burned alive.

Radama became the first man to be recognized as 'King of Madagascar', when Britain exchanged consular instruments with him. The great reformer forced his reluctant subjects into Anglican schools with such vigor that it is thought possible that, at the time, there were more children at school in Madagascar than in Africa. From his sergeants-general, Radama learned English and French, and had Malagasy transliterated into the Latin alphabet. He read the Bible, was impressed, and decreed that henceforth capital punishment in Madagascar would be by crucifixion. He abolished slavery and set the punishment for slavers as . . . slavery. He abrogated ordeals by poison, and the sacrifice of 'ill omen' children. In 1828, he died, aged thirtyfive, worn out by work, wars, women and local whisky. Twelve thousand Spanish doubloons were hammered flat to make his silver coffin, and another ten thousand to make its pedestal. The treasure buried with Radama included his twelve favorite warhorses and his eighty London-made uniforms. Twenty thousand oxen are said to have been slaughtered to feed his mourners; the chronicler says that his coffin was borne over prostrate acres of weeping women.

For the rest of the 19th Century, Madagascar was ruled by Queens, some of whom, like a redoubtable number of Asian and African Queens, were renowned for their cruelty. Radama's widow, who took the throne name of Ranavalona, widened capital punishment crimes to include Christianity, restored slavery and reputedly executed two hundred thousand people in thirtythree years of gory government. Some were burned alive, some crucified, some hurled off cliffs.

Ranavalona was short and fat and was – like the wife of President Roberts of Liberia – noted for her close resemblance to Queen Victoria. She had twelve husbands and numerous lovers, and was insanely superstitious, reactionary and xenophobic. The one exception to her racial and religious chauvinism was Jean Laborde, a simple young French blacksmith, who was shipwrecked on a Malagasy beach around 1828 and lived on the island for about fifty years until his death, becoming a Malagasy citizen and nobleman. Working from encyclopedias and simple manuals, he built an industrial complex at Mantasca – a spot favored by ample, swift-flowing water supplies, iron deposits and fine forests. Using two hundred thousand forced labourers, he mined and smelted iron and steel, produced glass, pottery, chinaware, bricks, tiles, cement, sulphuric acid, dyes, soap, potash, sealing wax, silk, ribbons, straw hats (still basic clothing in the island), paper, ink, rope, cloth, guns, cannon, grenades, cartridges, gunpowder and swords. He refined sugar, distilled rum, cultivated novelties like vanilla and grapes, improved the island's cattle, pioneered fish-farming. For the Queen, whose lover he is believed to have been, he built a new palace, with swimming pool, fish pond and zoo.

When the ardent old shrew died in 1861, after the island's longest reign, her sensitive son, Radama II, a bastard fathered by his mother's prime minister, abolished the barbarities associated with the previous tenant of the throne. He installed a sort of idealistic anarchy. He was soon strangled on the orders of his wife. She took the throne under the name of Rasoherina, and put the public executioners back in business.

Her successor, a cousin who called herself Ranavalona II, was crowned in 1868 carrying a Bible, a gift from Queen Victoria. She married and converted to Christianity her predecessor's prime minister, thus obliging him to abandon a dozen other wives, by one of whom he had nineteen children. Ranavalona II is chiefly famous for having employed Trader Horn as a high seas tax-collector.

The premier, Rainilaiarivony, introduced a code of laws which is partly still extant, reformed the kingdom slowly and lastingly, and played France and Britain off against each other. He drafted a consular treaty with the United States in 1867. During this reign, nearly all the Merina converted to Anglicanism, leaving the later, Catholic missionaries to concentrate on the serf and slave classes of Malagasies, and the backward bush and coastal peoples: this religious division is still sharply evident in Malagasy politics today.

When Ranavalona II died of gout at the age of fiftyfour, her all-powerful premier-widower selected her pretty twenty-two-year-old cousin to succeed to the throne, and married her too. Perhaps to avoid murmuring the wrong name in his sleep, this Malagasy mixture of Talleyrand and Don Juan gave her the throne name Ranavalona III.

Southern Africa

THE HISTORY OF THE SOUTHERN TIP OF AFRICA is directly linked, at the start, to the opening up of the Cape of Good Hope route to southern India. In 1652, the Dutch East India Company set up a watering-station on the Cape for the long-distance clippers, known then as Indiamen. The indigenous people of the Cape were scant in number, and composed of two curious subsidiary peoples in evolution, the Bushmen and Hottentots. After some initial raids, they proved to be easy, gentle, good-humored neighbors for the pioneers.

The Bushmen and Hottentots lived off cattle-raising and hunting; only to a limited degree were they suitable as labor in the Europeans' settlement. Their resistance to disease was poor. Even the limited numbers that existed then have been disappearing ever since.

Thus, in most of what is today Cape Province, the European population can assert – as of course it does assert, in rejecting certain claims of African nationalism – to be, to all intents and purposes, the indigenous tribe. East of the Kei, however, in areas known today as TransKei, Natal and Pondoland, tribes had migrated South from the Zimbabwes and from what is today Moçambique. These were the Nguni ancestors of the modern Zulu, and peoples who seem to correspond to those known now as the Xhosa, the Pondo and the Tembu.

These African groups of settlers were only interested in the high-rainfall lowlands – modern Natal and its neighboring lands. The Bushmen-Hottentot hunters and pastoralists clung to what is today called the Western Cape. The high veld was almost uninhabited. It was late in the 18th Century that the white colonists, advancing inland, first met 'Bantu' tribesmen near the Great Fish River, about five hundred miles East of Cape Town.

When it set up its watering station, the Dutch Company

had no real colonization intention, no interest in the interior. But to ensure defense of the settlement, and food for its members and the ships, farmer-colonists were sought. Cape Town, with its fine warm-temperate climate, its fertile soil, ample rainfall, and impressive natural beauty of mountain and coast, drew more and more settlers. By the time the Company decided to check further immigration, the immigrants already established were chafing against the restrictions imposed on their activities and area of settlement by the Company – and the inadequacy of Cape Town and its ships as a market for the expanding generations of white market-farmers.

During the 18th Century, many of these land-hungry people, generically described as Boers (peasants), trekked off into the interior, away from the Company – and from any world authority. They farmed and traded their produce with the Hottentots for cattle, then became stock-breeders themselves. Like the Hottentots before them, they found the immense plains better suited to cattle than to most crops. Many trekked on further East in search of better rainfalls.

A sturdy, immensely courageous people, the Trekboers pioneered and tamed vast expanses of what is today South Africa. Owing no allegiance to Holland, they came to be called Afrikaners (Africans), and their simplified version of Dutch became 'Afrikaans'. Their indomitable spirit, like that of the early pioneers of North America, was religious. Like the Puritans, they spurred their swords with piety, and reaped their harvests with a strong measure of primitive devotion and devout thanksgiving. Calvinists, they came to believe they were a sort of chosen people, whose industry and courage had been rewarded by God himself with a gift of this great new country, in which no recognized power contested their suzerainty. In this exalted context, they saw the 'heathen' around them as enemies, not just of God's elect, but of God himself, and therefore shorn of any rights which God's 'chosen' need respect. As well as their European skills, and industrious European dynamic, they possessed the precious Western ethic of rugged individualism.

To begin with, the Boers went East more than North. They erased Bushmen communities, and drove off the pastoral Hottentots. In 1779, they reached the Great Fish River, then the frontier of the 'Bantu' tribes with the Hottentots. The more advanced tribes they now encountered had broadly similar cultures; all their languages were rooted in nearly identical laws of syntax and pronunciation, with similar prefixes, suffixes and infixes. In most of the languages, 'man' was 'muntu'; from the plural of this, 'bantu', came the local generic term for all black Africans who are not Hottentots or Bushmen.

The encounter of 1779 indirectly caused the first of the numerous inter-tribal 'Kaffir Wars', the name being taken from the term used by the Arabs in East Africa for an infidel – *kafir*. (The word, which Arabs used to apply to all non-Muslims, was inherited by the Portuguese and then the Boers – who did not know that, as Christians, they were *kafiri* too.) These wars were to be a source of embarrassment to the faraway authorities in Cape Town, and to lead to closer administration.

During the Napoleonic Wars, 1793–1815, the Cape passed from Dutch to British ownership. With this change came still greater measure of control over the far-flung Afrikaner realms. In 1795, just as Company government was drawing to a close, the two Boer communities of Swellendam and Graaff Reinet declared their own independent republics out on the frontier – in much the same way as breakaway groups of 'other' African tribes traditionally founded chiefdoms. Britain, however, managed to reassert control. In 1820, London sent in some five thousand Britons, mostly ex-soldiers and their families, and gave them land near the frontier of white expansion: this was partly to assume defense of the dispersed territories against invasions by the Bantu, partly – in one historian's words – to 'provide a British leaven in the Boer mass'.

Until this period, the Bantu tribes living on the monsoon coastal plains of Natal had been able to expand as generations required, either into uninhabited territory or, like the Afrikaners, by killing off Bushmen or Hottentots. Now the arrival of white trekkers provided a new and more difficult challenge, just as the presence of Bantu settlers posed a new problem for the Boers. One result, on the more rapidly proliferating Bantu side, was to touch off the 'Kaffir Wars', with larger tribes seeking to oust weaker ones from their lands.

About the time of the arrival of the '1820 Settlers', the Zulu clan of the Nguni was falling under the influence of a rising military leader called Shaka; this forceful figure formed the traditional warrior age-groups into a sort of permanent army, which he taught to fight at close quarters, using the assegaï as a bayonet, not a throwing-spear. When the Nguni Chief Dingiswayo died in 1818, the Zulu clan became a sort of independent warrior nation, headed by Shaka, ultimately absorbing its other Nguni brethren by force. For ten years, the Zulu ravaged, plundered, and constructed a Natalian empire. Shaka, notorious in history for his cruelty as well as his skill, was finally murdered by his half-brothers in 1828; one of these, Dingaan, inherited the leadership. He proved as strong and ruthless as Shaka; what had formerly been the lands of tribal neighbors became almost uninhabited Zulu grazing grounds, fringing a wide Zulu empire.

Zulu rapine inspired similar movements among those the Zulu had defeated, but who felt strong enough to conquer weaker tribes. A Sotho warrior leader called Sebetwaan took a group, the Makololo, northward to conquer and rule Barotseland on the upper Zambezi. The main legion of the Sotho, under Mantatise, went West into Bechuanaland, plundering widely, and finally quarrelling violently and self-destructively among themselves. In what is now known as Swaziland, an established ruler, Sobhuza, and his successor, Mswazi, absorbed the refugees of Zulu attacks to forge a kingdom that blocked further Zulu advance in that quarter. The southern Sotho king Moshesh managed to forge a strong kingdom similarly, out of war refugees fleeing into his territory. Some Zulu leaders who had quarrelled with the tyrannous Shaka also struck out on their own and set up realms on the frontiers of Shaka's lands, fighting off their attacking brethren.

Soshangaan went North into Gazaland with his Shangaan people and absorbed the Tonga. Zwangendaba and his *impi* swept like locusts through the highlands of the Limpopo-Zambezi watersheds and finally settled around Lake Nyasa. Mzilikazi led the Ndebele – now usually called the Matabele – across the Drakensbergs, acquiring modern Matabeleland in Rhodesia's West; he scattered, in his march, the TransVaal Sotho – West toward the Kalahari, South toward

Basutoland-Lesotho. Into this holocaust of 'Kaffir wars' came the Great Trek – an ever-growing stream of tough, primitve, illiterate Boers who had set out from Cape Colony in 1836, fleeing, as Alan Paton has put it, 'from British liberal ideas'.

*

It was in 1825 that the British administration at Cape Town began enacting laws to protect the territory's non-Europeans. The colony was now less of a military concept, and there were elementary democratic institutions. Military commitments were reduced, and new sources of revenue were sought, to try to balance the still heavily subsidized budget. One obvious source of revenue was to regulate land owner-ship, thus raising its value. This struck an obvious blow at the Afrikaner farmer.

But what alienated Boer opinion most was the concept, in British law, of individual rights – and in particular the Aboli-tion, in 1833, of slavery in the British Empire. There were at the time twenty thousand Malay slaves in the Cape, imported because of the unsuitability for labor of Bushmen and Hottentots; the descendants of these Malays, plus per-sons of mixed Eurasian and Eurafrican stock, and some Euro-Hottentots and Malay-Ntots, form today's one and three quarter million Cape Coloreds.

The infant Legislative Council reacted to the wave of London liberalism by making a law removing some of the democratic protections provided for non-whites; this was vetoed in 1834 by the Colonial Office. In 1836, some land annexed to Europeans, for reasons of security, on the eastern frontier, was returned to Bantu ownership – a British decision taken in the interest of economics.

By then, Boer land hunger was very real, and in the pre-vailing conditions in the interior a family was said to need *about six thousand acres*: the 1834 and 1836 decisions con-firmed Boer opinion that the English were allying themselves, politically, with the black settlers against the white ones. A convoy of wagons, the first of many, set out across the Orange River. Piet Retief, the pioneer hero of the early Great Trek-kers, made no bones about the Afrikaner intention – to set up realms, to be run on strict, 'traditional' Afrikaner principles, beyond the reach of British liberal interference.

The first move was across the High Veld, where the Boers dispersed the Matabele North across the Limpopo; (there they established a power relationship over Mashonaland, the Mashona having been shattered by Soshangaan and Zwangendaba). But the main trek was into Natal. At first, Dingaan seemed peaceable, but soon the *impi* attacked. Retief was killed and a new leader, Pretorius, emerged. Like the pioneers in North America, the Boers used their wagons to form stockades, called *laagers,* and organized commandos to retaliate. Outnumbered, but better in firepower and mobility, the Boers crushed Dingaan, and in 1839 Pretorius proclaimed the Peasant Republic of Natal.

Although the Boers had crossed the Cape frontier, Britain insisted they were still British subjects. London was unwilling to leave these rebellious citizens, now a hopelessly moronic sub-group of the western culture, in control of Indian Ocean harbors. Boer expansion was creating African land hunger, and the wars thus engendered would be a constantly recurring defense problem for the Cape. British troops landed at what is now Durban, and Natal was annexed to the Crown in 1845. The obstinate Boers, foreigners to the British by language and mentality, naturally resented this new frustration, and many trekked back across the Drakensbergs.

For a while, each separate Boer community existed autonomously, under rugged, democratically chosen leaders; but before long the Boers began to feel that unity was essential against the political incursions of the British and the slaughtering incursions of the neighboring Bantu. Two independent states were formed: the South African Republic – modern Transvaal, between the Vaal and the Limpopo – and the Orange Free State, between the Vaal and the Orange. A male electorate chose *Volksraads* (Peoples' Councils) who in turn gave great powers to the Presidents in times of emergency – which were frequent. Thus was born something different from the (in many other ways similar) pioneer experience of North America: a drift toward dictatorship, or totalitarian authority, emerged early among the Afrikaners. Since both Boer republics lacked a viable economy, and since their proper administration would be costly, Britain refrained from absorbing them, and recognized their independence in 1852 and 1854 respectively.

In contrast with these poor but independent zones Cape Colony began to become prosperous in the 'Sixties, from sugar and sheep. Indian indentured labor was brought in for the plantations. Cape Colony then had about a quarter of a million whites, compared to forty thousand in the Transvaal, thirty thousand in the OFS. These two republics of undefined frontiers were soon unable to defend themselves from the continual warring brought about by their own expansions: the great tracts of cattle range necessary for a viable European farm made the issue one of dramatic proportions, and these small, veld communities wrote chapters in brutal courage. But they also raised problems of general peace which Great Britain was obliged to solve.

At the request of the great Moshesh, who had become Paramount of the Basotho in 1818, had united all the tribes of the Lesotho nation, and had been in power ever since, what the Europeans called Basutoland was brought under British control in 1868. Moshesh died in 1870. Partly to protect the eastern Cape frontier, partly to guarantee the harassed OFS, Basutoland was annexed to Cape Colony in 1871. The same year, Britain acquired Griqualand West, where diamonds had been found. The Griqua people, Hottentots with a long association with the Cape and with many Europeanized mores, welcomed the occupation, which saved the land from a Boer invasion.

The problem of the land-locked Afrikaner republics, still economically unviable, hard to defend from invasion, and cut off from the outside world except by slow ox-wagon trails, remained entire. Boer autonomy was a source of internecine African warfare, and it subverted the power for law and order of the chiefs. It was by then historically clear that a solution in the whole area would have to look upon all inhabitants of austral Africa, black and white, as citizens of the same country, with basically interdependent interests and problems.

In 1872, Cape Colony, whose economy was rising fast on diamonds, was granted self-government, with ministers responsible to a parliament, elected by all adult males without distinction as to race. Britain's hope was that, with this as an example, it would be possible to forge a self-governing, self-financing federation of the Cape, Natal and the Boer republics, leaving London to concern itself only with the Cape naval base. But there was at once strong opposition from the Cape itself.

The population there had no wish to share its diamond money with the degenerate Afrikaner peasants in the outback. Nor did they wish their racially balanced society, in which whites and Coloreds outnumbered Bantu, upset by the absorption of an illiterate horde of tribal voters. The OFS, poor but proud, was still smarting about the annexation of the diamond fields, but with a little persuasion could have been absorbed if the Cape had been willing. As it was, Cape opposition blocked progress in that direction. Natal was still a direct colony. This left the SAR (Transvaal), which was bankrupt – and oppressed by Zulu and Swazi incursions.

Urged on by Britain's consular agent, Sir Bartle Frere, Britain annexed the Free State – and found itself at war with the Zulu. Frere had promised internal autonomy for the Transvalers, on lines similar to the Cape, but London reneged on this. Soon Britain was not only at war with the formerly friendly Zulu, but at loggerheads with the suspicious whites – who, impressed by an early defeat of British regulars by the *impi*, themselves attacked the British Army and defeated it at Majuba in 1881. The independence of the Transvaal was then recognized once more, with Britain retaining only foreign affairs and the right to guard the long frontiers. Says a recent history: 'All Britain had succeeded in doing in the ten years since 1871 was to revive and increase the antagonisms which had first led the Boers to make the Great Trek.'

The Boers, with their own brand of 'elect' Christianity, also clashed with the missions, who tended to concentrate on areas outside Boer influence: this often stiffened Muntu resistance to Boer advances. Only among the Zulu were the missions notably unsuccessful, until the Nguni military systems were defeated in the 1890s. Moffat (later Sir Robert Moffat) of the London Missionary Society established a close relationship with Mzilikazi in the Transvaal, however, and this later permitted the LMS to christianize Matabeleland. The mission's influence was also great among the Basuto and the Griqua. Independence for the Transvaal checked the Christian advance northward, except between the Transvaal and the Kalahari – the narrow inhabited area of Bechuanaland (Botswana), where the King of the Bamangwato, Khama, was converted.

The 'missionary trail' northward had also led traders, concession-seekers and hunters, in the 'Sixties and later, up from the Cape as far North as Barotseland. It was from the LMS station at Kuruman – established by Moffat in a part of Botswana territory now annexed by South Africa – that Livingstone, who later became Moffat's son-in-law, had set out on his first journeys.

Livingstone's coast-to-coast trek with Makololo porters 1853–56 had disclosed the presence of a chain of Portuguese forts leading from the Angolan coast, from which mulatto *pombeiros* ranged far in search of slaves and tusks. He also found vast areas war-wracked to provide slaves for plantations in lowland Moçambique and on the Lower Zambezi. Livingstone concluded that only a substantial British presence in these areas would save the total break up of African tribal society. On his second major expedition, 1858–64, up the Zambezi and the Shire, he had laid the groundwork for penetration; but to begin with, in the 'Seventies, only more missionaries followed.

When, in the 'Eighties and 'Nineties, Britain moved in officially, to support the missions in Nyasaland, most of the resistance was Portuguese. But Portugal's dream to establish an ocean-to-ocean link – an idea that was later to inspire Germany, also – fell before the ambitions of Cecil Rhodes, and the new and vigorous forces which followed his spearhead through the center of austral Africa, bringing the railroad up from the Cape to Matabeleland.

As well as South Africa, Rhodesia and Basutoland (which was detached from Cape Colony and placed under direct British administration in 1884) two other British protectorates were to emerge in the area – Bechuanaland and Swaziland. Mutswana autonomy from the surrounding South African territories partly reflected Moffat's influence. The mission had helped relieve the Bamangwato – the most important of the eight Batswana tribes – from the depredations of the Zulus, Boers and Ndebele.

293

Khama II, who had succeeded to the paramountcy of the Bamangwato in 1872, and who had inflicted several defeats on the Ndebele, appealed many times to the Cape for military and political aid. Finally, in 1884, John Mackenzie was sent as Administrator, with the title of Deputy Commissioner. 'Bechuanaland' became a Protectorate the following year. In 1895, Britain announced it would hand over the country to the British South Africa Company – but Khama and two other Batswana chiefs went to London with a successful protest.

Britain's direct connection with Swaziland dated from Swazi appeals for aid against the Zulu. In the 'Eighties, King Mbandzeni of the ruling Nkosi-Dlamini clan sold a number of concessions to Europeans, and a British Advisor was appointed to shield the realm from exploitation. In 1888, however, the settler community was allowed to form a legislature and voted for incorporation into South Africa. At a meeting of Swazi, British and South African representatives in 1890, a compromise was reached on some limited autonomy; South Africa annexed Swaziland four years later, but definitively lost the country in the Boer War.

*

The pattern in southern Africa, with Europeans extending their rule to areas not predominantly non-African in habitation, was significant: all over the black continent, Britons, Portuguese, Afrikaners, Italians, Germans, Belgians and Frenchmen were, in the final years of the century, consolidating real sovereignly held territories and staking out conflicting claims. The colonial era, Africa's greatest historic shock, was now at hand.

Select Bibliography

Part I

ADRISI, al-	Description de l'Afrique (translation)	Leyden, 1866
ARDREY, Robert	African Genesis	New York, 1961
BATTUTA, ibn	Travels in Africa and Asia (translation)	London, 1929
BAULIN, Jacques	The Arab Rôle in Africa	London, 1962
BAKRI, al-	Description de l'Afrique Septentrionale (translation)	Algiers, 1913
BOVILL, E. W.	Caravans of the old Sahara	Oxford, 1933
	The Golden Trade of the Moors	Oxford, 1958
DAVIDSON, Basil	Old Africa Rediscovered	London, 1959
FAGE, J. D.	West Africa	Cambridge, 1961
HAUKAL, ibn	Description de l'Afrique (translation)	Paris, 1842
KHALDUN, ibn	Histoire des Berbères (translation)	Paris, 1925
LEO AFRICANUS	History and Description of Africa (translation)	London, 1896
MONTEIL, Vincent	L'Islam Noir	Paris, 1964
MRABET, Fadela	La femme algérienne	Paris, 1964
POST, Laurens van der	The Lost World of the Kalahari	London, 1958
SA'ADI, es-	Tarikh es-Sudan (translation)	Paris, 1900
SMITH, Mary	Baba of Karo	London, 1959

International Anthropological and Linguistic Review
Nature
Présence Africaine

Part II

ADAMS, Captain John	Sketches Taken During Ten Years Voyages to Africa between the years 1786–1800	London, 1822

	Remarks on the Country Extending from Cape Palmas to the River Congo	London, 1823
BAIKIE, William Balfour	An Expeditionary Voyage up the Rivers Kwora and Binue in 1854	London, 1856
BAKER, Samuel White	The Albert Nyanza	London, 1866
BARTH, Dr. Heinrich	Travels in North and Central Africa	London, 1857–58
BOLD, Lieutenant Edward	Merchants and Mariners African Guide	London, 1822
BOSMAN, William	A New and Accurate Description of the Coast of Guinea (translation)	London, 1705
CAMERON, Verney Lovett	Across Africa	London, 1877
CLAPPERTON, Hugh	Journal of a Second Expedition in the Interior of Africa	London, 1829
DENHAM, Dixon and CLAPPERTON, Hugh	Narrative of Travels and Discoveries in North and Central Africa	London, 1822–24
DIKE, Dr. K. Onwuka	Trade and Politics in the Niger Delta, 1830–85	Oxford, 1956
DRYSDALE, John	The Somali Dispute	London, 1964
DUFFY, Dr. James	Portuguese Africa	Cambridge, Mass., 1959
FAGE, J. D.	West Africa	Cambridge, 1961
FAGE, J. D. and OLIVER, R.	A Short History of Africa	London, 1962
FORDE, Daryll	Efik Traders of Old Calabar and The Diary of Antera Duke (ed.)	Oxford, 1956
FYFE, Christopher	A History of Sierra Leone	Oxford, 1962
GAILEY, Harry	A History of the Gambia	London, 1964
GASKILL, Gordon	Madagascar; the Isle of Riddles	Unpublished manuscript
HOHNEL, Ludwig von	Description of Lakes Rudolf and Stefanie	London, 1894
HOLT, John	Merchant Adventure (reprinted)	London, 1936
JONES, A. H. M. and MONROE, Elizabeth	History of Ethiopia	Oxford, 1935
JOOS, Louis C. D.	Brève Histoire de l'Afrique Noire	Issy-les-Moulineaux, 1961
KINGSLEY, Mary	Travels in West Africa	London, 1897
	West African Studies	London, 1899
KRAPF, Rev. J. Ludwig	Researches and Missionary Labours	London, 1860
KUP, Peter	Sierra Leone, 1400–1797	Cambridge, 1961
LABOURET, Henri	L'Afrique précoloniale	Paris, 1959
LAIRD, MacGregor and OLDFIELD, R. A. K.	An Expedition into the Interior of Africa by the River Niger, 1832–34	London, 1837
LANDER, Richard and John	Journal of an Expedition to explore the Niger	London, 1833

296

LIVINGSTONE, David	The Last Journal of David Livingstone	Edinburgh, 1874
LEWIS, Roy	Sierra Leone	London, 1954
LUGARD, F. D.	The Rise of Our East African Empire	Edinburgh, 1893
MARINELLI, Lawrence A.	The New Liberia	New York, 1964
MOOREHEAD, Alan	The White Nile	London, 1960
	The Blue Nile	London, 1962
NEWBURY, C. W.	The Western Slave Coast and its Rulers	Oxford, 1961
PANKHURST, E. Sylvia	Ex-Italian Somaliland	London, 1951
PARK, Mungo	Travels in the Interior Districts of Africa	London, 1799
POPE HENNESSY, James	Verandah	New York, 1964
PORTER, Arthur	Creoledom	Oxford, 1963
SIMMONS, Donald C.	Grant's Sketch of Calabar (ed.)	Calabar, 1958
	Holman's Voyage to Old Calabar (ed.)	Calabar, 1959
SMITH, Captain John	Trade and Travels in the Gulf of Guinea	Boston, 1851
SMITH, Mary	Baba of Karo	London, 1959
SPEKE, John Hanning	Journal of the Discovery of the Source of the Nile	Edinburgh, 1863
	What led to the Discovery of the Source of the Nile	Edinburgh, 1864
STANLEY, Henry Morton	How I Found Livingstone	London, 1872
	Exploration Diaries	London, 1961
THOMSON, A. A. and MIDDLETON, Dorothy	Lugard in Africa	London, 1959
THOMSON, Joseph	To the Central African Lakes and Back	London, 1881
	Through Masai Land	London, 1885

Index

299

301

306

317

318